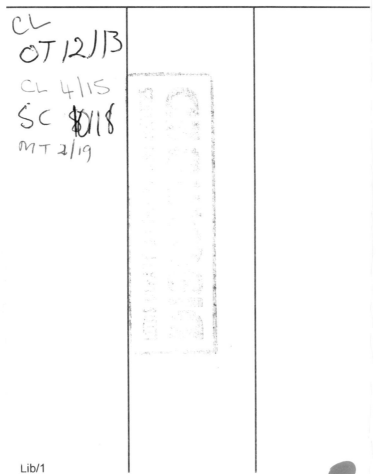

Great Lives:
PIVOTAL MOMENTS

Lauren SEGAL and Paul HOLDEN

JACANA

First published by Jacana Media (Pty) Ltd in 2008

10 Orange Street
Sunnyside
Auckland Park 2092
South Africa
(+27 11) 628 3200
www.jacana.co.za

© SAHA, 2008

ISBN 987-1-77009-592-2

Set in Baskerville and Frutiger
Printed and Bound for Imago Productions
Job no. 000762

See a complete list of Jacana titles at www.jacana.co.za

SAHA/SUNDAY TIMES HERITAGE PROJECT

FOREWORD

The heart of the South African History Archive's mandate is to document and disseminate stories and archival materials relating to historical and contemporary struggles for justice in South Africa. This includes recording the experiences, not only of the icons and well-known heroes of our past, but also of ordinary people whose life experiences are often ignored or airbrushed out of history.

Great Lives, Pivotal Moments presented SAHA with a unique opportunity to fulfill its mandate. The stories and images in this book provide readers with a chance to broaden their appreciation of both ordinary and extraordinary people and events that have shaped South Africa's past. Importantly for SAHA, the book is also a magnificent showcase for hitherto unseen archives that usually remain hidden in dusty basements. By weaving the archives into the life histories, *Great Lives, Pivotal Moments* brings documents, newspapers, memorandums and government gazettes to new audiences who do not often access this type of information.

We are also very excited about having had the opportunity to collaborate with the *Sunday Times* Heritage Project. It has been a unique experience for a small non-governmental organisation such as ourselves, to work with a national newspaper that has demonstrated a clear commitment to investing in our nation's collective memory.

Some may believe that vigorously engaging our past is counter-intuitive to the broader goals of reconciliation. SAHA, however, is convinced that exploring and sharing our histories is essential for building the foundations for a deeper understanding and appreciation of where we have come from.

We believe that this will provide us with opportunities to explore our commonalities and differences. These are the essential ingredients of South Africa's national slogan, *Unity through Diversity.*

We hope that you will enjoy reading this book and seeing through the window into aspects of our unique history that this publication opens.

Dumisa BUHLE NTSEBEZA
South African History Archive (SAHA) Chairperson

INTRODUCTION

On Thursday 9 March 2006, a life-size bronze statue of Brenda Fassie was unveiled outside the Bassline club in Newtown, Johannesburg. Well, Brenda wasn't a Big Man, and she's not on a horse. Still, there's no getting away from it: she is a figurative statue and she's cast in bronze. Inspired by José Villa Soberon's bronzes of John Lennon on a park bench and Ernest Hemingway propping up a bar – both in Havana – Brenda's creator Angus Taylor has made an unconventional memorial that is every bit as inviting and playful. At the time of her death on 9 May 2004, Fassie was this country's top selling local artist. She may not have been everyone's idea of a role model, but then, this is not a project about role-models. Brenda Fassie was a stellar newsmaker. Her work is part of this country's musical legacy. This is why we chose her as our Poster Girl to launch the *Sunday Times* Heritage Project.

The *Sunday Times* turned 100 on 4 February 2006. As part of our centenary celebrations and under the baton of the paper's editor, Mondli Makhanya, we set out on an ambitious journey across what – for us – was virgin tundra. My brief was to "in some way" mark the spot where some of the significant news events of "our" century (from 1906-) took place, while also recognising the remarkable newsmakers who stood at the heart of these actions. The blue plaques that pepper the streets of London – "Sylvia Plath lived here" etc – were mentioned as a point of departure. But it was the far more engrossing "Memory" signs on the streets of Schoneberg, Berlin, which informed our early thinking. This memorial making was neither grimly explicit nor sentimental, and ideas began to swirl for what might inform the look and feel of our permanent and site-specific "narrative" memorials.

The decision to give a selection of local artists pretty much free rein to make their own unique pieces evolved over time and with the guidance of many people who know a lot more about art than we do – notably the arts management company we work with to source and manage the artists and the artworks.

> We wanted to show how today's news is tomorrow's history. We wished to add a small stitch to the fabric of dozens of streets and communities; to shine a light on a singular moment in 100 years of newstime which, subtly or significantly, helped to shape the diverse "us".

By no means was all of the news history we wished to mark shocking and painful. Our researchers set out to identify and develop a number of stories, characters and sites across the news board – Eureka! moments in science, the arts, sport, politics, and society. A range of memories, often proud, even playful.

Journalists are storytellers of a particular stripe. Typically, newspaper stories are personality driven and action-orientated. The *Sunday Times* is a popular paper, so our angle on these narrative memorials is to hook the viewer by making the news events we are asking people to remember worth remembering – not because we should, but because we can't resist a good story.

In the identification and development of these stories our dedicated team of senior researchers has trawled through books and theses; original court documents, inquest papers, letters, banning orders, manifestos and commissions of inquiry; they have triple checked facts and tracked down original sources; they have established exact sites where events happened and found and interviewed people who were there to make sure no version was left unturned.

Our newspaper is not in the business of revising history, especially not to make any earlier incarnations of this newspaper look better! What we are doing through this project is to look back at 100 years of South African news history from the paper's 21st-century perspective. And that, as for all South Africans since 1994, is a liberating experience. So, we have the story plaques, on or alongside each artwork, which briefly describes the action: the plaque text is as short, sharp and adjective-free as a good news report should be.

Then we have the memorials themselves: floor and wall pieces, signage, freestanding sculptures, etc. Each one is unique, our chief command to artists being that their artworks be made as time-proof, weather-proof and vandal-proof as possible.

The great thing about the memorials is that they are all freely accessible and visible to the public. If our story site is a school, we installed our memorial outside the gates. Several times we had to resist the temptation to place a memorial inside the gates at the invitation of the building owners who were, if anything, more worried about vandalism than we were.

Getting the necessary permission, buy-in and blessings to erect 40 public memorials across the country was a massive and delicate undertaking. We are proud to boast a total of 35 out of 40 of our proposed memorials, considering the vast number of stakeholders' permission was necessary in order to proceed.

There was never a question of the *Sunday Times* imposing its will and foisting unwanted memorials on resistant communities: we would simply not be allowed to. But mostly the officials we've met have liked the project and taken great pains to help us make it happen in their neck of the woods. Ethically speaking, we decided that without the support of this project's "first ring" of custodians – the families, immediate communities and our chief protagonists who are still living – we would drop it.

But we have made a start. This is our contribution to storytelling our heritage, one we'll continue through 2007 and beyond. We believe these memorials and the sites where they live will add a valuable stitch to the fabric of their immediate surroundings and communities, animating the past in ways we can make sense of today.

Our starting point was that, in order to promote a national identity, we must first acknowledge the complex range of South African voices and experiences that have, in some way, shaped our heartlines, faultlines and achievements. On behalf of us all who worked on this unique project at the *Sunday Times*, we would like to pay particular tribute to the families of the extraordinary men and women who are the heart of our project. We thank them for their generosity towards us and their willingness to share with strangers their memories and experiences, joyous and painful, so that we might better know and understand what drove the people and events which have influenced who we are, and who we may still become.

Charlotte BAUER
Former Director of the *Sunday Times* Heritage Project

ACKNOWLEDGEMENTS

This book is the product of an extensive collaboration between researchers, writers, artists and managers from the South African History Archive (SAHA) and the *Sunday Times* Heritage Project.

The idea for the stories and memorials was shaped by the dynamic hands of the Director of the *Sunday Times* Heritage Project, Charlotte Bauer. She and her team of researchers chose the lively range of subjects that appear in this book. With great journalistic acumen, they researched and found documents and information that make the memories of these people and events sing on the page. We drew extensively from the profiles written by Sue Valentine, Gillian Anstey, Janette Bennett and Shelley Seid. Lomin Saayman, who was tasked with creating the *Sunday Times* website, and Lesley Perkes, who was responsible for the memorials themselves, were both very helpful along this journey.

Under the extremely able stewardship of Piers Pigou and the South African History Archive, the stories created by the *Sunday Times* were augmented with audio, photographs and other archival treasures. Our thanks to Marion Isaacs, Theresa Collins, Tshepo Maloi, Jane Sathekge, Katie Mooney, Tymon Smith and Nhlanhla Mthethwa, who spent days sifting through the archive to extract the gems that appear on the pages of this book.

We would like to thank all those at Wits Historical Papers, the Alan Paton and Struggle Archives (KZN), the National Archives, Manuscripts and Archives at the University of Cape Town, Bailey's African History Archives, Mayibuye, Liberation Archives, the Cory Library at Rhodes University, the Military Museum and the Avusa Library for their patience and cooperation in this process.

Professor Phil Bonner, Dr Noor Nieftagodien and Professor Cynthia Kros steered us in the right directions and brought their fine historical rigour to bear.

The text has been enriched by the inclusion of quotes from audio interviews conducted for a radio series by SAHA. Sue Valentine oversaw the radio production. We thank her and the other producers - Carolyn Dempster, Michelle Constant, Ocean Ngobeni, Tando Ntunja and Simon Hill for their skills and talent in bringing alive stories from the past.

A special thanks to Seitiso Mogoshane, Tshidi Semakale and Plantinah Dire for running the SAHA office and holding together the multiple threads that were woven into this book.

This project would not have been possible without the vision of the Editor and CEO of the *Sunday Times*, Mondli Makhanya and Mike Robertson, who took it upon themselves to celebrate the 100th birthday of the *Sunday Times* in a highly creative way. Nor would it have been possible without the generous support and vision of *The Atlantic Philanthropies* and its director, Gerald Kraak. It is rare for a philanthropic funder to broker a collaboration between an NGO and a media powerhouse. We believe that this book is a rich record of this unusual but rewarding experiment.

Our thanks also to Maggie Davey and Bridget Impey of Jacana Media. We began our relationship over a slice of chocolate cake and all our subsequent interactions proved equally enriching. As always, Sandy Shoolman brought her fine editorial eye and attention to detail to bear.

Carina Comrie's design ability to make historical information leap from the page is unparalleled.

Thanks to Mia, Josh, Johnny and Katya for the endless cups of coffee, tea and loving support.

Lauren SEGAL and Paul HOLDEN

Great Lives:
PIVOTAL MOMENTS

1 PORTRAITS OF COLONIALISM

1867 - 1923

This section explores some of the great lives and events of the colonial period in South African history. The stories we explore are from the second half of the 1800s up until about the mid-1920s, when the new Union government was taking the first steps to formalise racial segregation.

1867   Diamonds were discovered on a farm near Hope Town in Griqualand West in the Northern Cape. This led to a massive diamond rush.

1879   The British government invaded the independent nation of Zululand and defeated the Zulu army. The invasion was almost certainly linked to a desire to force black residents in the area to provide labour on the Kimberley diamond mines.

1883   Olive Schreiner published her first novel, *The Story of an African Farm*, under the pseudonym Ralph Irons.

1886   The main reef of the Witwatersrand Goldfields was uncovered on the farm of Langlaagte. This discovery led to another massive rush for riches, and Johannesburg was born.

1899   The South African War was fought between the British and the Boer Republics. The British Empire wanted control over the recently discovered goldfields. Large portions of South Africa were devastated and the war led to tension between English and Afrikaans South Africans that lasted nearly a century.

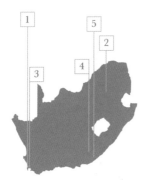

SAHA/*SUNDAY TIMES* MEMORIAL SITES:

>> ·

1 Olive SHREINER
Main Road, Kalk Bay, Cape Town

2 Mohandas GANDHI
Hamidia Mosque, Jennings Street, Fordsburg, Johannesburg

1908 The Draft Asiatic Bill stated that all 'Asiatics' in South Africa over the age of 8 were required to register their presence in the country. Gandhi burnt his registration card in protest.

1910 South Africa was declared a Union. The country would now be run by an internal government under the watchful eye of the British Empire. The declaration deeply upset black South Africans who had hoped that they would be given the vote.

1912 The South African Native National Congress was formed. This organisation, initially led by middle-class and educated black South Africans, later became the African National Congress (ANC).

1913 The 1913 Land Act set aside only 7.5% of all South African land for black ownership.

1914 The First World War was declared in Europe. South Africa entered the war on the side of Britain. In protest, Afrikaner generals pulled out of the ruling South African National Party and formed the National Party.

3

21 February **1917** The *SS Mendi* sank, staffed by black members of the South African Native Labour Corps.

1918 The Great 'Flu epidemic killed millions worldwide soon after the world confronted the horrific destruction at the end of World War I.

4

24 May **1921** The South African Police attacked the Israelite camp in Ntabelanga. After twenty minutes of battle, at least 171 Israelites lay dead. The Israelites were a religious group led by the Reverend Enoch Mgijima.

5

7 April **1923** Nontetha Nkwenkwe, a preacher in the Eastern Cape, was arrested on charges of treason and public disturbance. The authorities declared her mentally insane and transferred her to the Mental Hospital in Fort Beaufort. In fact, they were worried about her growing influence in the region. She was later transferred to Weskoppies Mental Hospital in Pretoria, where she remained for the rest of her life.

1923 The Native (Urban Areas) Act divided cities and towns along racial lines. Municipalities were forced to establish 'locations' on the periphery of white towns for the housing of black residents.

3   Isaac WAUCHOPE / SS Mendi
World War I Training Ground,
University of Cape Town

4   Enoch MGIJIMA / Bulhoek Masacre
Israelite Temple, Queenstown

5   Nontetha NKWENKWE
Magistrate's Court, Alexandra Street,
King William's Town

Olive SCHREINER

"It is delightful to be a woman, but every man thanks the Lord devoutly that he isn't one."

Olive SCHREINER, *The Story of an African Farm*

01

During the first decades of the 20th century, Olive Schreiner spoke and wrote passionately in support of the Women's Enfranchisement League, which met in homes and halls throughout the city of Cape Town, including at the English Church schoolroom that once stood on Main Road, Kalk Bay. Though the author of the feminist classic Women and Labour, and the best-selling *The Story of an African Farm*, was a major force in the worldwide struggle for women's suffrage, by 1912 she had quit the League she had helped establish because it refused to campaign for the vote for all women in South Africa. White South African women received the vote in 1930; black women, and men, waited until 1994.

Text from the Sunday Times memorial plaque

01 As a young woman, Olive Schreiner defied the conventions of her family and society by refusing to accept Christianity and by campaigning for women's rights.

02 Olive Schreiner's first novel, *The Story of an African Farm*, was initially published under the pseudonym Ralph Iron. Schreiner believed that the novel would not be taken seriously if it was published under a woman's name. Schreiner's identity as the book's author was only revealed when a second edition was published in 1891 as shown on opposite page.

THE STORY OF AN AFRICAN FARM

A NOVEL BY RALPH IRON

(OLIVE SCHREINER)

CENTURY HUTCHINSON
Johannesburg

A WOMAN AHEAD OF HER TIME

Olive Emilie Albertine Schreiner was born in Wittenbergen in the Cape to missionary parents Rebecca and Gottlob Schreiner. She was the ninth of twelve children. Schreiner's early life was hard, as her father lost his job with the London Missionary Society after allegations of corrupt business activity. His attempts to start his own business were disastrous. Schreiner's father died in poverty after his various business ventures failed, and the family was left destitute. Olive was forced to live with her brother, Theophilus, the religious headmaster of a school in Cradock, along with some of her other siblings.

Schreiner wrote *The Story of an African Farm* when she was a 21-year-old governess working in the Karoo. Some years previously, diamonds were discovered not far from where she was working. A rush to the diamond fields followed. Signalling her independence, Schreiner refused to go and live with her brother and his family when they left for the diamond mines to seek their fortune. She remained a governess in the Karoo. During these times, she would have witnessed how the government attempted to strip African people of their freedom in order to ensure cheap labour for the mines.

Olive Schreiner not only lived in a world where race relations were hardening. She lived in a world where all women, black and white, were treated as second-class citizens. Strict Victorian codes of morality attempted to 'keep women in their place'. Women were denied the right to vote and were regarded as 'pretty niceties', whose job was to marry when told, to produce children and feather the nest.

Schreiner was, however, a woman ahead of her time. She fiercely resisted the strictures of Victorian morality and advocated equality of the sexes, women's rights and independence as well as equality between white and black South Africans.

The Story of an African Farm gave voice to her ideals. It is an indictment of the government's cruel and unequal treatment of black people. The novel's protagonist is the independent-minded Lyndall who famously declares:

>> . . . .

1855   Olive Emilie Albertine Schreiner was born in Wittenbergen in the Cape.

1876   Schreiner's father died in poverty, leaving the family destitute. Olive went to live with her brother in Cradock.

1881   Schreiner went to England to train as a nurse but her severe asthma forced her to abandon her studies and return to South Africa.

Dear old Edward Carpenter

...A man and a woman stand in the same relation to each other as a white man to a black man...It would not do for the black man to be dependent on the white because at least in this country there are centuries of tradition of the inferiority of the black and the superiority of the white: of submission on one side and masterhood on the other; and these traditions...have affected both...I believe a friendship of true equality would be impossible between the two. Just so with a man and a woman, with 2,000 years of slavish submission on one side and animal dominance on the other...they can neither of them afford anything which tends to keep up those traditions.

With regard to my own marriage, dear, I will only say it is an ideally happy one...

Love to all the friends at Millthorpe

Olive

"When I am strong, I will hate everything that has power, and help everything that is weak." Although it was immediately recognised as a highly influential novel, Schreiner could not publish the novel under her own name. Instead, as can be seen from the cover on the previous page, the book was first published under the pseudonym Ralph Iron. It was only when the second edition was published in 1891, that Schreiner revealed her own name.

A "BARBARIC INSTITUTION"

A year after Schreiner wrote *The Story of an African Farm*, she agreed to marry Samuel Cronwright - despite having declared that marriage was a "barbaric institution". In this letter to her good friend Edward Carpenter, she compares marriage to the difficult relationship that existed between black and white people in the country at the time. The old ways of thinking and the habit of imagining that one person was superior to the other, she says, made these relations hard to change. She probably agreed to get married because Cronwright supported her ideals and her feminism and even took on her surname.

01 Olive Schreiner (centre) with her family in 1881. To the right of Schreiner stands her brother, William, who later became deeply involved in Cape politics. Also pictured are Schreiner's brother Fred, his wife Emma and son Wilfred.

02 Olive Schreiner's older siblings Theo and Ettie in the early 1870s. As a young woman, Schreiner distanced herself from her family.

03 Olive Schreiner with her husband Samuel Cronwright-Schreiner.

1883 *The Story of an African Farm* was published. Because of the highly conservative climate at the time, Schreiner published the book under a male pseudonym, Ralph Iron.

1894 Schreiner married Samuel Cronwright who was equally committed to promoting feminism.

1903 Schreiner met the British writer Emily Hobhouse who came to South Africa to report on the horrors of the British concentration camps during the South African War. Both were committed to feminist ideals and this was the start of a lifelong friendship.

THE RIGHT TO VOTE

Schreiner wrote a lot about, and fought hard for her ideals. She joined the women's suffrage movement which campaigned for the right of women to vote. In 1907, she became one of the Vice-Presidents of the Women's Enfranchisement League of the Cape Colony. The League's aims were simple: "The object of this society is to promote an intelligent interest in the question of the political enfranchisement of women in the Cape Colony, and to advocate for the granting of the vote to them on the same terms as men." Schreiner soon ran into conflict with some of the League's more conservative members as her scrawling over this pamphlet below shows. Olive wanted all women to be able to vote – not just white women. In December 1913, Schreiner resigned from the organisation, and moved to England. The League's committee begged her to stay, writing: "If we could make you realize all we feel in losing you, we are convinced you would not refuse our request." But Schreiner could not be swayed.

SCHREINER'S DEATH

Olive Schreiner moved to England, just before the outbreak of the First World War when England was fighting against Germany. It was a difficult period for Schreiner, as she suffered from poor health, writer's block, and was discriminated against because of her German surname. She returned to South Africa after the war when she sensed she did not have much time left. Schreiner struggled with ill-health for most of her life, and died in 1920. She was buried in this stone tomb in the Karoo according to her strict instructions, along with her only daughter, who died soon after Schreiner gave birth to her. She had always mourned the death of her baby and was not able to have more children. Her dog was buried with her.

Schreiner's wish for women to get the right to vote only came true many years after her death. White women in South Africa got the vote in 1930; black women in 1994.

01

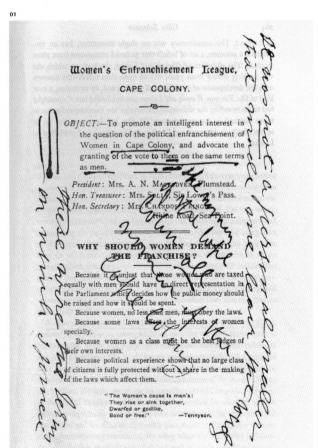

02

01 Schreiner's handwritten notes on the constitution show how she became frustrated with the League's approach to race relations. She scribbled in the left margin: "These were the terms on which I joined" and in the right margin: "It was not a personal matter that made me leave the society." In the centre she wrote: "The women of the Cape Colony <u>all</u> women of the Cape Colony."

02 Olive Schreiner was buried in this stone tomb in the Karoo along with her dog and her only daughter, who died as a baby.

1911 Schreiner published *Women and Labour*, a harsh attack on the place of women in modern society. It became required reading for the feminist movement. Three years later, she resigned from the Women's Enfranchisement League because of its unwillingness to promote a non-racial franchise. She moved to England, and remained there until World War One ended in 1918.

1920
11 December Schreiner died in South Africa. Thousands lined the railway track to watch her funeral procession.

"What is left of this wonderful woman is *The Story of an African Farm*. The great influence she had is hidden from us in the events she helped to shape."

Doris LESSING

ADDRESS > Main Road, Kalk Bay, Cape Town

The Olive Schreiner memorial is a tribute to Schreiner's fight for racial and gender equality. The artist, Barbara Wildenboer, wanted the crosses on the artwork to remind people of the crosses that voters place on a ballot paper next to the person they vote for. They represent Schreiner's fight to secure the vote for all women – both black and white. The artist says the round structure represents the dams that are dotted all over the Karoo, a part of the country that Schreiner loved. The Karoo is where Schreiner lived for a period and where she wrote *The Story of an African Farm*. The memorial is in Kalk Bay because the Women's Enfranchisement League often met in the English Church schoolroom that once stood on Main Road in Kalk Bay.

Mohandas GANDHI

"Truly speaking, it was after I went to South Africa that I became what I am now. My love for South Africa and my concern for her problems are no less than for India."

Mohandas GANDHI

01

On August 16, 1908, 3 000 Muslims, Hindus and Christians led by Mohandas Gandhi, a Hindu, gathered outside the Hamidia Mosque and burned their passes, documents all people classified 'non-white' by the government were forced to carry or face imprisonment. The huge bonfire, lit in a cauldron, marked the first burning of passes in South Africa and the beginning of Gandhi's *Satyagraha*, or passive resistance campaign.

Text from the Sunday Times memorial plaque

01 During his time in South Africa, Gandhi grew from a shy and struggling lawyer into a highly successful attorney and powerful political leader.

02 In 1906, the government introduced the Asiatic Law Amendment Ordinance which forced all 'Asiatics' to carry a registration certificate like this one or else face fines and imprisonment. Gandhi believed that the "Black Act (was) not the last step, but the first step with a view to hound us out of the country."

Serial N.º 7391   C.S.O. 187.

V 6615.

Transvaal Asiatic Registration Certificate.

Name in full... Jooma Cassim..

Race... B. Indian................... Age... 30... Height... 5' 9½ boots

Description... Mole right forearm. Slightly pockmarks

....

....

Registrar of Asiatics.

Date of Issue... 21st May 1908..........................

Holder's Signature ....

Name of Wife... Assa................ Residence... Boksburg

SONS and MALE WARDS under the age of 16 years.

NAMES.	AGE.	RESIDENCE.	RELATIONSHIP TO GUARDIAN.
Allibhai	11	India	Son
Hussambhai	1½	Boksburg	do
Abdul Hamid	4½	Boksburg	Son

GANDHI'S TRANSFORMATION

Mohandas Gandhi is one of the most important figures in modern history. He is mainly remembered for his acts of extreme self-sacrifice and for his rejection of violence during the struggle for Indian independence from British colonial rule. Less well-known is the fact that Gandhi's political transformation began in South Africa. Indeed, it was in this country that Gandhi developed his famous philosophy of *Satyagraha* - the adoption of passive resistance as a political tool. It was also in South Africa that Gandhi took the vow of *Brahmacharya* (celibacy and poverty) and committed himself to a life unfettered by the distractions of modern convenience and comfort.

It is hard to believe that when Gandhi started practicing law, he was so shy that he couldn't make a speech. In his first court case in Bombay, he was so overcome by nerves that he didn't ask the witness a single question!

When Gandhi arrived in South Africa in 1893, he refused to move from the 'first-class' carriage which was reserved for whites. He was thrown off the train at the station in Pietermaritzburg. Soon after this, he became involved in fighting for the rights of Indians. Gradually, he gained confidence in speaking out and leading delegations against the government. Speaking about his time here after he had returned to India, Gandhi said:

> "I was, with my countrymen, in a hopeless minority, not only a hopeless minority but a despised minority. If the Europeans of South Africa will forgive me for saying so, we were all Coolies (a negative slang word for Indian people). I was an insignificant Coolie lawyer. At that time we had no Coolie doctors. We had no Coolie lawyers. I was the first in the field. Nevertheless, [I was] a Coolie."

01-02 Indian Hawkers in Johannesburg, early 1900s

03 Gandhi, seen here to the left of the main group, stands with other *Satyagrahis* at the entrance to Johannesburg's Old Fort prison near modern-day Braamfontein or Hillbrow.

>> . . . .

1869 Mohandas Gandhi was born into a Hindu family in Porbandar, India, where his father was the *diwan* (Prime Minister). Gandhi married Kasturba Makhanji in an arranged marriage when he was fourteen years old. They had four sons: Harilal (1888), Manilal (1892), Ramdas (1897) and Devdas (1900).

1893 Gandhi completed his law degree at Oxford and set up legal practices in Rajkot and Bombay. He was invited to Durban to assist in a legal trial for Dada Abdullah and Company. He founded the Natal Indian Congress and became its first secretary. He was also enrolled as an advocate of the Supreme Court of Natal, the first Indian to achieve this honour.

THE LAUNCH OF *SATYAGRAHA*

In 1906, Gandhi's political involvement escalated. This was the year that the government introduced the Asiatic Law Amendment Ordinance which required that all 'Asiatics' over the age of eight were to sign and fingerprint registration cards. This was the government's first attempt at racial classification and registration in South Africa.

The Act – refered to as the 'Black Act' – was seen as deeply humiliating since it strictly limited where Indians were able to trade and live. For the first time, Gandhi espoused his philosophy of *Satyagraha*. *Satyagraha* is an amalgamation of two Gujarati words – *satya* (truth) and *agraha* (taking, seizing, holding) – the implication being that one seizes hold of the truth. For Gandhi, achieving political freedom was only half of the battle. *Satyagraha* was also about achieving inner freedom and following an inner truth. It was as important for Gandhi to follow his conscience and teach others to follow theirs as it was for him to win political campaigns.

Gandhi and his colleagues launched the Indian non-violent resistance campaign on 11 September 1906 at a mass meeting in Johannesburg's old Empire Theatre in Fordsburg, near Newtown. Three thousand Indians from all over the Transvaal gathered, together with a Chinese delegation. Gandhi stirred the crowd with these words:

"Let the accusation of breaking the law fall on us. Let us cheerfully suffer imprisonment. There is nothing wrong in that…If the government sends us to gaol, I shall be the first to court imprisonment. And if any Indian is put to trouble because of his refusal to register…I will appear in his case free of charge."

GOING TO JAIL

Hundreds of Indian and Chinese people supported Gandhi's call and refused to register for passes. Many were arrested and imprisoned at the Old Fort in Johannesburg as well as in other jails in Natal. The conditions in the Old Fort were appalling but Gandhi treated jail as a time to meditate and reflect. He welcomed the lack of comforts and the poor food. As a *Satyagrahi*, he believed that physical suffering would make him stronger and more determined in the struggle. All in all, Gandhi ended up spending 2 338 days in jail in South Africa and India.

1902 Gandhi returned to India following the South African War but was called back by South African Indians to help fight against anti-Asiatic legislation in the Transvaal.	1903 Gandhi was admitted to the Supreme Court of the Transvaal and opened law offices in Johannesburg. He founded the influential newspaper, *Indian Opinion*, to agitate against anti-Asiatic laws. Three years later, Gandhi launched his famous *Satyagraha* method of protest.	1910 Gandhi founded Tolstoy Farm as a base for the *Satyagraha* movement. Residents were committed to living a disciplined life which embraced labour and vegetarianism.

It was during his first imprisonment at the Old Fort in Johannesburg, that Gandhi entered into negotiations with the South African Prime Minister, General Jan Smuts. Smuts proposed that if Asians agreed to register voluntarily, he would repeal the Act. Gandhi felt that indeed, voluntary registration would be less humiliating and Gandhi, Thambi Naidoo and Leung Quinn (leader of the Chinese delegation) signed the compromise letter.

PASS BURNING

Gandhi was bitterly disappointed when Smuts reneged on his agreement to repeal the 'Black Act'. Gandhi re-launched the non-violent resistance campaign. On 16 August 1908, Gandhi led over 3 000 disgruntled 'Asiatics' in burning their registration cards outside the Hamidia Mosque in Newtown. Indians also defied the ban on immigration to the Transvaal. Hundreds of *Satyagrahis* were imprisoned. Many more suffered by having their trading licences taken away.

01   On 16 August 1908, Gandhi led the crowd in setting alight their registration certificates in a large three-legged pot. This pot stood on a raised platform and can be seen on the right of this photograph.

Eventually, the determination of the Indian community, together with pressure from India and Britain, forced General Smuts to back down. Gandhi and Smuts signed an agreement on 30 June 1914, seven years after *Satyagraha* began. This was passed into law as The Indian Relief Act. The Act scrapped a heavy three-pence tax on Indians, legalised Hindu and Muslim marriages, and allowed for the free entry of educated Indians into the country.

RETURN TO INDIA

Gandhi left South Africa in 1914 and returned to India a hero. He looked very different from when he arrived. He had given up western dress and wore only a covering of woven cotton cloth.

Just before he left the country, he sent Smuts a pair of sandals as a present. Gandhi had made these sandals on Tolstoy Farm where he had lived a life of hard work and religious discipline. Smuts wore the sandals for 25 years and then returned them to Gandhi in India saying,

"I have worn these sandals for many a summer, even though I may feel that I am not worthy to stand in the shoes of so great a man."

1913   Gandhi led the Great March of 2 000 Indian workers and their families from Newcastle in Natal to the Transvaal Border. Gandhi was imprisoned for the fourth time and sentenced to nine months hard labour. However, Jan Smuts released Gandhi early. A year later, Gandhi negotiated a settlement with him regarding the position of Indians in South Africa.

1914   Gandhi left South Africa. He went on to lead India to independence from Brittain in 1947. But this man of peace was assasinated a few months later on 30 January 1948.

"The Gandhian philosophy of peace, tolerance and non-violence began in South Africa as a powerful instrument of social change. This weapon was effectively used by India to liberate her people. Martin Luther King used it to combat racism in the United States of America...The spirit of Gandhiji that is, the *Satyagraha* conceived and tested in Africa at the beginning of this century - may well be a key to human survival in the twenty-first century."

Nelson MANDELA

ARTIST > USHA SEEJARIM

ADDRESS > Hamidia Mosque, Jennings Street, Fordsburg, Johannesburg

"It was difficult to conceive of an idea for the memorial because I felt like it was such an important story. The idea is when the wheel beneath the cauldron spins, the word truth appears and the viewer sees an image of a pass burning."

GANDHI

Reverend Isaac WAUCHOPE
THE SINKING OF THE *SS MENDI*

"You are going to die, but that is what you came here to do... Let us die like warriors, the sons of Africa."

Reverend Isaac WAUCHOPE

Early on the morning of February 21, 1917, a month after leaving Cape Town harbour, the troopship *SS Mendi* was rammed in thick fog in the English Channel. She sank in 20 minutes. On board, the Reverend Isaac Wauchope rallied the servicemen to support the war effort in Europe: "You are going to die, but that is what you came here to do... Let us die like warriors, the sons of Africa." This was the last contingent of the South African Native Labour Corps to fight in Europe. Wauchope was among the dead that morning. Of the 895 on board, 647 lost their lives, among them 607 black troops.

Text from the Sunday Times memorial plaque

01 Reverend Isaac Wauchope, the first published Xhosa-language prison poet, spoke with great bravery to soldiers of the South African Native Labour Corp during the sinking of the *SS Mendi*.

02 Three days after the sinking of the *SS Mendi*, the South African government headed by Prime Minister Louis Botha received its first report of the disaster.

SECRET

UNION OF SOUTH AFRICA

Secret

PRIME MINISTER'S OFFICE
CAPE TOWN
24th February, 1917

Minute No: 763

MINISTERS have the honour to inform His
Excellency the Governor-General that a telegram
has been received this morning from the Record
Officer, South African Native Labour Contingent,
London, reporting/the arrival at Portsmouth
(I)
Hospital of fifteen Native Privates who are
described as "survivors from the transport "Mendi"
and (2) the death on the 21st instant as the result
of shipwreck in the English Channel of one European non-commissioned officer and eight Native
Privates who embarked on the transport "Mendi"
which left here on the 16th ultimo.

MINISTERS will be glad if His Excellency can,
as a matter of urgency, obtain by cable full
particulars of the disaster to which the report
refers.

Louis Botha

DISASTER!

Early one morning, when a thick fog had settled over the English Channel, the captain of the *SS Mendi* reduced speed and repeatedly sounded the foghorn. His warnings were in vain. The *SS Darro*, an empty meat-packing ship destined for Argentina, ploughed at full-speed into the *Mendi* and tore a huge hole in the ship's side. In only 20 minutes, the *SS Mendi* had sunk.

Most men aboard the damaged ship were asleep in their bunks when they heard the shouts to come up to the deck. In the panic and confusion that erupted, Reverend Isaac Wauchope emerged as an important leader. He calmed the men with his stirring words of patriotism and bravery. The men sang and stamped together as the *Mendi* sank into the bitterly cold sea.

'Be quiet and calm my countrymen, for what is taking place now is what you came here to do...Brothers, we are drilling the death drill. I, a Zulu, say here and now that you are all my brothers...Xhosas, Swazis, Pondos, Basotho and all others, let us die like warriors. We are the sons of Africa. Raise your war cries my brothers, for though they made us leave our assegais back in the kraals, our voices are left with our bodies...' *Reverend Isaac Wauchope*

Few made it to the lifeboats. Those who did, risked their lives to save others as Dr le Hertslet recalled at a memorial service for the disaster many years later:

01

>> •

1852   Isaac Williams Wauchope was born in Doornhoek, near Uitenhage in the Eastern Cape, into a prominent mission-educated family.

1888   Wauchope enrolled at Lovedale College, a bastion of black education in the Eastern Cape.

"I hear myself say, 'Goodbye, my strength is gone', and then I feel the strong hands of a Native gripping my wrists and holding me up. Then several others catch me round the chest and shoulders and drag me, nearly dead, into the boat, and so I am saved."

"[Stump] made no inquiries and took no steps... to ascertain the result of the casualty; remaining in the vicinity and doing nothing for, in all, nearly four hours. In the opinion of this Court, his inaction was inexcusable."

Many more troops could have been saved had the master of the *SS Darro*, Henry Stump, acted appropriately. Stump refused to lower lifeboats from his ship and he made no attempt to rescue those on board the *Mendi*. According to evidence later provided to an official enquiry, Stump seemed unconcerned about the potential loss of life:

01 The *SS Mendi* carried troops during World War One. It travelled much of the world. Here, the Mendi was about to leave Port Calabar in Nigeria after picking up soldiers to be taken to the Western Front.

02 The *SS Darro* weighed over 10 000 tons, while the Mendi weighted only 4 230 tons, and this difference in size meant maximum damage when the two ships collided.

02

'SONS OF AFRICA'

The South African Native Labour Contingent (SANLC) was formed during World War I to provide essential labour services such as digging trenches, felling trees, loading ammunition and building roads and railways, as can be seen in this series of photos. Since black troops were not allowed to carry weapons of any kind, these jobs were very dangerous.

Despite this, 25 000 black South Africans responded to the call for help and volunteered to serve in the First World War. Some were attracted by the high wages on offer while others felt committed to the cause. The recruitment of black troops proved a controversial decision. Some white South Africans worried about the impact of introducing "raw Natives" into the hurly-burly world of Europe. An editorial in *The Star* of November 1916 noted:

> "It is highly undesirable to introduce raw Natives into civilised countries since they cannot be exposed to liquor and women without danger…Natives going overseas for non-combatant service would be contaminated and would return to South Africa to spread contamination among their own people and to prove a fertile source of trouble and friction in their relationships with whites…"

01 The government advertised widely for African recruits to assist in the war effort.

02 SANLC troops, pictured here in France, were often viewed with curiosity as they were the only black troops mobilised for the Allied Forces. In this photo taken in 1917, they are being inspected by King George.

03 SANLC members operating in East Africa provided essential support as transport drivers, often putting themselves in considerable risk as enemy troops would attack these vehicles.

1910   Wauchope was found guilty on one count of fraud after a parishioner alleged that he had altered the will of an individual under his care. He was sentenced to two years in prison where he wrote a series of letters and poems. They appeared in the Xhosa language newspaper *Imvo*, making Wauchope the first published author of Xhosa prison literature.

1912   Wauchope was released from prison due to his impeccable disciplinary record and because members of the public, both black and white, petitioned for his release.

The conditions for SANLC troops were much the same as for migrant labourers on South Africa's gold mines. The troops were housed in compounds, forced to carry passes, and were not allowed to interact with any Europeans. The handbook provided to the white officers leading the SANLC, entitled 'Appendix to Notes for Officers of Labour Companies (South African Labour)', set down strict rules for how SANLC troops were to be treated in France:

> "Compounds should be surrounded by an unclimbable [sic] fence or wall, in which all openings are guarded…Under the conditions under which they are living in France, they (the Natives) are not to be trusted with white women, and any Native found wandering about without a pass and not under escort of a white N.C.O. should be returned to his unit under guard, or failing this, handed over to the military police."

It was this treatment that made the SS Mendi tragedy that much more poignant – not only did over 600 SANLC members die, but they died taking part in a war in which they were treated like second-class citizens.

04   Members of the SANLC, pictured here in East Africa, assisted allied troops by performing manual labour such as loading transport trains.

05   SANLC member felling trees.

06   SANLC troops digging trenches.

1914
28 July   Over 21 000 members of the SANLC left South Africa to provide support to British troops in France. These black South Africans were not armed, and were housed in separate compounds from Europeans, lest they became infected with "the sin of self-confidence".

1916
September   The SANLC began recruiting 'Native' soldiers to provide labour on the war-front. It attracted a huge number of volunteers. By January 1918, over 25 000 black South Africans had joined.

A CALLOUS RESPONSE

It took three days for the first report of the SS Mendi disaster to reach the South African government. 649 men died, of whom 607 were black. Prime Minister Louis Botha recognized the valuable work done by the 'Native' soldiers on board the *SS Mendi*. He led members of the all-white Parliament in a minute's silence. This tragic incident was, however, forgotten in the months and years to come by all but the survivors and the friends and families of the victims. This letter of condolence, sent by the Wesleyan Methodist Church of Kimberley, is an example of the outpouring of grief expressed mainly by black South African organisations at the time.

This letter pledged solidarity with the Union and argued for the SANLC to remain active: "Though disaster has overtaken us…we do not intend to hold back, but to go forward, and assist our Sovereign in any capacity that may be allotted to us, to uphold the flag under which we enjoy liberty."

Despite these pledges of solidarity, the government disbanded the SANLC. The announcement was met with dismay, especially amongst black South Africans, who felt that this act undermined their rights to defend their own country. Even more shocking, the Union government refused the British government's offer of £50 000 for medals for African combatants in World War I. Survivors went without honour or medals for the rest of their lives. It was only after apartheid ended, that the story of the *Mendi* was retold. A new corvette ship bought for the SA Navy was named the *Mendi* to commemorate the tragedy.

Resolution I.

We have heard with deep sorrow, of the loss of the Transport Ship "Mendi", on which a large number of our countrymen were sailing to join the members of the Labour Contingent, and who lost their lives by the collision in the English Channel on the 21st February 1917.

We extend our sympathy to all the bereaved, and pray that they may be sustained and comforted by the thought that their loved ones lost their lives while in the execution of their duty, for King and Empire.

Resolution II.

We, the Native members of the Wesleyan Methodist Church, Kimberley, assembled in our Centenary Church, on the occasion of the Memorial Service for our fellow countrymen who lost their lives in the transport "Mendi", while on their way to assist the Empire in the great struggle for freedom, desire to express our unswerving allegiance to the King, and our loyalty to the Government of our country.

Though disaster has overtaken us by the loss of so many of our people, we do not intend to hold back, but to go forward, and assist our Sovereign in any capacity that may be allotted to us, to uphold the flag under which we enjoy liberty, and where so many opportunities are given to us for self-improvement, and advancement.

We pledge ourselves to use our influence in urging our young men to assist our Empire in any capacity, to bring the war, by Divine help, to a successful issue.

1916-1918	Over 21 000 SANLC members left South Africa to provide support to British troops in France.	
1917 February	The *SS Mendi* collided with the *SS Darro*. The Mendi sank over the course of the next few hours.	

"These people (the Natives) said: 'This war is raging and we want to help', and in so doing they have shown their loyalty to their flag, their King, and country, and what they have done will redound to their everlasting credit."

Prime Minister General Louis BOTHA,
in a speech delivered in Parliament in 1921 to mourn the Mendi disaster.

· ·

ARTIST > MADI PHALA

· ·

ADDRESS > World War I Training Ground, University of Cape Town

This sculpture is set on a grassy embankment on the middle campus of the University of Cape Town. This was the site, some 90 years ago, where troops of the South African Native Labour Contingent gathered before marching to Table Bay harbour and embarking for France on the SS Mendi. The sculpture evokes, in Phala's words, "the history of the people - the black corps, the officers and the crew members".

Phala said his brief was to avoid anything "epic or monumental", which posed a significant challenge in developing the piece:

"It was very limiting. I think in epic and monumental terms, but the joy of it was the challenge...It's not like you look at it and you've got the answers, you'll still want to talk to me, you'll want to ask me questions...It's not all about what I'm saying, it's about how you perceive it. That's very important."

Enoch MGIJIMA

BULHOEK MASSACRE

"You are informing me that you are coming out with an adequate force. Do you mean that you are coming out to war against the God of Israel? If you then Sir, Mr Truter, are coming out to make war please inform me. I shall then write or say my last word before you destroy me."

Enoch MGIJIMA
in a letter to Colonel Theo Truter, days before the Bulhoek massacre

01

On May 24 1921, police killed at least 183 Israelites – followers of the prophet Enoch Mgijima – in a 20-minute battle at Bulhoek near Queenstown. About 500 white-robed men, armed with sticks and spears, challenged the machine guns of an 800-strong police force brought in to remove the Israelites who had settled at the holy village of Ntabelanga, or Bulhoek, to pray. Mgijima was charged with sedition and imprisoned. On his release in 1924, he and other survivors started building this tabernacle, where the massacre is commemorated annually by the Church of God and Saints of Christ, as the Israelites are now known.

Text from the Sunday Times memorial plaque

01   Enoch Mgijima, pictured here in Israelite regalia, was an imposing and charismatic figure. He attracted over 3 000 followers from around the country to his tabernacle in Bulhoek.

02   The reaction to the Bulhoek Massacre was instantaneous and overwhelming. The Communist Party, who issued this flyer, condemned the massacre as a heavy-handed attack on black freedoms.

9/85 3/20

MURDER!   MURDER!!   MURDER!!!

THE BULLHOEK MASSACRE

CHRISTIANS SLAUGHTER THEIR CHRISTIAN BRETHREN
GREAT EMPIRE DAY CELEBRATION.

How appropriate and how much in keeping with the Matabele Massacre, and other of their brutal Empire building tactics.   And the Bullhoek tragedy was either by fate or circumstances enacted on their very Empire Day.

We accuse the responsible Government, whose forces are headed by a brutal assassin, of murdering unarmed strikers in Johannesburg 1913,— slaughtering unarmed natives in Port Elizabeth 1920,— and their latest debauch is the gruesome mutilation of hundreds of natives who were Christians and passive community.

Hence, this brutal invasion is truly symbolical of Governmental tyranny in their hysterical efforts to exploit the workers, irrespective of their particular colour or religous beleifs, and to maintain their position functioned by an idle and parasitic class; their armies are ever available to suppress any liberterian effort from the oppressing yoke of Capitalism.

A condemnation meeting will be held on the Parade at 11 a.m Sunday morning.

Sunday evening Adderley Street.

St. Marks Schoolroom, Tennant Street, Monday evening 30th at 7.30 p.m.

Published by The United Communist Party, 20 Plein Street, Cape Town, and printed by The Commercial Press, 64 Sir Lowry Road, Cape Town.

THE MFENGU PEOPLE

Enoch Mgijima was the youngest of nine children. His father – the farmer Jonas Mgijima – was one of the Mfengu people who had received land from the British in Ntabelanga or Bulhoek, meaning 'mountain of the rising sun'. The Mfengu, a largely Xhosa-speaking group, had come to the Eastern Cape between 1820 and 1840 after fleeing the Zulu kingdom during the *Mfecane* - a period of turmoil in the interior of the country. Finding themselves caught between the hostile Zulu army on one side, and the British army on the other, they decided that their best bet was to side with the British. The land they accepted was in return for the Mfengu's support in the white settler 'frontier wars' against African communities along the Eastern Cape frontier.

The Mfengu adopted a Christian way of life. They wore Western clothing, built square houses and attended mission churches. The Mfengu were a relatively prosperous community at first. But in 1896/7, an outbreak of rinderpest decimated their herds of cattle and this was followed by a severe drought. White government laws undermining independent black farmers, especially the 1913 Land Act, took a heavy toll on the Mfengu.

Mgijima grew up in a Wesleyan Missionary household. He left Bulhoek at the end of Grade Five to study at Lovedale but returned home due to chronic headaches. He became a small landowner and hunter. He also became a member of the local Wesleyan Methodist Church and worked as a lay preacher and then as an evangelist in his region.

AN ANGEL APPEARS

One day, when Mgijima was nearly 40 years old, he had a vision that changed his whole life. He was out hunting when an angel appeared before him. The angel told him to educate his people and lead them back to the "old ways of worship". He felt very confused by this at first and decided to leave the Wesleyans to join a small church from America. Shortly, Enoch started his own church group called the Israelites.

Many people decided to join Mgijima's church especially after he predicted the end of the world. This was in 1919, just after the First World War. The Mfengu faced many difficulties at this time. The Great 'flu had killed more than a 1 000 people in the area. A very bad drought had destroyed the crops and killed the cattle. Mgijima brought a message of hope and comfort. He promised his followers that they could become God's chosen ones. He called them to gather and pray at his tabernacle in Ntabalenga. Robert Edgar, a scholar who has written much on Bulhoek, comments:

> "Mgijima's prophecies offered one alternative - of dramatic change, hope, salvation, comfort, solace – that was extremely attractive. The outside world might be antagonistic and hostile, but at Ntabelanga, Mgijima promised a reversal of roles. The outcasts were now God's chosen and blessed ones." *Robert Edgar, Because they Chose the Plan of God.*

01

>> •

1868   Enoch Mgijima was born in Bulhoek, 25km south-west of Queenstown.

1907   While out hunting, Enoch Mgijima had his first prophetic vision.

'WE WON'T MOVE'

That year, the Israelites decided not to leave Ntabelanga as they usually did after celebrating Passover. By 1921, 3 000 followers had gathered at Bulhoek. Brick houses, streets and a courthouse, the signs of permanent settlement, emerged despite Mgijima's reassurances to the local inspector of African locations that this was a temporary gathering. The government accused the Israelites of squatting illegally, and tried to persuade them to leave. Some of the people who were already resident in the area also didn't want the Israelites to stay as they claimed the Israelites were using their grazing land. Repeated delegations, including black leaders, urged the Israelites to leave the land. Mgijima's brother Charles declared: "God sent us to this place. We shall let you know when it is necessary that we go." The Israelites refused to leave.

CONFLICT LOOMED

After heated communications between the Israelites and the authorities, violent conflict seemed inevitable.

In early May 1921, Colonel Theo Truter gathered the largest police contingent ever assembled in South Africa in Queenstown, near Ntabelanga.

Truter shared little sympathy with the claims of the Israelites. He issued the ultimatum below to the Israelites telling them that he was there to remove them from Ntabelanga, and warned them "that any resistance to lawful authority will be drastically dealt with".

02

```
To.
      ENOCH MGIJIMA and ALL associated  with him and styling
themselves "ISRAELITES" at NTABELANGA.


      YOU ARE HEREBY NOTIFIED that upon instructions of the
Government, I have come to Queenstown and will arrive at
Ntabelanga on Monday the 23rd instant with adequate force
to carry out certain orders which are detailed hereunder
namely:-

   1.  To arrest certain men against whom warrants have been
       issued in order that they should be dealt with accord-
       ing to law.

   2.  To see that all unauthorized residents leave Ntabelanga
       and go back to where they came from.

   3.  To destroy all houses erected without authority.

   4.  On completion of these operations a Force will be left
       on Ntabelanga to prevent any unauthorised resident
       squatting there.

      Every one's person and property will be respected.

      YOU ARE WARNED however that any resistance to lawful
authority will be drastically dealt with.



                                        Commissioner,

                                        South African Police.

Queenstown
   21st May 1921.
```

01 Enoch Mgijima called over 3 000 Israelite followers to his tabernacle, a collection of patchwork tents in Ntabelanga, after he had a vision in which he foresaw the end of the world.

02 Colonel Theo Truter, head of the South African Police Force gathered near Bulhoek, issued this ultimatum three days before the massacre. It ordered the Israelites to vacate the land peacefully.

1910 Mgijima predicted that a star would appear in the east. In April, Haley's comet streaked across the sky and this helped him to gain respect as a visionary preacher.

1912 Five hundred African Christians left the Wesleyan Church to join Mgijima. Mgijima began baptising members of his church in the Black Kei River in Ntabelanga

Ntabelanga,

Cape Province,

22nd May 1921.

To Theo T. Truter,

Commissioner,

South African Police,

Queenstown.

Sir,

Yours of the 21st. instant duly to hand, I feel glad that to-day I am able to express myself to you, how God has sent me to his people. On the 19th April 1907, the Lord God had appeared to me by a vision. I was only a hunter of game and a sinner before God, but the God of Heaven and earth appeared to me and sent me to His people and whosoever shall hear his word, saying do you hear the sound from the west. The Lord informed that the war will began in 1914, and from thence there shall be no peace on earth. The Lord God also informed me from what side it shall appear when it comes in Africa. You are just on its track, as you now stand. This war is not for the kings nor the rulers of this world, but it is the war of the Lord God of Israel. I the servant of the Lord do inform you therefore. That this war is not caused by me nor any earthly kind.

I understood that you Sir, intent to come out to Ntabelanga with an adequate force, may it therefore be known by you and all, that the armies and forces shall be ruled by God. As for myself, I am a messenger before the blood. The whole world is going to sink in the blood. I am not the causer of it but God is going to cause it. I am a man of blood, said the Lord. Th Lord of hosts is his name. The time of Jehovah has now arrived, all nations are invited to the marriage of the Lord God of heaven and earth and also to the sacrifice of the God of Heaven and Earth Rev.19:17-18 Ezek 39:17-20. God has now taken kindness away from human

human being.

(1) In reference to your letter, as to arrest certain men, this has already been replied to the Magistrate and to Native Superintendent of Locations, Kamastone.

(2). As to unauthorised residents to leave Ntabelanga, this point has been often replied to even at the meeting in which you were present in December last, at last with the commission of three men.

(3) As to destroy houses erected. All houses were erected with the permission of the Authorities. This point has also often replied to. I understood that you sir, were coming out with an adequate force, and if resisted will drastically deal with. We are here praying to the God of our fathers, therefore we do not believe that Jehovah will allow it. I have been praying the government about this matter for a very long time, until now, and am still praying the Government to allow the Israelite to pray their God. You are informing me that you are coming out with an adequate force. Do you mean that you are coming out to war against the God of Israel?. If you then Sir, Mr Truter, are coming out to make war please inform me. I shall then write or say my last word before you destroy me.

Yours faithfully,

(sd) E.J. Mgijima.

GOD'S SERVANT

Mgijima, who saw himself as God's servant, told Truter that he could not move, asserting as seen in the letter to the left: "I am a messenger before the blood. The whole world is going to sink in blood…"

Mgijima had another vision of people falling and the police coming from many directions. He gathered his followers and told them they should leave. They chose not to.

Colonel Truter had lost patience, as he made very clear in his letter to the Secretary of Justice, seen on the right. All attempts, he claimed, would be made to avoid bloodshed but, if "resistance is offered there will be no alternative and the Israelites will have to be taught a lesson."

01 Mgijima's response to Colonel Truter's ultimatum informing Truter that he refused to move the Israelites from Bulhoek and that he could not control the wishes of God.

1919   Enoch predicted the coming of a cataclysmic millennium. He urged all his followers to gather at Ntabalenga. By 1921, over 3 000 people had settled around the Israelite Tabernacle in Ntabelanga. The gathering upset local administrators, who urged the followers to vacate the land, or face violence.

1920   The Superintendent of Locations met with Mgijima over his concerns at the number of followers gathered at Ntabalenga. Mgijima promised that his followers would leave after a service on the 18th of June. This did not happen. Tension mounted between the Israelites and local authorities.

SOUTH AFRICAN POLICE
ZUIDAFRIKAÄNSE POLITIE.

S.A.P. 50.

DEPARTMENT OF JUSTICE
RECEIVED
MAY 26. 1921
CAPE TOWN.

Queenstown,

23rd May 1921. ——191—

The Secretary for Justice,
Parliament Street,
Cape Town.

SUBMITTED TO
MINISTER.
26/5/21

Re "ISRAELITES AT NTABELANGA"
))))))))))))))))))))))))))))))))

I have the honour to advise you for the information of the Minister that I arrived at Queenstown with Deputy Comm- issioner Trew on Tuesday the 17th instant. The various detachments of Police ordered to Queenstown were still arriv- ing from day to day and mobilization was completed on Friday the 20th instant. The Force consists of:-

Mounted; 30 Officers and 586 other ranks.
Foot: 112 other ranks.
Machine Gun Troop: 1 Officer and 41 other ranks, with three Maxims.
Artillery: 2 Officers and 55 other ranks with 2 Guns.
Medical Staff: 1 Officer and six other ranks.

Opportunity was taken whilst mobilizing to train the men to work together, an opportunity they have never had before. On Saturday morning, the Force was given Regimen- tal Drill with Machine Gun detachments and did very well.

General Van de Venter expressed himself very satisfied.

On Friday afternoon, after consultation with the Magistrate and the Secretary for Native Affairs, I addressed a letter to the "Prophet" a copy of which is attached, I also gave it publicity in the local press.

This was done to give the Israelites and the Natives generally an idea of what is intended to be done so that they should not have any reason, subsequently, to excuse resist- ance (if any) to ignorance of what was intended.

In reply I received a communication from Enoch Mgijima a copy of which I attach, to which I replied as per further copy attached, at the same time warning the messenger (a most intelligent native) that we did not come to war on them but that resistance to lawful authority would entail most serious consequences.

The Force consisting of :-
Mounted: 22 Officers and 590 other ranks.
Maxim Gun Troop: 1 Officer and 42 other ranks with 3 machine guns.
Artillery: 2 Officers and 55 other ranks with 2 guns.
Medical Staff; 1 Officer and 6 other ranks, left this morning and will encamp on the farm Potgieters Kraal to- night where General Van De Venter and I will join it.

(2)

A sufficient force consisting of 112 other ranks of foot Police, in addition to those usually stationed here, have been left in Queenstown for eventualities.

Tomorrow, Tuesday the 24th instant, we shall commence dealing with the Israelites at Ntabelanga.

I trust that the steps I have taken will have the approval of the Government and, I can assure the Minister that every- thing possible has been arranged to prevent any bloodshed. If, however, resistance is offered there will be no alternat- ive and the Israelites will have to be taught a lesson.

Commissioner,
South African Police.

1921 24 May	Eight hundred policemen attacked 500 Israelite men. After a battle of 20 minutes, at least 183 Israelites were left dead. Enoch Mgijima and his brother Charles were arrested.
1921 December	Mgijima was sentenced to six years hard labour for sedition after a highly publicised trial.

04

SPECIAL EDITION
TEN MINUTES OF TRAGEDY.
FULL STORY OF BULLHOEK FIGHT.
THE CHARGE OF THE WHITE-ROBED FANATICS.
A BLOODY ENDING TO A MAD ESCAPADE.
CASUALTIES NOW ESTIMATED AT 200 TO 250

In last evening's issue of The Argus a brief account appeared from our Queenstown correspondent of the grim tragedy which occurred at midday yesterday outside the Israelites' camp at Ntabalanga. To-day our correspondent sends the appended detailed story of the fight, which presents a vivid picture of what happened when the fanatical Israelites made their mad charge on to the loaded rifles and fixed bayonets of the police. In this narrative our correspondent gives a later estimate of the casualties amongst the Israelites, which are now put at between 200 and 250, including over 100 dead.

01 In the aftermath of the massacre, the Eastern Cape scrubland in Bulhoek was dotted with the bodies of the fallen Israelites. Here, a surviving Israelite stands next to one such body, draped in a white sheet.

02 An Israelite in full regalia speaks to mounted members of the South African Police Force. In the wake of the massacre, nearly 150 Israelites were arrested and transported to Pretoria for a mass trial.

03 Both Enoch (right) and Charles Mgijima (centre, with a bandaged leg) were arrested after the massacre. After a highly publicised trial, both were sentenced to six years hard labour.

04 This special edition of *The Argus* newspaper carried a full report of the massacre the following day.

BLOODSHED

At 9 a.m. on 24 May, 800 policemen formed into five detachments on the slopes overlooking Ntabelanga. Charles Mgijima acted as commander of the Israelites and divided 500 of the strongest men into five age regiments armed with *knobkieries* and spears. The women and children sat and prayed by the tabernacle. How the massacre actually began is disputed. The outcome, however, is not. Dressed in white robes, the Israelites were conspicuous targets as they ran towards the police lines. The police fired a few shots over their heads, but then they found their range and began killing mercilessly. The rifles and machine guns sliced through the Israelite men. Despite the odds, the Israelites kept on charging. They yelled at the police, '*Magwala*' (cowards) and 'You will all die here'.

After 20 minutes, the battle was over. After the massacre, the Israelite men began to dig mass graves to bury the dead while the police tore down the Israelites' makeshift homes.

AN UNBROKEN SPIRIT

The judge found Mgijima and the other arrested men guilty of sedition and declared it "a crazy notion that the black man would have his freedom". After six years of hard labour, Mgijima was released from prison due to poor health, and settled in Queenstown. His spirit was not broken. After his release, he rebuilt the tabernacle at Queenstown. He died two years later on 5 March 1926. Queenstown became the centre of the Israelite Church. Today, there are Israelite congregations throughout the Eastern Cape.

1924   Mgijima was released from prison due to poor health, and settled in Queenstown.

1926
5 March   Mgijima passed away in Queenstown. He had attempted to rebuild the Israelite Tabernacle in Queenstown for the final two years of his life.

"This was one of the first times after the union of South Africa that the white government used police and army troops to crush a group of Africans who would not obey its laws. Unfortunately, it has not been the last."

Robert EDGAR

ARTIST > MGCINENI SOBOPHA and MICHAEL BARRY

ADDRESS > Israelite Temple, Queenstown

The cenotaph - memorial column - created by Mgcineni 'Pro' Sobopha and Michael Barry recalls a tragic episode in South African history that was kept hidden during the decades of apartheid.

Sobopha says the Bulhoek massacre "raises issues around forced removals, land and colonialism" and "intersects the areas of religion and politics". Religion, he adds, often became the place to which African people turned, while being stripped of their land and their rights.

The story of Enoch Mgijima and the Israelites evokes a spirit of defiance and survival - the church is thriving today. The artwork reflects this abiding strength. Sobopha and Barry repaired the fence around the Israelite temple and incorporated the cenotaph as a special feature of the new fence.

Nontetha NKWENKWE

"We are not making war against you; we are your servants living in this place for the purpose of praying and fearing God's wrath which is coming upon the whole world...We humbly beg you to give us a chance to pray."

Delanto QUASHE,
follower of Nontetha Nkwenkwe, in a letter to the Minister of Native Affairs

01

On December 6, 1922, at the King William's Town magistrate's court, the prophetess Nontetha Nkwenkwe was committed to Fort Beaufort mental hospital for "medical observation" as hundreds of her followers sang hymns outside. Nkwenkwe had begun having visions and preaching temperance after surviving the 1918 'flu epidemic. Authorities feared her growing popularity would threaten white rule and the established churches. After she was moved to Weskoppies hospital in Pretoria two years later, 36 of her followers walked there on a 55-day 'pilgrimage of grace'. Nkwenkwe died at Weskoppies in 1935. In July 1998 her body was exhumed and returned - via the pilgrims' route - to her home. The Church of the Prophetess Nontetha survives to this day.

Text from the Sunday Times memorial plaque

01 There are no photos of Nontetha Nkwenkwe. This is an artist's rendition of Nkwenkwe derived from contemporary descriptions. It was painted by Lizo Pemba, the grandson of George Pemba.

02 Nkwenkwe's followers continuously wrote to the colonial government requesting that Nkwenkwe be released from her imprisonment at Weskoppies Mental Hospital. They were unsuccessful in their attempts.

Qekwane
Tamacha P.O,
King Wms Town
10th Jan, 33

Dear Sir

I ask you to allow me to repeat my
words to you. Our application to you is to ask you
to release the prophetess on leave, and if you
don't please point out the reason why you
should not let her out because first Government
sent out ministers of the Gospel to preach it
among the people now when the prophetess
also came by the same way you imprisoned
her and said she's mad? Now I ask
from our Authorities to point us out what is
truth and what is error because I think if
what she preaches is an error
the whole world must also be the same
Dear Sirs if our Authorities have sympathy
with us must also realise all these expenses
of coming up there yearly. Awaiting your
reply

yours obedint Servant

Delanto Qoshe &co.

THE BIRTH OF A PROPHETESS

Nontetha Nkwenkwe was born in a village near King William's Town in a rural area of the Ciskei. She was illiterate her whole life. Her husband, a migrant worker in the Western Cape, died shortly after the last of Nkwenke's ten children was born. Nkwenkwe took on the responsibility of supporting an extensive family.

During the Great 'flu epidemic of 1918, Nkwenkwe caught the 'flu. She went into a deep coma. While she lay unconscious, God spoke to her. He told her that she must become a religious leader and educate her people to stop abusing alcohol. Zakile Jati, the bishop of Nkwenkwe's Church, told the story of her vision that has passed down through the years:

> "When she was asleep she saw two men. They took her to a beautiful land with beautiful houses...Then there comes a word from a cloud. This word says go back to the earth and stop the coal fires because God couldn't see the earth because of the smoke from the fires on which people were brewing African beer."

Nkwenkwe wrestled with this calling. In her further conversations with God, she was told that if she did not agree to preach, this task would fall to her daughter. Nkwenkwe wanted to protect Nokazi and approached traditional chiefs and their counsellors for help. They gave her permission to preach.

Nkwenkwe cut a very dramatic figure in a white robe and head-dress with a white sash wrapped around her waist. She carried a long black stick. Her male converts were equally striking in white coats and shoes. During her services, she would ask her followers to sit in a semi-circle in front of her and to come forward and kneel on her white sash so that they could ask for unity and for their hearts to be as white as her belt. Because she could not read, she held her hands open, looking into her palms as if she was reading from the bible. Sakomzi Tole, an evangelist of the church, describes Nkwenkwe's message:

> "She was saying, 'ibumbaya manyano' which means 'unity' in English. Her message was, "If you are united the Devil cannot destroy you..."

At first, she had an avid local following of about five hundred people and the colonial authorities welcomed her preaching. She did not call on her followers to rise up against the government in any way. They saw Nkwenkwe as helping in the conversion of Africans to Christianity and in promoting temperance.

IMPACT OF BULHOEK

The Bulhoek Massacre in May 1921 changed everything. The site of the massacre, where the Israelites had been moved down for refusing to leave the land, was not far from where Nkwenkwe lived. As the historian Robert Edgar comments,

> "The colonial authorities now had a very keen eye out for any prophet, any religious leader who was operating in that region of the Ciskei and Transkei. They very much wanted to keep a lid on any religious figure because they didn't want a repeat of Bulhoek, and that's when Nontetha came to their attention."

Nkwenkwe was not preaching anything radical at the time. She did not call on her followers to rise up against the government. Indeed, her message was very moderate. But her support base was growing and the magistrates in Fort Beaufort and King William's Town made up their minds that she was a destabilising influence in their area. The problem for them was that Nkwenkwe was not violating any law and they had no pretext to arrest her. Robert Edgar describes how the authorities dealt with this conundrum:

> "Rather than bring her up on a trumped up charge, they decided to silence her by defining her as mentally insane. They said that she's hearing voices from God, therefore she must be crazy."

1875 Nontetha Nkwenkwe was born.	**1918** The Great 'flu epidemic spread rapidly through South Africa. In the same year, the Medical Disorders Act was passed and empowered magistrates to order the detention of people suspected of mental disorder if there were two supporting medical certificates.	**1922** After the Bulhoek Massacre, authorities became more concerned about religious movements in the Eastern Cape.

A DISTURBING ELEMENT

On 6 December 1922, the authorities committed her to Fort Beaufort Mental Hospital for observation. Here, she was diagnosed with schizophrenia. She was released on 6 January 1923 but was ordered to refrain from preaching or else face arrest.

Nkwenkwe refused to stop preaching. Police spies from King William's Town monitored her activities and relayed the message that she was a trouble-maker to the authorities. The letter below shows how the authorities increasingly tried to portray Nkwenkwe as a "disturbing element among the natives" whose teachings needed to be "carefully watched".

01

No. 139/23.

SOUTH AFRICAN POLICE.

KING WILLIAM'S TOWN.
29th APRIL 1923.

The Deputy Commissioner,
    South African Police,
        GRAHAMSTOWN.

NATIVE UNREST ON THE KEISKAMA.

With reference othe attached reports of Sub-Inspector Norman, No. 1600(M) Sergt. Searle A.B. and No. 1875 (M) L/Sergt. Wagenaar, J.A. I have the honour to inform you that I went into this matter thoroughly with the persons named and the Magistrate and Superintendent of Natives at Middeldrift. It appears that the Prophetess Nonenta or Nonteto first commenced her disturbing influence amongst the natives in May 1922 at the Newlands Location, East London. She was ejected there and resumed her preaching at Tamacha Location from whence she was placed under restraint in the Mental Hospital, Fort Beaufort on the 6th December 1922. She was released by the Superintendent of the Fort Beaufort Mental Hospital on six months probation early in January 1923 and in February resumed her preaching, being again arrested and confined in the Mental Hospital, Fort Beaufort on the 7th instant.
        She is of the Tribe of Chief Gangalizwa (Magquakwebes) of Ngabassa Location and gives out that she died and a vision appeared to her telling her to return to her tribe and prepare them for the downfall of the Europeans when they will come into their rights again. She appeals only to the red kaffirs preaching against their drinking kaffir beer and buying the white man's drink. They have first and foremost to abandon their native dress red blanket and adopt the European attire, both males and females. She has also told her followers that they must not go to the mines to work nor do any manual labour in their lands. This is however disputed by the Superintendent of Native Locations, Middeldrift who informs me that since she started preaching the young men and girls of the Tribe do the coffling of the lands instead of the old women. The Chief Gangalizwa and the Petty Chief Tamsanga Lutuli of Ngabassa Location are both favouring and encouraging this woman's doctrine against the Tribe. Up to the time of her arrest (7th instant) she had a following of 150 to 200 men and women and at each meeting the kraals used to supply goats for slaughter to feed her followers, 10 to 15 goats being slaughtered at a time and sometimes a beast. This naturally appealed to a large number of natives who attended the meetings knowing they would be well fed. Owing to her instruction in regard to clothing the traders have reaped a golden harvest in the sale of men's clothing and women's dress material as also shawls and in a number of instances natives have disposed of cattle to the traders to get the money to purchase clothing.
        Since her arrest her mantle has descended on a young

2.

        This is a disturbing element amongst the natives and the movement will have to be carefully watched. It would be fatal were the Prophetess Nontenta allowed out again and the Magistrate of Middeldrift has requested the Superintendent of the Mental Hospital, Fort Beaufort not to liberate her without giving him prior warning. The natives areas yet, even in the Ngabassa Location, very divided in opinion as to the Prophetess and this new form of religion, some holding it as nonsense while others think that there must be something in it. She informed her followers that the recognised churches were only money making concerns and that they must not have anything to do with them. With the incarceration of the Prophetess it may die out but I have instructed Sergeant Searle and L/Sergt. Wagenaar of Fort White to keep in touch, by the aid of the detectives named with the movement and keep your office and that of the Magistrate of Middeldrift fully advised. The Magistrate of Middeldrift (Mr. John Tudor) wished me to bring to your notice the promptness and dispatch with which the apprehension of this woman was effected by L/Sergt. Wagenaar of Fort White. Within five hours approximately of the receipt of the telephonic warrant she had been apprehended and escorted into Middeldrift, a distance of approximately 30 miles having been travelled on horseback and by cart in the performance of this duty.

        I consider that pressure should be brought to bear on Chief Gangalizwe and Petty Chief Tamsanga Lutuli whose encouragement of the movement is only adding fuel to the flames.

        Your complete file No. 139/23 herewith.

                sgd E?Tomley Hutchone. Major.
            DIVISIONAL INSPECTOR. S.A POLICE.
            EASTERN CAPE DIVISION.

COPY/.

01 In this letter, it is claimed that Nkwenkwe's preachings were causing political disturbance.

1922 6 December	Fearful of Nkwenkwe's growing following, the authorities had her committed to Fort Beaufort Mental Hospital for observation. She was diagnosed with schizophrenia.	1923 7 April	Nkwenkwe was arrested, held at Fort Beaufort Hospital, and later moved to Weskoppies Mental Hospital in Pretoria, after refusing to stop preaching.

SEDITIOUS! INSANE!

As the weeks went on, the accusations against Nontetha became more dramatic. Sergeant JA Wagenaar managed to extract this damaging statement, shown below, from Sergeant Sinono Maneli. Nkwenkwe was arrested on 7 April 1923, held at Fort Beaufort Hospital, and later moved to Weskoppies Mental Hospital in Pretoria - thousands of kilometres away from her family and her church followers. The authorities hoped this would be the end of the story. Little did they know what lay in store.

Nkwenkwe was held under atrocious conditions. The image of a comfortable mental hospital could not be further from the truth. Robert Edgar noted that mental hospitals, which were racially segregated, were seen as "place(s) of confinement for hopeless, incurable cases". They were overcrowded, had "desperately inadequate" food supplies and sanitation, and lacked full-time medical supervision. The mental hospitals in which Nkwenkwe was interned, reportedly operated under conditions of "sheer poverty and neglect".

01

As these meetings which they pretend to be religious as merely a blind, as you Nonteta's people discuss secretly certain seditios subjects, i.e. that the black race must combine to throw over the Europeans, (2) that the existing churches are money making concerns under the control of the Europeans (3) the existing Bible is a fraud (4) that the American Negroes are coming who will cut the throats of the Europeans and converted natives who are converted underthe existing churches; these are the things that will cause trouble and is causing trouble.

The Chief Tamsanga Kama had ordered that all these seditios meetings must cease, what power have you Non-teta's followers to oppose his order. They did not reply to this and went to their repective homes. I was under the impression that the matter will cease, but I found that they are still holding their meetings secretly at night.
sgd SINONO MANELI.

Statement taken by me at Ngcabassa on this 15th day of May 1923.

sgd J.A. WAGENAAR. L/SGT.
S.A. POLICE.

01   Over time, the government distorted Nkwenkwe's messages. Although she explicitly rejected the teachings of prophets such as Enoch Mgijima, and welcomed the European presence in South Africa, the authorities portrayed her as seditious and treasonous.

02   Nontetha Nkwenkwe was interned at Weskoppies Mental Hospital

'PILGRIMAGES OF GRACE'

Upset by the internment of their leader, Nkwenkwe's followers refused to allow the matter to rest. They organized a series of 'pilgrimages of grace' to Pretoria to demand her release. Denver Webb, Director of Museums in the Eastern Cape, describes one such pilgrimage:

"One elderly gentleman said to me, 'Every day we prayed, every morning we prayed and we would get to a farm and they would give us a barn to sleep in and a sheep to slaughter.' So they saw this as some sort of mission in going all the way to Pretoria."

On 10 February 1927, the *Rand Daily Mail* reported these events:

"PROPHETESS" AMONG PHILISTINES

NATIVE FOLLOWER'S PASSIVE RESISTANCE

To rescue Nonteta, their prophetess, from the hands of the "Philistines," her followers have shown that they are prepared to endure insults, hardships and tribulation, and are now busy in demonstrating to the authorities in Pretoria the extent to which they are prepared to sacrifice personal comfort and convenience for the sake of what is to them an ideal.

1926	Nkwenkwe's followers undertook a	1930	Nkwenkwe's followers launched a second
23 November	'pilgrimage of grace' to Pretoria to have their leader freed. They arrived 55 days later, in mid-January 1927.		'pilgrimage of grace' to secure her release. The police were tipped off about the march, and the followers were arrested for not having passes to enter the Orange Free State.

36 : 37

The article continued:

> "Nontetha...is in the Pretoria Mental Asylum, and recently 36 of her followers arrived from King William's Town, having walked all the way, to try to secure her release.
>
> The authorities have proved adamant, and the latest development in this curious battle is the adoption of passive resistance tactics by Nontetha's followers. They definitely refuse to leave Pretoria until Nontetha is released.
>
> As a result, twelve were arrested and charged under the pass-laws on Monday, being fined £1 each, the sentence to be suspended for 24 hours on condition that they left Pretoria. Late yesterday afternoon the period of suspension terminated, but they were still in Pretoria. They will now be arrested, and will probably be charged under the Urban Areas Act."

THE RESPONSE OF THE AUTHORITIES

Persistent appeals for Nkwenkwe's release forced Dr J T Dunston, the Commissioner for Mental Hygiene, to re-assess her case in 1928. Although he conceded that she did not pose a threat or danger to anyone, he nevertheless recommended to officials that they forbid any further contact between Nontetha and her followers. He claimed that "visits from her relatives and followers have a very disturbing influence and make her mentally worse".

Undeterred, her followers again tried to see her in 1930. This time, the government stopped them at Aliwal North, arrested them for travelling out of their area without passes, and sent them home. But these protest actions again forced a medical examination to clarify the situation and justify Nontetha's continued incarceration. On 2 June 1930, FD Crosthwaite, Physician Superintendent in the Office of the Mental Hospital in Pretoria, wrote, the letter seen on the right, to JT Dunston.

F.N. 859

Office of the Mental Hospital,
Pretoria.
2nd June, 1930.

The Commissioner for Mental Hygiene,
Union Buildings,
Pretoria.

With reference to the detention at this Hospital of Female Native patient Nontete, No. 859, I have the honour to report as follows:-

At a Conference held at this Hospital on May 1st, 1930, Nontete was seen by all the medical staff, who were unanimous in the opinion that the patient was mentally disordered and properly detained in the Mental Hospital on the grounds that the following symptoms have been repeatedly and constantly observed during her detention here:-

1. Acute hallucinosis.
2. Delusions of a grandiose nature.
3. Delusions of poisoning.
4. Emotional attitude of religious exaltation with a state of restless excitement.

The following questions may arise and I have endeavoured to answer them:-

1. Is there any reason why Nontete should not be allowed conditional discharge to specified relatives?

   Nontete is not a danger to herself, and there is no reason why she should not be so discharged having regard only to her mental condition.

2. Is Nontete likely to again prove herself a source of disturbance, and possibly, danger to the preservation of order amongst her people, if discharged conditionally?

   The answer to this question must be "yes". Not much encouragement would be needed I fancy to rekindle her activities in the direction of her mission, and it is very difficult to estimate the probable strength of the restraining influence exercised by her knowledge of what would happen if she broke the conditions of discharge.

3. Is it advisable to refuse a conditional discharge and to bring the matter to the length of a Judicial Enquiry?

   Yes.

(sgd) F.D.Crosthwaite.
PHYSICIAN SUPERINTENDENT.

| 1930 June | Nkwenkwe's case was reassessed by Dr FD Crosthwaite. He classified her as a paranoiac, in the sub-group "prophets, saints and mystics". | 1930 -1935 | As a result of the assessment by Dr FD Crosthwaite, Nkwenkwe was kept at Weskoppies Hospital until her death. | 1935 20 May | Twelve years after she was first admitted to hospital, Nkwenkwe died of liver and stomach cancer at Weskoppies. |

A PAUPER'S BURIAL

On the basis of Crosthwaite's report, JT Dunston wrote to Major Herbst of the Department of Native Affairs on 11 June 1930. His words sealed Nkwenkwe's fate.

> "Dear Major Herbst...I forward herewith a copy of a report by the Physician Superintendent of the Pretoria Mental Hospital...I would add that I know Nontetha personally and am well acquainted with her case and I would express my opinion more strongly than Dr Crosthwaite has. I feel sure that if she is discharged there will be a repetition of all the troubles which occurred before she was sent to a mental hospital. Her hallucinations and delusions have never changed in character. They are only less prominent at the moment because she has not an opportunity of feeding them on the credulity and admiration of her followers."

In the end, Nkwenkwe was never released, and died alone in Weskoppies on 20 May 1935. She was buried in an unmarked pauper's grave:

> "The sad aspect of the whole thing was that long after she died, they sent a telegram to Fort Beaufort which was then presumably the nearest magisterial post or address and only a long time afterwards was delivered to the community, by which time she'd been given a pauper's burial... Typically these paupers' graves had two, three people buried in the same grave, and of course there were no grave markers. It was an open field." *Denver Webb, Director of Museums in the Eastern Cape*

Some 55 years later, after much groundwork to find where her remains were buried, researchers Bob Edgar and Hilary Sapire organised for Nkwenkwe's remains to be returned to the Eastern Cape. On a Sunday in October 1998, Nontetha Nkwenkwe was laid to rest next to her church in her home village, Kulile.

Still today, in houses all around the Eastern Cape, men and women gather each Sunday for worship. Their uniforms are white and black, with a sash over their shoulders and across their chests. The preaching is intense and when the congregation stands to sing, their voices engulf the room. They are part of the congregation of the Church of the Prophet Nontetha – a church which now claims a following of some twenty thousand people throughout the country.

1998
July
The American academic, Robert Edgar, discovered and exhumed Nkwenke's remains after an intense investigation to find her grave.

1988
October
Nkwenkwe's remains were returned to her followers. She was buried at her home in a grand ceremony.

"What made her story very poignant was the way she was treated. Unlike some of the other people who might have been leading resistance movements, they didn't give her her moment in court. By not doing this…she was rendered ineffective and taken out of circulation."

Denver WEBB, *Director of Museums in the Eastern Cape*

ARTIST > LENNLEY WATSON

ADDRESS > Magistrate's Court, Alexandra Street, King William's Town

Lynnley Watson feels a personal connection to the story of Nkwenkwe. "I had an emotional, gut reaction to the story as soon as it was relayed to me. It felt as if the commission had been tailor-made for me as it fitted in so well with my current work. My work centres on women's issues, particularly women from disadvantaged backgrounds, who have contributed to society, often under very challenging circumstances." Watson has also completed a large sculpture of the Xhosa prophetess Nongqawuse and a work about Aids called *Altered States*.

Watson sculpted Nkwenkwe holding her staff and praising God.

2 SEGREGATION AND EARLY APARTHEID

1930s -1951

This section investigates the impact of racial segregation - how people dealt with their frustrations and how they tried to bring the evils of the system to the attention of the world. The stories begin in the 1930s and end in the early years of apartheid when a string of new discriminatory laws were imposed.

Early 1930s The South African Communist Party (SACP) led the way in the adoption of a more aggressive form of protest against segregationist laws.

1934 Jan Smuts (of the South African Party) and Barry Hertzog (of the National Party) joined forces to form the United Party. More hard-line members of the National Party left in disgust and formed the 'Purified' National Party.

1935 Albert Luthuli was elected Chief of the Groutville Mission Reserve.

1936 The small number of black people who could still vote, lost their right. In a conciliatory gesture, the government reviewed the Land Act and provided additional land for black people. It was still only 13% of SA and no land could be purchased outside of the 'Native reserves'.

1937 Pirates soccer club, the forerunner of Orlando Pirates, was formed in Soweto.

1938 Cissie Gool was elected to the Cape Town city council, becoming the first black female city councillor in the country.

SAHA/*SUNDAY TIMES* MEMORIAL SITES:

1 Albert LUTHULI	2 Orlando PIRATES	3 Cissie GOOL
International Conference Centre, Durban, KwaZulu-Natal	*4503 Khunou Street, Orlando East, Soweto, Johannesburg*	*Long Market Pedestrian Mall, between Buitenkant and Plein Streets, Cape Town*

1940-1946 Mass-based resistance grew. Anti-pass protests, bus boycotts and squatter movements sprung up in urban and rural areas. These struggles often attracted younger people.

1943 A more radical group formed in the ANC, including Mandela, Sisulu, and Tambo. They formed the ANC Youth League and called for more militant action.

[4]

11 February 1948 Alan Paton's most famous novel, *Cry, the Beloved Country*, was published.

28 May 1948 The Purified National Party bitterly opposed Prime Minster Smuts' decision to take SA into the Second World War on the side of Britain. They developed the idea of apartheid and promised to solve the "native problem" by limiting all contact across the colour line.

1948 The National Party (NP) came into power in the 1948 elections under the former Dutch Reformed *Dominee* (Reverend) DF Malan. The NP controlled the country for the next 46 years.

1949 Racial segregation hardened. The Mixed Marriages Act of 1949 was the first act to be passed followed by the Immorality Act of 1950. The laws prohibited inter-racial marriage and sex.

December 1949 The ANC adopted the Programme of Action which spelled out a more aggressive form of resistance. The ANC Youth League replaced the more conservative Dr Xuma as ANC President with James Moroka.

[5]

1950 The Population Registration Act enforced the classification of people into four racial categories – white, Coloured, Indian /Asiatic and Native. A Registration Board was set up to judge cases where there were disputes about a person's racial identity.

1950 The government used the Suppression of Communism Act to silence political leaders. Many were banned from speaking in public or from attending political gatherings.

1951 In 1951, Coloured people lost their limited rights to vote through the Separate Representation of Voters Act.

1951 The "most shameful session" of the all-white Parliament placed some 75 pieces of racist legislation on the statute book in a single sitting. The ANC launched a campaign of non-violent resistance later called the Defiance Campaign.

[6]

19 December 1951 Bessie Head was informed of her mixed race heritage, and was barred from returning to live with her adoptive family.

---

[4] Alan PATON
Ixopo High School, 1 Lewis Drive, Ixopo, KwaZulu-Natal

[5] Race CLASSIFICATION
High Court Annex, Queen Victoria Street, Cape Town

[6] Bessie HEAD
Werda Hoerskool, 90 Parkside Road, Hillary, Durban, KwaZulu-Natal

Albert LUTHULI

"I, together with thousands of my countrymen, have in the course of the struggle for these ideals, been harassed and imprisoned, but we are not deterred in our quest for a new age in which we shall live in peace and in brotherhood."

Albert LUTHULI, *Nobel Peace Prize Acceptance Speech*

Chief Albert Luthuli was the first African recipient of the Nobel Peace Prize. As a lay preacher, teacher, president general of the ANC and an international statesman, he spent most of his adult life fighting for the freedom and human rights of the majority of South Africa's population. Despite the apartheid government's attempts to silence and isolate him from public and political life, Luthuli retained his role as leader of the ANC for 15 years, until his tragic death on July 21 1967. It was on this day that Chief Luthuli was found injured next to a railway bridge. He died of a cerebral hemorrhage and contusion to the brain at about 2.25pm that afternoon. As a banned person, he could not be quoted at his own funeral.

Text from the Sunday Times memorial plaque

01 Albert Luthuli at home in 1964 during the time of his banning.

02 This document shows how the government limited Albert Luthuli's power as a chief. He was unable to hear legal cases ranging from murder to "suspected witchcraft".

02

N.A. 117.

Telegrafiese Adres:
Telegraphic Address:
"NATIVES."

UNIE VAN SUID-AFRIKA.

UNION OF SOUTH AFRICA.

DEPARTEMENT VAN NATURELLESAKE,
DEPARTMENT OF NATIVE AFFAIRS.

Posbus
P.O. Box } 384,

PRETORIA.

No. 188/53.

21 SEP. 1950

Chief Albert Lutuli,
C/o The Chief Native Commissioner,
PIETERMARITZBURG.

Greetings,

    With reference to your appointment as Chief of the abasemaKholweni tribe resident in the district of Lower Tugela, I have to inform you that the Honourable the Minister of Native Affairs has approved, with effect from the 1st December, 1943, of the conferment on you of jurisdiction to try and punish according to Native Law and Custom any Native who has committed, in the area under your control, any offence punishable under Native Law and Custom except the following offences which should be referred to the Police:-

        Treason; Sedition; Public Violence; Murder; Culpable Homicide; Rape; Robbery; Assault with intent to commit murder, rape or robbery, or to do grievous bodily harm; Indecent assault; Arson; Theft of Stock; Sodomy; Bestiality; Perjury in a Court other than a Chief's Court; Offences committed against persons or the property of persons not being Natives; Pretended Witchcraft; and any conspiracy, incitement or attempt to commit any of these offences.

    In the exercise of this jurisdiction you may impose a fine not exceeding five pounds upon any person convicted by you of any such offence.

    A copy of the regulations made by the Minister of Native Affairs for the guidance of Chiefs in the exercise of criminal jurisdiction is attached for your information.

Greetings,

SECRETARY FOR NATIVE AFFAIRS.

HUMBLE BEGINNINGS

Albert Luthuli's parents, John Bunyan Luthuli and Mtonyi Gumede, were married in Groutville, a small town near Stanger in KwaZulu-Natal. They later moved to Southern Rhodesia (now Zimbabwe) where his father was an evangelist and interpreter at a mission station near Bulawayo. It was here that Albert Luthuli was born, the third son in the family. "I cannot be precise about the date of my birth", Luthuli wrote in his autobiography, *Let My People Go* "but I calculate that I was born in the year 1898, and certainly before 1900." When Luthuli was about ten, his father passed away and his family returned to Natal. He lived with his uncle, Martin Luthuli, the chief of Groutville. Luthuli began his schooling at the local mission school and went on to take a teacher training course at a Methodist institution in Pietermaritzburg. After his graduation, he returned to his rural roots to run a small primary school in Natal and it was here that he became a lay preacher.

Religion was a powerful force in Luthuli's life. The teachings of the Congregational Church in which he was raised, strongly influenced his political commitment and his dedication to non-violence and human rights. In a speech he made much later in his life, Luthuli stated,

"We should rest content in the conviction that we are performing a divine duty when we struggle for freedom." Speech to the first Natal Congress of the People in Durban, 5 September 1954

A TEACHER AT HEART

Luthuli was recommended for a government bursary to further his teacher training at Adams College in 1920. On completing the two-year course, he was offered a job at the College - the second African to be offered a teaching position. He stayed in this job for the next 13 years. It was here that he met and married Nokukhanya Bhengu, one of his students and later also a teacher at Adams. Together they had seven children.

Whilst teaching, Luthuli was elected Secretary of the African Teachers Association in 1928, and President in 1933. This was the start of a long and illustrious political career.

In 1933, Luthuli's life reached a turning-point. The tribal elders of Groutville asked him if he would replace the incumbent Chief. Luthuli delayed responding to this request for two years. He felt that he was a teacher at heart. He was also troubled by the notion that Chiefs would be authorised by the Native Affairs Department, paid a salary, and limited in their power.

01

ON HIS DISMISSAL FROM THE CHIEFTAINSHIP OF THE ABASE MAKOLWENI TRIBE IN THE UMVOTI MISSION RESERVE, GROUTVILLE, LOWER TUGELA DISTRICT, NATAL,

by

ALBERT JOHN LUTULI,

18th November, 1952,

P.O.Groutville Mission, Natal.

What have been the fruits of my many years of moderation? Has there been any reciprocal tolerance or moderation from the Government, be it Nationalist or United Party? No! On the contrary, the past thirty years have been the greatest number of Laws restricting our rights and progress until to-day we have reached a stage where we have almost no rights at all: no adequate land for our occupation, our only asset,cattle, dwindling, no security of homes, no decent and remunerative employment, more restrictions to freedom of movement through passes, curfew regulations, influx control measures, in short we have witnessed in these years an intensification of our subjection to ensure and protect White Supremacy.

>> . . . .

A SERVANT OF THE PEOPLE

In 1936, Luthuli finally agreed to stand and was elected Chief of the Groutville Mission Reserve in 1936. He explains his change of mind:

> "I think that perhaps all the emphasis which Adams (College) had placed on service to the community bore fruit. I recognized now that the call of my people was insistent, and the reasons I gave for declining the request of the tribal elders seemed to me to be excuses for not going to their aid."

Luthuli assumed his duties in the context of a rapidly segregating South Africa. Much of his work was as a petty administrator, running the affairs of his 5 000 constituents. He was given jurisdiction to try court cases according to "Native Law", but was strictly limited as to exactly what cases he could hear, as seen in the letter from the Ministry of Native Affairs on the opening page. However, Luthuli achieved some successes for those who fell under his chieftainship.

During his tenure as Chief, Luthuli's eyes were opened to the harsh realities of South African life. In his biography he wrote, "Now I saw, almost as though for the first time, the naked poverty of my people". He also reflected in a speech

in 1952, how Chiefs were put in an "invidious" position. As a "servant of the people", a Chief needed to look out for their constituents' interests. But as government-appointed bureaucrats, Chiefs were forced to institute government policy, which was aimed at subjugating their own people:

> "Any Chief worthy of his position must fight tirelessly against such debasing conditions and laws. If the government should resort to dismissing such chiefs it may find itself dismissing many Chiefs..."

Luthuli's relationship with the Native Affairs Department became increasingly tense as his involvement in politics grew. He became a member of the Institute of Race Relations as well as the Christian Council of South Africa. In 1944, he joined the ANC. He played a key role in the launch of the Defiance Campaign in 1952. The Native Affairs Department demanded that he either resign his chieftainship or resign from the ANC. After a tense meeting with the Native Affairs Department Secretary, Dr Eiselen, Luthuli refused to budge and he was subsequently 'relieved' of his position. But Luthuli remained a Chief in the eyes of many and was always referred as Chief Albert Luthuli.

Laws and conditions that tend to debase human personality- a God-given force- be they brought about by the State or other individuals, must be relentlessly opposed in the spirit of defiance shown by St.Peter when he said to the rulers of his day "shall we obey God or man?". No one can deny that in so far as non-Whites are concerned in the Union of South Africa, laws and conditions that debase human personality abound. Any Chief worthy of his position must fight fearlessly against such debasing conditions and laws. If the Government should resort to dismissing such Chiefs

it may find itself dismissing many Chiefs or causing people to dismiss from their hearts Chiefs who are indifferent to the needs of the people through fear of dismissal by the Government. Surely the Government cannot place Chiefs in such an uncomfortable and invidious position?

What the future has in store for me I do not know. It might be ridicule, imprisonment, concentration camp, flogging, banishment and even death. I only pray to the Almighty to strengthen my resolve so that none of these grim possibilities may deter me from striving, for the sake of the good name of our beloved country, the Union of South Africa, to make it a true democracy and a true Union in form and spirit of all the communities in the land.

01   Luthuli wrote this statement of protest after being requested to resign from the ANC or lose his position as Chief. He emphasised the impossible position of Chiefs since the government was making them enforce apartheid laws.

1933   Luthuli was elected President of the African Teachers Association. In 1935, Luthuli was elected Chief of the Groutville Mission Reserve.

1944   Luthuli joined the ANC. In 1951, he was elected President of the ANC's Natal Division.

BECOMING PRESIDENT OF THE ANC

A month after Luthuli was dismissed as Chief, he was elected President of the ANC, a position he held until he was killed in 1967. The government immediately banned Luthuli from addressing or attending public gatherings. When his first ban expired, he was banned again. His ban was finally lifted in 1956, Luthuli travelled extensively and made several public appearances. But his freedom was soon curtailed again. In December 1956, he was arrested along with 155 other comrades and imprisoned in the Old Fort in Johannesburg. The charges of treason against him and 64 others were ultimately dropped. However, Luthuli was banned once more and confined to Groutville for a period of five years. "I was back in Groutville, with the prospect before me of five years of isolation and frustration. It was a bleak outlook."

After Sharpeville, Luthuli publicly burned his pass and called for a national day of mourning. He was arrested amidst the government clampdown on political activity and the banning of the ANC and PAC. He spent five months in detention and was kept in the prison hospital because of his high blood pressure.

A NOBEL LAUREATE

Luthuli's tireless contribution to the fight for freedom and human rights was finally acknowledged when he received the Nobel Peace Prize in December 1961. Grudgingly, the government gave him a travel visa. His acceptance speech in Oslo was a rousing call for the continuance of non-violent protest against apartheid. He returned from Oslo to a life of virtual imprisonment and went back to writing his biography and managing his land.

AN UNTIMELY DEATH

On a cold winter morning, while walking from his farm stall to his home across the railway line, Luthuli was struck by a train. The train's engineer phoned the station manager who ran to the scene and recognised Luthuli at once. The manager called for an ambulance but it was too late. The hospital pronounced Luthuli dead. His burial service in the graveyard of the Groutville Congregational Church was attended by over 7 000 mourners and lasted four hours. Rousing eulogies and tributes were paid to this great leader of the struggle.

01  02

03

01 Chief Albert Luthuli (on right) with Dr Moroka in 1952, after he was appointed president of the ANC.

02 Chief Albert Luthuli and his wife Nokukhanya in London on their way to collect the Nobel Peace Prize, 7 December 1961.

03 The finding of the inquest made no mention of any other possible causes of Luthuli's death and cleared the South African state of "any criminal culpability".

1952   Luthuli played a key role in leading the Defiance Campaign. When he refused to resign from the ANC, the government revoked his chieftainship of Groutville. In December 1952, Luthuli was elected National President of the ANC.

1953   Luthuli was banned and prohibited from attending any political gatherings. Three years later, he was arrested as part of the Treason Trial.

"They took away his chieftainship but he never ceased to be the Chief. They took away his temporal power, but he never ceased to have the spiritual power. They took away his freedom but he never ceased to be free. He was, indeed, more free than those who had bound him."

Alan PATON

ARTIST > NOTOBEKO NTOMBELA and MONLI MDANDA

ADDRESS > International Conference Centre in Durban

The artists pay tribute to Chief Luthuli through a memorial displaying unity amongst people who are demonstrating their support for him. The artists explain: "This is a symbolic walk to the place where Chief Luthuli was injured. The railway line suggests the location. The cylindrical plinth suggests the structure built by the apartheid resistance movement with the Chief's influences. The circular railway track suggests the circle of life."

1960   After the Sharpeville Massacre, Luthuli publicly burned his pass. He was served with a banning order that confined him to Groutville.

1961 December   Luthuli travelled to Oslo to receive the Nobel Peace Prize.

1967 12 July   Whilst walking to his home in Stanger, Albert Luthuli was hit by a train. He died later that day.

LUTHULI

Orlando PIRATES

"In their wildest dreams they did not imagine Pirates to be the Pirates it is today…a big corporate and everything like that. For them it was getting the little boys in Orlando off the streets, playing and socialising. It progressed because of their popularity. People came and came…"

Ralph HENDRIKS,
one of the first so-called 'Coloureds' to join Pirates

In 1939, an eager band of schoolboys was transformed into one of South Africa's most formidable soccer teams, Orlando Pirates. This house (at 4503 Khunou Street, Orlando East, Soweto) was the home and headquarters of the team's first President, Bethuel Mokgosinyana, who turned the boys into professionals. He gave Pirates their 'colours', the black and white kit they wear today. Every Wednesday, for 10 years, the boys gathered to discuss game strategy; Mokgosinyana always opened and closed these marathon sessions with a prayer. On Fridays before matches the chosen team 'camped' here all night.

Text from the Sunday Times memorial plaque

01   Jomo Sono, one of Orlando Pirates' greatest players, leaps into the air after scoring a goal for Pirates in front of a packed stadium in Soweto in December 1979.

02   There were few avenues for leisure in the townships in the 1950s and 1960s. Being a soccer fan was one of the ways that residents enjoyed their spare time.

PASSION IN THE DUSTY STREETS

Orlando Pirates is far more than just a soccer team. It is an institution, a religion, a symbol of Soweto's vibrant urban culture and a testimony to the power of sport to overcome racial divisions.

Orlando Pirates' history is closely linked with the history of Soweto. In 1904, the government burned down the so-called Coolie Location (where Braamfontein stands today) on the grounds that it was a health hazard. What the government really feared was the inter-racial mixing; "the promiscuous herding of Indians, Malays, whites and Kaffir people" in this inner-city slum. The Johannesburg City Council removed the African population to a tented camp called Klipspruit, 13km from the centre of Johannesburg. Klipspruit was the nucleus of

01   This picture, taken in the early 1960s, shows a typical street scene in Orlando East. Orlando Pirates offered a chance for supporters to transcend these bland surroundings.

02   1960s Soweto was filled with stylistas emulating the style of black consciousness leaders overseas. Here, a stylish Sowetan shows off an African print miniskirt and a well-kept Afro.

03   In 1969, the apartheid state blocked an exhibition match between the top-ranked black side, Pirates, and the top-ranked white side, Highlands. These two teams were only able to face each other for the first time in 1982, as shown here.

Soweto. Further townships were built around Kliptown to accommodate Johannesburg's expanding black population. In 1935, the government built Orlando East. The township was named after a councillor in the Native Affairs Department, Edwin Orlando Leake. Conditions in Orlando were bleak: there were no roads, no parks, no lighting, no sanitation and no shops.

It was here that SA's most formidable soccer club had its roots. The Orlando Pirates Boys Club was established two years after the first residents moved into tiny matchbox houses in Orlando. This Boys Club was part of a network of recreational clubs that black people established at this time. It became a meeting place for students from surrounding schools and provided an escape from the monotony and dangers of township life. But it was missing something vital, as Sam 'Baboon' Shepherd Shabangu, one of Pirates' original players, recalls: "At the Boys Club we had everything - table tennis, physical culture, weight lifting, boxing...except football. So we asked: 'Why don't we have a football team of our own?' We called ourselves Orlando Boys Football Club." Their first coach, Pele Pele Mkhwanazi, was the local boxing instructor. Mkhwanazi wanted to prevent the boys from becoming *tsotsis* (gangsters) by giving them something fun and constructive to do. A year later, the team joined the Johannesburg Bantu Association despite competing barefoot and without a kit.

>> ·

1873   Members of the Orlando Boys Club organised themselves into an official soccer team. Two years later, some players left after a fight over stolen funds and formed a new team which they called, 'Pirates'. 'Orlando' was added to the name ten years later, at the same time as the famous skull and crossbones became the club's insignia.

1945   Orlando Pirates was promoted to the Johannesburg Bantu Football Association's First Division, South Africa's strongest league.

A LEGEND IS BORN

The arrival of Bethuel Mokgosinyana on the scene changed the fortunes of the club. Mokgosinyana was a relatively wealthy factory foreman, a devout Christian and, most importantly, a keen footballer. He joined forces with Mkhwanazi and became President of the club. He donated the club's first kits - a black top emblazoned with the letter P and white pants and provided boots for the players. The club also took on its now iconic name. Inspired by the Errol Flynn movies showing at the local movie theatres, the club was called Pirates. A legend was born as described by *Drum* magazine in June 1980:

'Mokgosinyane, a self-appointed social worker and keen footballer, invited a group of boys to his big yard at No 4305 Orlando East. The yard became theirs for football practice…this is how the mighty Orlando Pirates was born.

"Ya, those were the days," Mokgosinyane reminisces. "Yes, today Pirates players drive snazzy cars and jet all over for their matches, but things were tough in those early days. We used to walk from Soweto to George Goch for our games. We had guys like the legendary Isaac 'Rocks' Mothei, 'Baboon' Shepherd Shabangu and 'Buick' Buthelezi."

At first, only boys from Orlando were allowed to play for Pirates. Sam 'Baboon' Shabangu, tells how, "We were very selfish and didn't want people from outside to play for the team. We wanted children of Orlando to grow up with the name of the club on their lips. We had a team of 11 with only one reserve. And as a result we grew together and developed a very good understanding." James 'Hitler' Sobi, another player, remarks:

"In our era, the difference was that we had passion. It was the only thing for young boys to do. There was no TV. The highlight for every boy growing up was to be able to play soccer. Nowadays, there are so many distractions and only the real few who are dedicated go and play soccer. But then, virtually every young boy was passionate about soccer."

DIVIDE AND RULE

By 1942, Pirates had become the top team in Johannesburg. When semi-professional soccer came to South Africa in 1960, Pirates joined the non-racial South African Soccer League (SASL). But the League was not allowed to use municipal grounds because it was against government policy to have Africans, Coloureds and Indians playing together. In the late 1960s, the apartheid government tightened its control over sports. In 1969, it banned the much-awaited friendly game between Pirates and a white team, Highlands Park, which was to be part of independence celebrations in Swaziland. There was a huge outcry. Then in 1970, the government banned all racially mixed teams. Ralph Hendriks, a Coloured member of Pirates, remembers how,

"In 1970, the Chairman of the soccer league got a directive from the government that the races should not be integrated on the soccer fields. It was that divide and rule tactic of the old regime. So he sent out the decree that no Coloured or Indian players can play for black teams. There were five of us at the time playing for Pirates and we were then forced to leave or rather, Pirates was forced to let us go."

| 1952 | Pirates won every competition that it entered. It repeated the feat in 1972. |
| 1969 | Kaizer Motaung split from the team to form the Kaizer XI team (later Kaizer Chiefs). |

FAITHFULS

The phenomenal growth of Pirates from its humble beginnings is not just a story about soccer. It is also a story of how a new popular culture was forged as more and more black people settled in Soweto and created their own fashions, social rituals, ways of talking and musical styles. Soccer was at the centre of the new urban black identity. Professor Phillip Bonner comments:

"...the rise of Orlando Pirates symbolizes the growth and establishment of an African urban population. Orlando Pirates gained their support from that community and you can see it clearly: they gained mass support as Africans became settled in Soweto."

Pirates became known as 'The People's Club' and was affectionately called 'the Buccaneers' because of its skull-and-crossbones logo. By the early 1960s, the games drew huge crowds and soccer players and team managers became celebrities. Sport editor, Lesley Sehume, recalls: "These people were icons. They were role models. They inspired the local people."

Irvine Khoza, current chairman of the club, adds that not only were Pirates icons, but were also trendsetters:

"By association with club members and followers, people from outside the city would get a feel of the kind of dress sense that was required for one not to be detected as an

---

1971   Orlando Pirates won the National Professional Soccer League, and dominated club football for much of the decade. The team won the title four times in 1971, 1973, 1975 and 1976.

1976   Irvine Khoza, who played a key role in South Africa's 2010 Soccer World Cup bid, was appointed administrator of Pirates. He later became its owner and runs the club today.

outsider. In terms of being *klever* (street wise) and fashionable and buying the right records, it helped to be a Buccaneer faithful."

Fans became enthralled at the games and the team had to win at all costs. Supporters gave inspiration to players through the famous song 'Congo'. Mike Tseka comments that, "Remember the DRC war? That's how the song started because to Pirates every match was like a war that had to be won. Congo was where Pirates fans were. Even the players sang it as they went onto the ground to inspire themselves."

Pirates functioned as a social club that protected its members. Pirates supporters who worked for the local government went so far as to secure passes and urban residency rights for newly-arrived Pirates supporters. At one stage, the club had its own funeral *stokvel*, as Lesley Sehume recalls:

> "It was an institution. It was a great thing for you to become a member of Pirates. In fact, they started a burial society and you know, once a member or supporter died they even had a choir who would come to the funerals."

'PIANO AND SHOESHINE'

At a time of great repression in the townships during the 1960s and 1970s, Pirates managed to create a sense of power amongst the black community. Pirates' attractive brand of football, known colloquially as 'piano and shoeshine', was the ultimate statement of black beauty and ability. John Perlman, an avid soccer commentator, agrees:

> "If they're doing their tricks and sticking it to someone on the pitch, it's a glorious thing. It's saying, 'We do have something. Our community has something.' I really enjoyed it when a clever black player made an onrushing white player fall on his arse. That was me, as a white liberal, getting the thrill vicariously, so you can imagine how much it must have meant to the black player himself."

Pirates' distinct playing style was based on Brazilian football using short passes, creative flicks and big dollops of pace rather than the more stolid British style of long balls played to strikers adopted by white South African football teams. Peter Alegi, a prominent soccer historian claims that, "Pirates became black football's trailblazers." On and off the field, Pirates continuously charted new territories of success.

In 1952, Pirates won every competition it entered. But it was in the 1970s that Pirates really began to dominate local soccer. In 1971, Pirates won the National Professional Soccer League title. It repeated the feat in 1973, 1975 and 1976.

After the June 1976 student uprising, the team supported the youths who had taken to the streets to protest against Afrikaans as a language of instruction in schools. Donald Dliwayo, a former chairman of the club, organized a tour of the club in Botswana to help raise funds to assist young leaders to leave the country and join the ANC in exile.

01 Orlando Pirates No. 1 fan, Nale 'Mzayoni' Mofokeng, shows how support for Pirates could take over one's style of dress.

02 A white guard watches over exuberant Pirates fans during a match against Dynamos in 1979.

1976 Following the Soweto uprising, FIFA banned South Africa from international competition.

1979 It is unclear exactly when soccer became desegregated. This was an informal process but, from the pictures we have, mixed-race teams seem to have been commonplace by 1979. In 1981, the National Premier Soccer League formed the Zambuk division, which was multiracial. In 1982, Pirates and Highlands faced each other for the first time.

TRAIL BLAZERS

Over the years, acrimonious splits from Orlando Pirates led to fierce rivalries with other teams. Black soccer fans became divided. The most famous split was in 1969 when Kaizer Motaung, one of Pirates' best-known players, formed Kaizer Chiefs. This created great bitterness in the soccer world and Motaung was threatened more than once as a result of his action.

In 1982, a second team emerged out of Pirates. Cosmos was formed by Matsielela 'Jomo' Sono, son of the famous Pirates player, Eric 'Scara' Sono. Jomo, as he was known, gained his nickname from Jomo Kenyatta, the 'spear of Africa'. It was believed that Jomo Sono had the same leadership skill as this famous Kenyan leader.

In the post-apartheid period, Pirates again blazed the trail for South African soccer. In 1995, a year after South Africa's first democratic elections, the team won the premier African soccer competition, the African Champion's Cup. Pirates beat the Ivory Coast giants ASEC Mimosa in a tense match. By doing so, it became the first and only South African team to win an African title. The following year, Pirates contributed key players to the South African national team, known colloquially as Bafana Bafana, which won the first African Nations Cup South Africa had ever entered. As South Africa moves towards the hosting of The Soccer World Cup in 2010, cheering every goal and mourning every game lost, there is no doubt that soccer is the game of our country's people.

01 The exceptionally talented Jomo Sono
dribbles his way past two Durban City
defenders. A year after this game, Jomo
Sono split from Pirates to form his own club.

02 Eric 'Scara' Sono (right) would have been
proud of his son's achievements in soccer, even
though he eventually left the Orlando fold.

1982   Matsielela 'Jomo' Sono, one of Orlando
Pirates' key players, purchased the once
successful Highlands Park soccer team and
renamed it 'Jomo Cosmos'.

1985   After winning its first league title in decades the
previous year, Orlando Pirates won the African
Champions Cup. It was the first South African team
to win an African title.

"I think to Pirates fans it's not soccer, it's a religion:
I firmly believe that once a Pirate always a Pirate."

Ralph HENRICKS

ADDRESS > 4503 Khunou Street, Orlando East, Soweto, Johannesburg

Jazz, improvisation, collage and an enduring passion for the Bucs all contributed to Sam
Nhlengethwa's Orlando Pirates memorial.

"From a little boy of five years old, I've been a Pirates fan. I used to keep A3 foolscap exercise
books at school, and at the end of the year make that my album of Orlando Pirates."

Sam Nhlengethwa says his Pirates artwork was inspired by three visual references: the exterior of
Bethuel Mokgosinyana's house in Orlando East, Soweto, where the work is to be erected; a picture
of Mokgosinyana himself; and several news pictures of Pirates' supporters.

The figure of Mokgosinyana stands at the end of a group of posed players who were drawn
without any identifiable features.

Cissie GOOL

"Millions of people have died in the war against Nazism and Fascism...the battle for freedom is only beginning in this country. It must go from passive resistance to active resistance, then to strike action, until the whole economic machine of the country is paralysed."

Cissie GOOL, *Cape Times*, 22 July 1946

01

In August 1938, Cissie Gool was elected to the Cape Town City Council, the first black woman in the country to serve in local government. Known as the "Jewel of District Six" she represented the people of that constituency in the council until 1951. The daughter of city councillor and political leader Dr Abdullah Abdurahman, she was a founder and leader of the National Liberation League and the Non-European Front in the 1930s, and was active in the fledgling passive resistance movement. In 1962 Gool became the first black woman to be called to the Cape Bar.

Text from the Sunday Times memorial plaque

01   Cissie Gool was renowned for being exceptionally striking. As Amy Thornton, a political activist who knew Gool, has noted: "Cissie was quite a firebrand as a young woman, and apparently a great speaker and beautiful."

02   Cissie Gool was a revolutionary candidate for the Cape Town Municipal Council. Her demands spoke directly to the needs of the people of District Six.

BC506 A5·5

MUNICIPAL ELECTION

WARD 7   5th SEPT., 1938

VOTE FOR

"The People's Own Candidate"

"The People's Own Candidate"

Mrs. Z. GOOL
M.A.

(PRESIDENT OF THE NATIONAL LIBERATION LEAGUE OF S.A.)

Who stands for

1   DECENT HOUSING AND SANITATION
2   ADDITIONAL REFUSE REMOVAL SERVICES
3   MORE CRECHES AND CLINICS FOR THE POOR
4   OPEN SPACES FOR CHILDREN
5   THE ABOLITION OF SLUMS AND THE REFORM PARTY
6   EQUAL OPPORTUNITY FOR THE EMPLOYMENT OF COLOURED PEOPLE IN THE COUNCIL
7   HIGHER WAGES FOR MUNICIPAL EMPLOYEES
8   RECREATION GROUNDS AND A SWIMMING BATH FOR WARDS 6 & 7
9   NO RESIDENTIAL SEGREGATION
10 THE IMMEDIATE CONSTRUCTION OF A PUBLIC HALL FOR WARDS 6 & 7

STEWART, CAPE TOWN

SOUTH AFRICA'S 'JOAN OF ARC'

Zainunnisa 'Cissie' Gool was dubbed 'Joan of Arc' by the South Africa press after the French martyr who led her people to battle against their enemies. Like Olive Schreiner before her, Cissie Gool was a woman far ahead of her time. She was born in 1897 in Cape Town to a prominent political family. Her father, Dr Abdullah Abdurahman, was the first black South African elected to the Cape Town City Council, a position he held until his death in 1940.

Her father ensured that Cissie had a good education. He hired both Mohandas Gandhi and Olive Schreiner to tutor her. In 1913, Dr Abdurahman, along with the father of Cissie's future husband, founded the Trafalgar School for Coloured Pupils. The school delivered outstanding education and Cissie studied there for two years.

Cissie's determination and independence were evident from a young age. At 13, she wrote a poem that later won the African People's Organization prize for best poetry in the Junior Division. Emblematically, the poem, on the opposite page, was about a mother who would not let her child be free and independent, and watched him die as a result.

At the age of 22, Cissie married Dr Abdul Hamid Gool and they had three children. Whilst raising her kids, Gool attended university and became the first black woman to receive a degree from the University of Cape Town. A year later, in 1933, she obtained a Masters Degree in Psychology.

OUT THERE

Gool became increasingly politically active. While her father was a moderate early 20th-century politician, she was far more radical. In 1936, she joined the Twenty Club, a discussion group for prominent socialist academics such as James la Guma, Sam Kahn and John Gomas. That same year, Gool played a key role in the formation of the National Liberation League of South Africa (NLL), which called for the end to racial segregation. She became president of the NLL in 1936, making her the first woman to lead a liberation movement in South Africa. As Justice Albie Sachs has noted: "At a time when woman's role was to be in the kitchen and to look after children, Cissie was out there."

Cissie snubbed social conventions in her private life as well. After being elected president of the NLL, she left her husband and moved in with the Jewish communist and co-activist, Sam Kahn. The move scandalised Cape Town's community, especially the Muslim community in which she was brought up. As Amy Thornton recalled in the SAHA radio documentary on Cissie Gool:

"She and Sam Kahn had this mad love affair. They must have been a very dramatic couple, because he was a handsome and poetic, brilliant, truly brilliant man, tall, and Cissie was a lot older than him, but everyone maintained she was the love of his life."

>>

1897 Zainunnisa 'Cissie' Gool (nee Abdurahman) was born into a prominent political family in Cape Town.

1912 Gool won first prize for a poem and a short story she submitted to a literary competition organised by the African People's Organisation.

HIS MOTHER'S BOY

Prize Poem

Miss Z. Abdurahman

His eyes were bright, his hair was fair,
  He was his mother's boy;
He was her pride, her only child,
  Her only loving Roy.

Around his neck in flaxen folds
  His golden ringlets fall;
His cheek was like the crimson rose,
  His eyes like the blue-bell.

She loved her child as life and death,
  No sweeter child could find.
Oft in the eve when all was still,
  She would instruct his mind.

They lived within a cottage small,
  Upon the lonely moor.
Both were proud, and spoke to none;
  Yet both were very poor.

When children sought his company
  On any summer's day;
She'd proudly check the little mites,
  And lead him then away.

None saw the boy, he, too, was proud.
  He was his mother's boy.
None but her proud and selfish self,
  His presence could enjoy.

A sad day dawned, and the happy lad
  Lay sick upon his bed;
His crimson cheeks, now turned white,
  His curls tangled on his head.

Both day and night she guarded him
  With deep maternal care;
She now looked on a faded flower,
  Once radiant, rich and fair.

She promised to give her boy to the world,
  If ever he recovered;
But one winter's night the hour came,
  Twixt life and death he hovered.

She knelt beside the pining child
  With anxious, tearful eyes.
Oh, God! her boy was sinking fast,
  Perhaps would never rise.

Lo! next day when the sun arose
  O'er snow-white clouds above,
An angel clad in heavenly robes,
  Descended crowned with love.

He smiled, and pointed to the bed,
  Where lay the dying Roy:
"Your God, he sends me," he gently said,
  "To claim your only boy."

All things seemed hushed at the voice of death:
  The angel shone with light.
He clasped his hands and gazed above,
  Then vanished out of sight.

She gazed upon her child's death-bed.
  Where God's gold light once shone;
His soul had passed from death the live,
  And she was left alone.

She bowed her head before the Lord.
  And yielded up her child;
Gone was her haughty, selfish spirit,
  She was humbled, meek and mild.

Anxious for a Prize.

[01] Cissie Gool's early writing reflected her
need to break free from the constrictions
of parental and social authority.

1913 Dr Abdurahman Gool founded the Trafalgar
School because of the lack of good schools
available for Coloured children in the Cape.

1919 Cissie married Dr Abdul Hamid Gool and
they had three children; Rustum (1923),
Shaheen (1926) and Marcina (1931).

A PASSIONATE ORATOR

Gool grew increasingly involved in politics. In 1937, the Cape Government tabled the Segregation Ordinance that introduced rigid residential segregation in Cape Town. The ordinance enraged Gool and her political colleagues. She organized a march on the Grand Parade in Cape Town under the banner of the NLL. This major event had a lasting impact on the politics of the Cape, as Yusuf Rassool, a relative, later recalled:

"I heard our Auntie Cissie rousing the crowds with her passionate oratory, and her singing in an electrifying soprano: 'We'll hang Oswald Pirow from a sour apple tree', to the tune of John Brown…We left for home before the end of the meeting when the crowd went on the rampage and Cape Town had a night of terror. Several constables' helmets were sent flying, and several heads were truncheon-bashed with the only weapon the police carried in those days. But the mass meeting had succeeded. The legislation was abandoned for the time being, but the police thereafter carried arms."

THE FIRST BLACK WOMAN COUNCILLOR

After two years as President of the NLL, Gool ran for a seat in the Cape Town Municipal Council to represent District Six. Her message, at the time, was revolutionary: poverty alleviation, social justice and an end to segregation. She made a major impact. She beat her rival, Mr MacCullum, by 280 votes. She was the first black woman to serve on the Cape Town Municipal Council. Her next election victory was even more impressive, as she beat her challenger, Dr Gow, by 644 votes.

01 This picture was taken at the first congress of the NLL held in 1937. Cissie Gool is in the centre of the front row.

02 Cissie Gool with other members of the NLL after she was elected President in 1936.

03 Cissie Gool was able to captivate crowds with a fiery passion and a deep commitment to the ideals of justice and equality.

1933   Gool enrolled at the University of Cape Town in 1918 for a Bachelor of Arts Degree. She completed her Masters Degree in 1933.

1936   Gool split from her father's political views and was elected president of the newly-formed National Liberation League (NLL).

Cissie Gool was an immensely popular councillor. She won the trust of her constituents, and made a real impact on their day-to-day lives, as these two quotes show:

"She was handing out tickets to kids in the street to go to the Star Bioscope up the road in Hanover Street, to see *Snow White and the Seven Dwarves*, in colour. It was like magic for us. It was those kinds of things that left an impression on me as a boy." *Stan Abrahams, former resident of District Six*

"Mrs Gool...hits straight from the shoulder, and is vigilant, fearless and uncompromising. She is a woman who has been consistent in her fight for the rights of all citizens. Whenever any threat of segregation appeared in any form Mrs Gool has been in the forefront to defeat it."

Letter to the Editor, Cape Standard, 29 August 1944

01 An intimate portrait of Cissie Gool, tagged with the word "me", taken a year after her election to the Cape Town Municipal Council.

02 Cissie Gool won the support of many members of the Cape Town local government, who saw her as a champion of their cause.

01

02

> BC 506 A2·18
>
> REPLY: BOX 1536.
>
> In reply please quote:
> Geliewe by beantwoording aan te haal:
>
> No._____
>
> ### UNION OF SOUTH AFRICA. - UNIE VAN SUID-AFRIKA.
>
> CIVILIAN PROTECTIVE SERVICES,
> BURGERLIKE BESKERMINGSDIENSTE,
> DEPARTMENT OF JUSTICE,
> DEPARTEMENT VAN JUSTISIE,
> OLD G.P.O. BUILDING, · OU H.P.K.-GEBOU,
> ADDERLEY STREET. · ADDERLEYSTRAAT.
> CAPE TOWN. · KAAPSTAD.
>
> 5th.Sept.,1944.
>
> Mrs.Z.Gool,
> 25 Exner Avenue,
> Vredehoek,
> CAPETOWN.
>
> CONGRATULATIONS.
>
> Dear Mrs Gool,
>
>   This is to congratulate you on your success in the contest against your opponent, Dr. Gow, in the event of the Council-election. We, the City Council's employees would be deeply sorry, like many other people, should you have missed your seat. As far as we concerned, we always wished you a successful win in this occasion only for your ir-racial and anti-National efforts in the interest of everybody's difficulties,especially the poor people. We have known you from pre-war days down to the present precarious period. Your assistance for the people needed a heavy support from all the electoral dimensions.These are the sort of people we want for representing the majority.
>   We again hope for your inexhaustible efforts with their events during the term of the Council and that you try as you did before, to give a help where it is necessary, especially for the Native folk who have caused a great confusion in the minds of the White. The Coloured folk looks up to you for their help as well.
>
>   Though I, personally, do not know your face, I have known you from the Press and have appreciated every motion from your mentality. But I will one day give me chance to visit you as I have from now known your address.
>
>   I beg to be sir,
>
>   Yours in the struggle,
>
>   Moses J.Dumalisile.

1938 Gool won a seat in the Cape Town Municipal Council as representative of District Six. She held the post until 1951.

1946 Gool became increasingly involved in the Passive Resistance Movement. This eventually led to her arrest in Durban.

In 1946, Gool joined the Passive Resistance Movement (PRM). The movement began after World War Two to fight the fascism that had threatened Europe. She quickly became a key player in the Movement and led several marches with Sam Kahn against racist merchants in Cape Town. In July, she was elected chairwoman of the Cape PRM. She held meetings throughout the country, and was encouraged by the success of the PRM in India that had led to the country's independence from Britain.

But her actions, now on a national scale, caught the attention of the police. She was arrested in Durban in 1946 for the first time. In 1951, she was again brought before a magistrate and fined for holding a public meeting. She resigned from the Cape Town Municipal Council as a result of this intimidation. She also resigned in protest at the apartheid government's newly passed Group Areas Act of 1950 which introduced strict racial segregation - something she had fought against her whole life. In 1954, Gool was banned under the Suppression of Communism Act. This ban effectively silenced her and ended her career as a political leader.

Gool refused to be cowed. She decided to gain legal expertise to continue her fight. In 1962, she completed a law degree at the University of Cape Town. She was called to the Cape Town Bar, becoming the first black woman advocate. She intended to continue her struggle from this new position of power.

Cissie Gool's hopes were tragically curtailed. In 1963, she died of a stroke. Her death caused deep grief in the community, as shown in the two newspaper articles below.

01

SHE'S NOW AN ADVOCATE

MRS. Z. GOOL, a non-White Cape Town City Councillor — and a grandmother — was admitted to the Bar as an advocate by Mr. Justice Hall in the Supreme Court, Cape Town, to-day.

Mrs. Gool, who was congratulated by the judge on 'a very meritorious achievement,' now becomes the only woman practising as an advocate in Cape Town.

02

THE CAPE ARGUS, THURSDAY, JULY 4, 1963

'JOAN OF ARC' OF COLOURED FOLK DIES OF STROKE

03

01 Cissie Gool received her second degree from the University of Cape Town.

02 When Cissie Gool died, it came as an immense shock to the entire population of Cape Town.

03 Hundreds of Moslems accompanied the funeral procession of over 2 000 people to Cissie Gool's grave in the Mowbray Cemetery. Here men carry the richly decorated bier on the first stage of the march.

1951   Gool was called before a magistrate in Cape Town for convening a public meeting and thus breaking her banning orders. She resigned her seat on the Municipal Council.

1954   Gool was named a communist under the newly promulgated Suppression of Communism Act.

"Cissie was one of the best-known personalities in Cape Town. She was a tremendous public figure. She had a marvellous presence, a great smile and was a powerful orator. People noticed her."

Justice Albie SACHS

ADDRESS > Long Market Pedestrian Mall, between Buitenkant and Plein Streets, Cape Town

"I'm not trying to shout out anything, I'm just trying to make something that quietly affirms the political career of a woman who did a great deal," says Cape Town artist Ruth Sacks about her design.

In the face of a character as charismatic, controversial, vibrant - and physically beautiful - as Cissie Gool, Sacks chose to focus on her commitment to improving the lives of Cape Town's common people. Sacks says that although Gool was criticized for being an attention-seeker and for not having a clear political philosophy, she was firmly committed to representing the city's poorer people. Each bollard is inscribed with text documenting aspects of Gool's political contribution. These include gathering money to take 2 000 children from her District Six constituency to see the Walt Disney film *Snow White and the Seven Dwarves* for the first time, fighting for a wage increase for firemen and for the right of people of colour to serve as traffic wardens.

"These things weren't really newspaper headlines, or wouldn't go down in the history books, but at the time they made a lot of difference," says Sacks.

Alan PATON

"Cry, the beloved country for the unborn country for the unborn child that is the inheritor of our fear. Let him not love the earth too deeply. For fear will rob him of all if he gives too much."

Alan PATON, *Cry, The Beloved Country*

01

Alan Paton taught maths and chemistry at Ixopo High School from 1925 to 1928. Paton met his first wife, Dorrie, in the town which was also the setting for his famous novel about racial injustice in South Africa, *Cry, The Beloved Country*. The novel, published in 1948 - the year the all-white National Party came to power - had sold 15 million copies by the time of Paton's death. It was made into two films and inspired a Broadway musical. The first film, made by Zoltan Korda in 1951, was shot around Ixopo. The lead US actors, Sidney Poitier and Canada Lee, were not allowed to stay at hotels in the town because they were black. In the end they stayed at Rayfield, a farm owned by Paton's family, and the film was shot in a fictitious village, built for the film, close by. Paton played a prominent political role. He was a founder member and President of the Liberal Party and he gave evidence in mitigation of sentence at Nelson Mandela's treason trial.

Text from the Sunday Times memorial plaque

01 Alan Paton, photographed here in an interview with *Drum* magazine, expressed his hope that race relations would improve following the publication of *Cry, The Beloved Country*

02 Alan Paton's novel, *Cry, The Beloved Country*, received rave reviews in both South Africa and abroad. It was considered moving and beautiful.

Pulled Up Barbed Wire

MR. ALAN S. PATON, "the man who pulled up the barbed wire at Diepkloof and planted geraniums" retired this month, at the age of 45, from the reformatory where he was principal from 1935 — the year that reformatories were transferred from the Department of Justice to the Department of Education—so that he could give all his time to writing. In his youth he finished two works of fiction—and threw them in the waste-paper basket. But he never lost the feeling that one day he would write something that he would want to keep. At Diepkloof there was no time to write the story that simmered at the back of his mind; he had to wait for a rainy night in Trondheim for an opportunity to begin. He made a tour of prisons and reformatories in Scandinavia, Britain and the United States.

Cry The Beloved Country

A Milestone In Literature

Sunday Tribune July 11, 1948

IT is a long time since I have read a new novel so moving and so beautiful as Alan Paton's **Cry The Beloved Country.**

Indeed, its publication seems to me to be an event of great importance, not only for South African literature, but for the whole future of the country.

Mr. Paton has attempted to do what must have seemed virtually impossible before he did it: to show in a literary work the complexity of human and racial relations in South Africa, and out of that tangled skein to weave a pattern of human sympathy.

The problem for a writer who attempts this is not only that he needs intimate knowledge of the problems that are involved—Mr. Paton has this knowledge at his finger-tips—but that he must be able to stand back from his theme and see South Africa in perspective.

Mr. Paton gained his knowledge from his South African upbringing and from his experience as Principal of the Diepkloof Reformatory; but his power of organising that experience and of giving it full literary expression is a power that knowledge alone will not give. It is the result of imagination, compassion, and intellectual integrity.

Simple Story

THE story of the novel is a simple one. A Zulu parson of a village near Ixopo receives a letter from Sophiatown to tell him that his sister is very sick, and that he should come at once.

He goes to Johannesburg, to find that his sister has become a prostitute and that his son has fallen into an evil way of life. While he is being sought by his father, the son murders a European whose house he is robbing.

The young European who is killed is the son of a farmer who lives near the Zulu parson's own village; he was an ardent reformer, and at the time of his murder was engaged on a study of the causes of Native crime.

The son is caught, found guilty of murder, and hanged; but not before the father of the murdered man has realised that the crime was the fault not of any one individual, but of the whole of society.

Says Professor Geoffrey Durrant

Watching The Dawn

BOTH the farmer and the Zulu parson return to the Ixopo district; and there the farmer does what he can to repair the ravages that ignorance, bad farming methods, poverty and malnutrition are causing among the Natives. The book ends with the Zulu parson watching the dawn from a hill-top on the morning when his son is hanged in Pretoria Jail.

The book is written in a rhythmic prose which has in it much of the lilt and balance of the Bible. It moves with a grave and quiet beauty, turning aside nowhere to avoid a bitter or painful truth, but taking in all the fear, the agony, the waste of human hopes and of human life, recording them not coldly, but calmly; and communicating to the reader not depression, but a kind of tragic exultation.

To give a broadly significant background to a story which in itself is significant, Mr. Paton sets it against such incidents as the Native bus boycott in Johannesburg and the erection of Shanty Town. These passages, and many others in the book, have the status of poetry.

Carries Reader Along

THE rhythmic repetition of phrases and ideas carries the reader along as on a wave, urging him almost irresistibly to see what he has in the past been deliberately blind to the suffering of mothers, the daily deaths of children from bad housing and lack of food, the corruption of men and women by an evil society, and above all the naked dignity of the human soul when it is laid bare by grief, whether it is the soul of Black man or White.

Lest some readers be alarmed, let me assure them that there is no easy sentimentality in Mr. Paton's treatment of the Native, and especially of the Native criminal. On the contrary, the evil that proliferates in the slums of Alexandra and Sophiatown is seen most vividly as evil; and the point of view of the European who believes that only suppression is of any use is fully recorded.

Mr. Paton does not question the justice of the court which sentences the Native murderer to death. Instead, he sees as one bright spot in a dark scene the existence of a judiciary with full freedom to administer the law to all races without fear or favour.

But his work goes deeper than these considerations. It does not set out to apportion blame, to advocate any simple "solution," to espouse any particular cause. It attempts instead, and with much success, to open our eyes to the monstrous nature of our present social arrangements, to show the fear that eats away the lives of men. It takes the South Africa that we know, the experience of our everyday lives, and illuminates these familiar events and places with a steady and searching light. Whatever the reader thinks about the "Native problem" when he takes up the book, it is safe to say that his attitude will be very different when he puts it down.

He is persuasive, and the book is moving, because he resists all temptations to rhetoric or to easy indignation.

Hopes Too Full

IT seems to me that Mr. Paton's hopes for a better human life in South Africa have led him into dwelling too fully, in the last part of the book, on the possibilities of a change of heart and a fresh start. He shows Jarvis, the farmer, returning to his farm and doing all he can by providing milk for the school children, a new church, and an agricultural instructor, to prevent the further decay of the Native life in his district.

This is not psychologically impossible, for there are many generous-minded men who, like Jarvis, need only to have their imaginations quickened.

But it seems to me that this part of the book weakens the tragic effect of the whole, and must to some extent dissipate the impression that the rest of the book makes. The reader may even feel in a vague way that somehow or other some Jarvis will appear with miraculous milk to save the children, and all will be well. Mr. Paton has, in this part of the book, indulged his hopes and diluted his vision of things as they are.

It is, however, a comparatively small fault, and the author's achievement remains. He has continued the work that was begun by Van der Post in his novel, "In a Province," but he has carried the work much further. He has created an image of South Africa that will impress itself deeply on the minds not only of South Africa, but of the world.

A LOVE OF BOOKS

Alan Paton is widely considered to be one of South Africa's most influential writers and important political figures. Paton's mother was an English schoolteacher and his father, a Scottish immigrant, worked as a shorthand writer in the local Supreme Court. His father instilled in him a love of books and nature but Alan resisted his father's strict disciplinarian conduct.

Paton left home after finishing school and studied for a Bachelor of Science Degree and a Diploma in Education. He became President of the University of Natal's Student Representative Council and began writing poetry in his spare time. He published his first poem, *To a Picture* in the university magazine.

After completing his diploma, Paton moved to Ixopo to teach science and maths at the local high school. He was drawn to the little town about 80km west of Pietermaritzburg, near the Eastern Cape border, by its sheer physical beauty:

> "The Ixopo countryside laid me under a kind of spell, and this was enhanced by the prevalence in summer of the mists that would descend on the village and hide it from the world."

Paton fell in love with the rolling hills of the area. *Cry, The Beloved Country* opens with the line, 'There is a lovely road that runs from Ixopo into the hills'. Here too, Paton fell in love with a woman, Dorrie Lusted. Paton remembered himself as very shy, while Dorrie, on the other hand, was "full of mischief and zest". Dorrie was married at the time of their meeting but her husband died of tuberculosis and she and Paton were married in 1928. They remained together for nearly 40 years, until Dorrie's death.

As a teacher, Paton was loathed by many of his pupils because ironically, much like his father, he was a strict disciplinarian. Harry Usher, one of his former pupils, later recalled a frightening incident:

> "A little girl in Standard V dropped a blob of ink on her page as he was passing, so he grabbed her by the head and bobbed her up and down on the bench. She was so scared of that man she would start shivering when he came into the class."

Paton admitted that some of his charges "hated him like poison". He soon moved on to teach at Maritzburg College, and had his first son David in 1930. His second son, Jonathan, was born in 1936.

01

02

>>

1903
11 January

Alan Paton was born in Pine Street, Pietermaritzburg. At the age of 15, he enrolled at the University of Natal and studied towards his Bachelor of Science Degree and a Diploma in Education.

1925

Paton left Pietermaritzburg to teach at the Ixopo High School for white students. This experience provided much of the inspiration for his novel *Cry, The Beloved Country*. He married Dorrie Lusted in Ixopo in 1928. They had two children, David (1930) and Jonathan (1936).

REVOLUTIONARY REFORMS

In 1935, Paton was appointed Principal of the Diepkloof Reformatory for young boys in Johannesburg. His felt a great sympathy for the children, as he later recalled:

"Of those four hundred boys, one hundred were children. The youngest was nine. The offences of these children were trivial. They should never have been there at all. They had pilfered from shops and fruit stalls and at the markets. One of them had been so foolish as to steal a tin of jam from the pantry of the magistrate's wife. Most of them were children in need of care, but what was to be done with them…"

Paton's harsh disciplinarian streak had faded and he introduced a series of revolutionary reforms. He tore down the bars and replaced the barbed wire with geraniums. He established open compounds for trustworthy students, which allowed them to leave whenever they wanted. These reforms were very successful - only 1% of all boys deserted during his tenure. He was deeply moved by the plight of the boys, and wrote his most famous poem, *To a Small Boy who Died at Diepkloof*. It begins:

"*Small offender, small innocent child*
With no conception or comprehension
Of the vast machinery set in motion
By your trivial transgression,
Of the great forces of authority,
Of judges, magistrates, and lawyers,
Psychologists, psychiatrists, and doctors,
Principals, police, and sociologists,
Kept moving and alive by your delinquency,
This day and under the shining sun
Do I commit your body to the earth
Oh child, oh lost and lonely one."

Paton wanted to become National Director of Prisons and Reformatories, and sold his life insurance policies to finance an international study tour of prisons. He left in 1945 on the second ever South African Airways flight to London.

CRY, THE BELOVED COUNTRY

One night, while he was in Norway, he started to write the book that became *Cry, The Beloved Country* in his hotel room. His son, Jonathan, says that his father was overwhelmed by homesickness at the time. The blurb on the back cover describes the novel as a record "of a simple Zulu parson's (Stephen Khumalo) search for his delinquent son in the maelstrom of Johannesburg". The harrowing portrait of the unequal race relations in South Africa was inspired by his experiences at Ixopo and Diepkloof. Kumalo expresses Paton's deepest fear:

"I have one great fear in my heart, that one day when they (the whites) are turned to loving, they will find we are turned to hating."

The novel ends with Stephen Khumalo praying for his son who is to be hanged at dawn, and for the country:

"For it is the dawn that has come, as it has come for a thousand centuries, never failing. But when that dawn will come, of our emancipation, from the fear of bondage and the fear of fear, why, that is a secret."

The novel was published in 1948 to rave reviews and was considered the most important South African novel since *The Story of an African Farm*. The reviews describe Paton's accomplishment in capturing the essence of the tragedy of a whole society through the story of two families. The reviews also applaud the "biblical simplicity of its style and drama".

After the book was published, Paton resigned from the reformatory to write full-time. By the time of his death in 1988, the book had been translated into 20 different languages.

01   Alan Paton with his family. From left: David, Dorrie, Alan and Jonathan.

02   Paton talking to Prime Minister DF Malan at the premiere of *Cry, The Beloved Country* in Johannesburg in 1951. Paton abhorred Malan's policies.

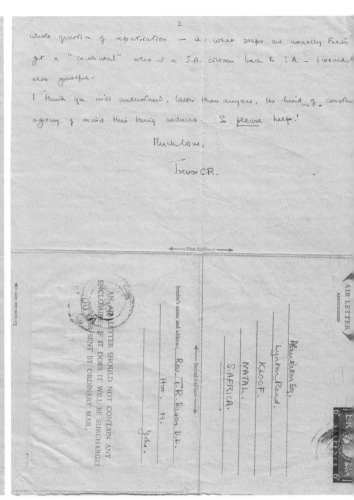

A FIERCE CRITIC

Paton became directly involved in politics in 1953 when he formed his own party, the Liberal Party. He continued to be politically active after the party was forced to disband because of its multi-racial membership. When the apartheid government arrested 155 political opponents and charged them with treason, Paton helped form the Treason Trial Defence Fund to provide financial assistance, moral support and day-to-day help to the trialists and their families. The correspondence above, between Paton and Reverend Trevor Huddlestone shows how Paton was a pillar of strength and wisdom for those involved in the struggle against apartheid.

Paton's outspoken approach to apartheid landed him in trouble with the authorities. In 1960, the government refused to renew his passport so as to stop him from travelling to New York to receive the prestigious Freedom Award. The authorities feared that Paton's acceptance speech would reflect badly on the country.

Widespread criticism from abroad, together with the actions of P.E.N (an international organisation staffed locally by Paton and other writers who fought for creative freedom), forced the government to issue Paton with a passport. He travelled to the USA and delivered a biting critique of apartheid, just as the government feared.

1953 · Paton formed the Liberal Party. He was the President until 1968 when the apartheid government banned the party for having both black and white members.

1956 · Paton helped raise the Treason Trial Defence Fund to assist the accused in the Treason Trial. Four years later, he became Vice-President of the International Defence and Aid Fund, which provided financial assistance for the legal protection of political activists.

Lynton Road,
KLOOF,
Natal, South Africa.

29th December, 1956.

My dear Trevor,

I did not feel able to consider your letter by myself, so got into touch with Ambrose. He does not exclude the possibility that your evidence may be necessary, but he says that this should be left to Counsel to decide and that if they think it necessary, you will be subpoenaed. Now the Bishop is not a lawyer, and I do not know whether this term can be correctly used of a person living in another country. It seems to me, then, that if the Bishop is approached for you to be made available, he will, in turn, approach the C.R., but he says, and I agree, that on no account should you contemplate disobedience.

It is not really for me to say what I am going to say now, but I only do it because you asked my advice. I think if you came out here without the authority of the C.R., and if, as a consequence, the C.R. disown you, and if, after the trials, the S.A. Government deport you, then your consequent position in England might be more frustrating than it seemed to be six or nine months ago. You would have robbed yourself both of your part in the South African struggle and of your part in the Community, and I dread to think of that. On the other hand, you may feel that the future must look after itself, or, alternatively, that God will look after it, in which case I would have no more to say. But all these possibilities point to the importance of your being sure of what you intend to do.

I am not quite sure of the point of your question in regard to repatriation. Do you mean what steps are necessary for you to take in England so that the South African Police would ask the British Police to arrest you and send you back to South Africa? It seems to me that this is not a question for a lawyer. It all depends on whether the S.A. Police want you back. My own guess is they do not. But if the question is still urgent to you, please state it more clearly.

I took the letters concerning Brother Jeremy and his own brother to Hector Carter, a young priest in Pinetown, who promised he would look into it at once. As far as I can see, Brother Jeremy wants his own brother to be converted, but there is no sign whatever in the brother's letter that he wishes to be. I honestly felt it was not a matter for me, and I am not sure it is a matter for Carter either, but I did the only thing

Alan Paton... "I'd rather have my views than my passport." The picture was taken last night.

ALAN PATON: GOVT. MOVE ATTACKED

THERE was swift reaction in Britain and the Union yesterday to the news that Alan Paton's passport had been withdrawn by the South African Government.

I could see to do under the circumstances.

Stephen, Joel, David and Edward came here on their last Sunday. They really seem to like coming here. Have you ever watched Joel listening to music? It has the most extraordinary effect on him, and he looks as though he will burst out at any moment into tears or what else, I am not quite sure.

We both send our love to you, and hope that the way will show itself to you more clearly. All good wishes for the New Year.

Affectionately,

01   Reverend Trevor Huddlestone asked Alan Paton's advice as to whether he should return to South Africa to testify in the Treason Trial as a defence witness.

02   Paton wrote back swiftly and warned Huddlestone against coming to South Africa for fear of arrest.

03   The apartheid government tried to block Paton from travelling to the USA to receive the Freedom Award by not issuing him with a passport.

1973   Paton published *Apartheid and the Archbishop*, a biography of Geoffrey Clayton, the former Archbishop of Cape Town. Over the next 15 years, he published a number of books, including a collection of short stories called *Knocking on the Door* (1975); the first volume of his autobiography, *Towards the Mountain* (1980) and the second volume, *Journey Continued* (1988).

1988
12 April   Paton died in his home at Lintrose, Botha's Hill, Natal, at the age of eighty-five as a result of cancer of the oesophagus.

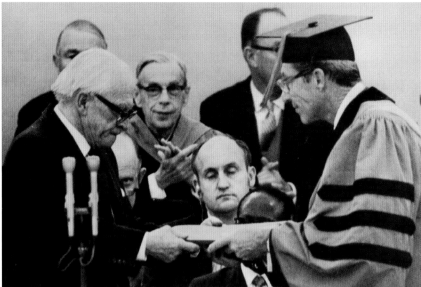

AN ILLUSTRIOUS CAREER

Paton was continuously recognised both at home and abroad as one of South Africa's leading figures in the fight against apartheid. "My whole life has been a struggle between the writer and the activist, and it has not stopped…", he reflected.

A year after his death in 1988, the *Sunday Times* started the Alan Paton award for non-fiction. The award encourages writers to pursue Paton's standards of excellence and commitment.

The Alan Paton award celebrated two forms of writing that Paton himself used: fiction and non-fiction. The first recipient of the award was Marq de Villiers for his book, *White Tribes Dreaming*.

01   Alan Paton married his secretary Anne Hopkins in 1969, two years after his first wife passed away. Here they are seen signing the marriage registry.

02   Paton receiving an honorary degree from Harvard in 1971.

03   Paton was constantly in demand as a speaker. This picture was taken during an interview a year before his death.

"One of South Africa's leading humanists, Alan Paton vividly captured his eloquent faith in the essential goodness of people in his epic work. A goodness that helped manage this small miracle of our transition, and arrested attempts by the disciples of apartheid to turn our country into a wasteland."

Nelson MANDELA, speech at world premier of *Cry, The Beloved Country*, 1995

There is a lovely road that runs from Ixopo into the hills .

ARTIST > ANDREW VERSTER

ADDRESS > Ixopo High School,1 Lewis Drive, Ixopo, KwaZulu-Natal

The memorial to Paton is made up of the first words of Paton's most famous book, *Cry, The Beloved Country*:

"There is a lovely road that leads from Ixopo into the hills..." These words are made of steel letters which are to be embedded into the pavement outside Ixopo High School. This is where Paton took up his first teaching post and taught science and maths.

Race CLASSIFICATION

"It was a total mix up. You don't know what you are. At the age of 23 I'd had three classifications. So what the hell am I? Today, the only people that can discriminate against me are blacks and Chinese, 'cos I've been everything else. It's tragic man, I tell you."

Vic WILKINSON

01

01 As a result of apartheid's race laws, all public amenities, such as this beach, were segregated.

02 The Population Registration Act of 1950 attempted to define the different racial groups in South Africa. These racial categories were changed, redefined and expanded throughout the era of apartheid.

In the 1960s, a room in what is now the High Court Annex (in downtown Cape Town) was the scene of formal hearings of the most bizarre and humiliating kind as ordinary people came before an appeal panel to argue about what "race" they should be labelled. Between 1950 and 1991, apartheid's Population Registration Act classified every South African as belonging to one of at least seven "races" and accordingly granted or denied them citizenship rights on a sliding scale from 'White' (full rights) to 'Bantu' (with the fewest). The classification was subjective, and families were split apart when paler or darker skinned children or parents – or those with curlier hair, or different features – were placed in separate categories.

Text from the Sunday Times memorial plaque

Act No. 30 of 1950.

ACT

To make provision for the compilation of a Register of the Population of the Union; for the issue of Identity Cards to persons whose names are included in the Register; and for matters incidental thereto.

(Afrikaans Text signed by the Officer Administering the Government.)
(Assented to 22nd June, 1950.)

BE IT ENACTED by the King's Most Excellent Majesty, the Senate and the House of Assembly of the Union of South Africa, as follows :—

1. In this Act, unless the context otherwise indicates—   Definitions.

   (i) "alien" means an alien as defined in section *one* of the Aliens Act, 1937 (Act No. 1 of 1937); (xv)

   (ii) "board" means a board constituted in terms of section *eleven*; (x)   Act No. 30 of 1950.

   (iii) "coloured person" means a person who is not a white person or a native; (iv)

   (iv) "Director" means the Director of Census appointed under section *four* of the Census Act, 1910 (Act No. 2 of 1910), and includes the Assistant Director of Census and any officer acting under a delegation from or under the control or direction of the Director; (ii)

   (v) "ethnic or other group" means a group prescribed and defined by the Governor-General in terms of sub-section (2) of section *five*; (iii)

   (vi) "fixed date" means the date upon which the census is taken in the year 1951 in terms of section *three* of the Census Act, 1910 (Act No. 2 of 1910); (xiii)

   (vii) "identity card" means the identity card referred to in section *thirteen* but does not include an identity card which has lapsed in terms of any regulation; (viii)

   (viii) "identity number" means the identity number assigned to a person in terms of section *six*; (ix)

   (ix) "Minister" means the Minister of the Interior; (vi)

   (x) "native" means a person who in fact is or is generally accepted as a member of any aboriginal race or tribe of Africa; (vii)

   (xi) "prescribed" means prescribed by regulation; (xiv)

   (xii) "register" means the register referred to in section *two*; (xi)

   (xiii) "regulation" means a regulation made under section *twenty*; (xii)

   (xiv) "this Act" includes the regulations; (v)

   (xv) "white person" means a person who in appearance obviously is, or who is generally accepted as a white person, but does not include a person who, although in appearance obviously a white person, is generally accepted as a coloured person. (i)

INVENTING RACE

South Africa was a deeply divided country long before apartheid was introduced in 1948. When the National Party came to power, it set about tightening the already existing policies of segregation. The Population Registration Act of 1950 lay at the heart of the apartheid enterprise. This Act defined South Africans according to three major racial groups: whites, Coloureds (who were "neither white nor Native") and Natives. Every South African over 18 years of age had to carry an identity document that stated their classification.

The Population Registration Act relied on the idea that there was a 'scientific' way of determining a person's race. In fact, the Act had to be amended six times to redefine what constituted race in South Africa. Initially, the act stated that a person's race was determined by their "general appearance". This was later changed to race being defined by how the "community accepted a person". If you looked black, and other people thought you were black, you were black. The Act was again amended to make heritage the key determining factor. According to this definition, if your parents were black you were black, even if the community accepted you as white. From the late 1960s onwards, new racial categories were added. You were not just black but were one of seven ethnic groups such as Zulu, Xhosa or Sotho. You weren't just Coloured but were Cape Coloured, Cape Malay, Griqua or Other Coloured.

These new racial categories were introduced at the same time as the declaration of the Bantu Homelands Citizenship Act of 1970. The Bantustans, which had been created in 1959, became 'independent states' for the different ethnic groups. Black people lost their South African citizenship and instead became 'citizens' of these Bantustans. They were forced to move to their new 'homes' and by the late 1980s, the government had forcibly removed roughly three million black South Africans into the Bantustans. This caused terrible upheaval and suffering.

The implementation of these Acts made apartheid the most systematic form of racial segregation in the world. As Deborah Posel, Director of the Wits Institute for Social and Economic Research, comments:

"In South Africa, a person's racial identity governed where they could live…where they could work, what kind of jobs they could take, where they could socialise, who they could drink beer with, what hotels they could or couldn't visit, which parks they could or couldn't sit in, and which part of a bus they could occupy.

From the outset, the legislation allowed for the possibility of appeal and a racial classification appeal board was constituted. It allowed somebody to dispute the terms of their classification, so it was indeed possible for somebody to change their race or have their race officially changed, odd as that sounds"

01 Ernest Holyoake stands in front of the Appeal Board sign. He had tried, unsuccessfully, to be reclassified as 'Coloured' after being classified 'Native'.

02 These men heard the cases of people who contested their racial classifications. Mr JJ Groenewald, Head of the Appeal Board, sits centre right, while Mr Treurnicht, Head of Census, is seated to the far left.

>> . . . .

1923   The Native (Black) Urban Areas Act prevented any unemployed 'non-white' South African from living permanently in any urban area.

1930   The Population Registration Act, Immorality Amendment Act and the Group Areas Act were passed and worked together to prevent any mingling of races.

THE APPEAL BOARDS

The first Appeal Board was established in Cape Town, presumably because of the large Cape Coloured community which, the Government believed, would contest its racial classification most often. The Board heard over 20 000 cases in its first years of existence.

The Appeal Boards were staffed by apartheid bureaucrats. The highest authority was the Head of the Census. The Head of the Census, as well as the Head of the Appeal Board, took part in each hearing. In 1951, the government ordered that everyone be classified in the course of the census. In other words, census takers became unofficial race classifiers.

Without a scientific means to judge race, the Appeal Board members would check a person's scalp, their fingernails, and the colour around their eyes. They used the absurd and degrading pencil and comb tests where a pencil or comb was inserted into a person's hair, and if it stayed in place, they were classified as 'Coloured' or 'Native'. Allegedly, people were deliberately injured so that the Appeal Board could test in which language they expressed their pain.

"Tan-coloured Johannes Maynard of Ophirton, Johannesburg, is another brand-new African. His parents were Coloureds, his grandparents were Coloured, and his great-grandfather was a Hollander who married a slave.

When Mynard got to the Native Affairs Department, he had to run a comb through his hair. The comb got tangled in his scant hair somehow and failed to drop as it should have. Then his skull was closely inspected and it did not show the 'accepted' characteristics. Something about the shape or texture of his ears seemed to be wrong, and so Mynard could not be declared Coloured. He was reclassified as an African – notwithstanding that he had been allowed into the Cape Coloured Corps during the last war." *Drum, October 1955*

1954   The first Race Classification Review Board was established to deal with individuals who contested their classification. The Board sat in Cape Town.

1959   The Review Board split. Specialist Appeal Boards were established in the Transvaal, Cape and Natal.

AFFIDAVIT

I, the undersigned,

███████ residing at 301, Albertus Flats, Westbury Extension

do hereby DECLARE

1. I was born on the 28th May 1938 at Umtata in the Transkei. My father was ███████ and my mother was ███████ ███ They were not legally married.

2. A Reference Book was issued to me on the 11th October 1958 containing the following personal data :

   Ethnic Group : Xhosa
   Tribe   : Xhosa
   Citizenship : South Africa
   N I Number   : ███████

3. I wish to submit that this classification was made in error and that for the following reasons I should be reclassified as a Coloured person :

4. I married a Coloured man, ███████ I D Number ███ in 1967 in the All Saints Cathedral Umtata. (ANNEXURE A).

   We took up residence in Norwood Coloured Residential Area. From this matrimonial unity two children have been born :

   1. ███████ on 11 July 1968 (ANNEXURE B)

   2. ███████ on 22 DECEMBER 1970 (ANNEXURE C)

   and both are classified as Coloureds.

5. A daughter ███████ was born out of wedlock on 18 April 1960. She was classified as a Coloured with I D Number ███████

6. In 1970 my husband and I took up residence in Johannesburg, residing at Coronationville for five years, whereafter we moved to Westbury, another Coloured residential area. At present I am residing in Westbury Coloured Residential Area where my children are educated at the Newclare Primary School No 2 as Coloureds in the Coloured Community. The Director of Coloured and Asian Affairs granted me permission to stay in Coloured Areas. (ANNEXURE I)

AFFIDAVIT :

7. In November 1977 my husband and I were divorced in the W.L.D. (ANNEXURE D) and I was granted the custody of the children by Court.

8. BEING ACCEPTED AS A COLOURED PERSON :

   8.1 I am accepted as a Colored in a Coloured Community, communicating and associating with Coloureds only from day to day.

   8.2 My home language is English. I myself learnt Xhosa as a child in Umtata but I do not use it now. My children cannot speak any Black language.

   8.3 My nieces and nephews are Coloureds. Our whole family structure is that of Coloured persons.

9. I attach hereto affidavits by members of the Community in which I live affirming that I am generally accepted as a member of the Coloured Community. These affidavits have been made by :

   9.1 ███████ (ANNEXURE E)
   9.2 ███████ (ANNEXURE F)
   9.3 ███████ (ANNEXURE G)
   9.4 ███████ (ANNEXURE H)

10. In 1974 I applied for a position as a Pupil Nursing Assistant at the Coronation Hospital. At that Time I was accepted as a Coloured by my employer. After being employed for three weeks enquiries was made into my identity documents. In lieu of the fact I being classified as a Xhosa as per my Reference Book I had to resign from this employment. Matron Carstens at the Coronationville Hospital assured me that I will be employed as soon as the dispute re my identification is settled.

11. At present my eldest daughter is supporting the family. She is working as a nurse at the Coronationville Hospital. I am not employed. I truly want to become a nurse, working in a Coloured Hospital with my people.

12. I humbly request to be reclassified as a Coloured to settle the dispute re my identification. I wish to take up employment as a Coloured and be allowed a honourable life as a Coloured in a Coloured Community.

TRAUMATIC DIVIDES

Hundreds of families were divided because members were classified into different racial groups. This was especially true for 'Coloured' families, an identity most difficult to define. This Act deeply affected these families:

"The 1950 Act affected my family so much... We had to forget about our white relatives... and they had to forget about us. Because either way, it was wrong to be mixing." *Zayne Adams*

"These bloody laws come out, so now, how do you fill in your forms? Who's going to disown whom? Who's going to lie, who's going to leave the country?" *Vince Kolbe*

"The big family break up happens then in all our families...my own family, my wife's family. And it happens in a whole variety of ways." *Crain Soudien*

1959 The Bantu Self-Government Act established ten Bantustans, mostly in poor agricultural areas. Every ethnic group was assigned a 'homeland'.

1967 The Population Registration Act of 1950 was amended so that a person's race would be determined largely by heredity, rather than by standards of community acceptance.

B E ë D I G D E   V E R K L A R I N G   ANNEXURE E

S W O R N   A F F I D A V I T

Ek ....█████████... PRIEST OF COR.VILLE COLOURED DISTRICT

Die ondergetekende, persoonsnommer
the undersigned, identity number   █████████

woonagtig te ....COR.VILLE JOH.BURG...
resident at

verklaar hiermee onder eed soos volg:
declare under oath as follows:

Ek beskou en aanvaar Mnr./Mev./Mej. ████████████
I regard and accept Mr./Mrs./Miss.

.... woonagtig te ...WESTBURY EXT. 2..
residing at
JOH.BURG

as 'n ⚹ dui ras aan ...COLOURED... en wel om die volgende redes:
as a ⚹ indicate race .... for the folowing reasons:

.....SHE LOOKS VERY COLOURED, LIVES AND ASSOCIATES ALWAYS WITH THE
....COLOURED PEOPLE, IS A MEMBER OF A COLOURED PARISH & COMMUNITY
....EVERYBODY ACCEPT HER AS A COLOURED, IS MARRIED TO A COLOURED
....HER CHILDREN GO TO A COLOURED SCHOOL, SHE IS WELL SPOKEN, AND
....WHEN EMPLOYED SHE IS EMPLOYED AS A COLOURED PERSON.

Verklaarder/Deponent

Die verklaarder erken dat hy/sy ten volle op hoogte is
van die inhoud van hierdie verklaring en dit begryp.

The deponent has acknowledged that he/she knows and under-
stands the contents of this affidavit.

Hierdie verklaring was beëdig/bevestig en onderteken
voor my te COR.VILLE ... op die 19.3...
This affidavit was sworn to/affirmed and signed before me
at ...JOHANNESBURG... on the ....
dag van
day of .MARCH... 19.80.

KOMMISSARIS VAN EDE/COMMISSIONER OF OATHS

DEPARTEMENT VAN BINNELANDSE
AANGELEËNTHEDE

Civitas, Strubenstraat
Privaatsak/Posbus   X114
PRETORIA
0001
REPUBLIEK VAN SUID-AFRIKA

VERW.   (B) 15853/80
REF.

BYLYN   260
EXTENSION

DEPARTMENT OF INTERNAL
AFFAIRS

Civitas, Struben Street
Private Bag/P.O. Box   X114
PRETORIA
0001
REPUBLIC OF SOUTH AFRICA

Republiek van Suid-Afrika
Republic of South Africa

NASIONAAL (012) 28-2551
NATIONAL
INTERNASIONAAL + 27 12282551
INTERNATIONAL

3-668SA   "INTERIOR"

BI 57

Hoek Street Law Clinic
P.O. Box 9495
JOHANNESBURG
2000

1982 -01- 2 0

Madam

APPLICATION FOR RECLASSIFICATION : ████████
YOUR REFERENCE : H510/80/LGB/im

With reference to previous correspondence, regarding
the above-mentioned matter, I have pleasure in advising
you that after careful consideration the classification
of the abovenamed has been amended to Cape Coloured
in terms of section 5(4)(c) of the Population
Registration Act, 1950 (Act No. 30 of 1950). Kindly
return her Reference Book to the Director, Reference
Bureau, Private Bag X200, Pretoria.

An identity document will be issued to her in due
course.

Yours faithfully

DIRECTOR-GENERAL
/cl

Address all correspondence to the Director-General and not to individual officers. Please quote the above reference number in your reply.

"We are God's creation, all of us man, Louis
Armstrong used to sing a song, "The only sin, was
in my skin that's why I was black and blue". And
that was so true, man, of what happened in this
country. It was so true." *Vic Wilkinson*

01 In order to convince the Race Classification
Appeal Board of the need to be reclassified,
individuals submitted affidavits like this
one. They tried to show that the community
accepted a person as belonging to a particular
racial group. Personal details have been
blacked out to respect the privacy of the
original applicants.

02 This supporting affidavit from Reverend
Molenaar was presented to the Appeal Board
to support the person's reclassification.

03 After an extensive process, this appellant was
finally granted a re-classification from the
group Xhosa to Cape Coloured.

1970 The Black Homelands Citizenship Act turned Bantustans
into sovereign states. Members of a particular black
ethnic group were considered citizens of their
homeland, and not of South Africa.

1986 The Prohibition of Mixed Marriages Act,
Immorality Act and all urban influx laws
were repealed.

THE SCARS REMAIN

Once a re-classification attempt was successful, people would be given new identification (ID) numbers. Under apartheid, people's ID number was determined by their gender and race. This meant that any apartheid bureaucrat could tell your racial group just by looking at your ID number.

The system of race classification collapsed in the late 1980s as apartheid began to crumble. In 1986, the most notorious race laws were repealed, including the Prohibition of Mixed Marriages Act, the Immorality Act, and the urban influx laws. In 1991, the Population Registration Act and the Group Areas Act were finally consigned to the dustbin.

But the scars of this law remain with South Africans today, as Zane Adams describes:

"It was the most destructive law ever to be passed because people had to take decisions: 'Am I gonna be white, or am I gonna be Coloured?' They had to make that decision and whichever decision they made was going to affect their whole lives. The scars, the broken hearts are still with us today, because idiots like the Verwoerds and those poeple of that time who enforced laws like that, didn't have any idea about what would happen today. They were only thinking about then."

B-(26085)   BUN 14069

REPUBLIEK VAN SUID-AFRIKA
REPUBLIC OF SOUTH AFRICA

Sy Ed., Prof., Dr., Ds., Mnr., Mev., Mej.   20/04/1982
The Hon., Prof., Dr., Rev., Mr., Mrs., Miss.

█████████████   *70*

C/O MRS███████████,
HOEK STREET LAW CLINIC,
P O BOX 9495,
JOHANNESBURG,
2000.

Neem asseblief kennis dat —
Please note that —

VAN
SURNAME   ██████████

VOORNAME
FIRST NAMES   █████████████

IDENTITEITSNOMMER
IDENTITY NUMBER   ████████████████

geklassifiseer is
has been classified

IN THE CAPE COLOURED GROUP

vir die doeleindes van die Bevolkingsregistrasiewet, 1950.
for the purposes of the Population Registration Act, 1950.

OP LAS VAN DIE SEKRETARIS VAN BINNELANDSE SAKE
BY ORDER OF THE SECRETARY FOR THE INTERIOR

01 To formalise a successful appeal, this person was re-issued with a new ID document that clearly stated that she now belonged to the Cape Coloured Group.

1991   The Population Registration Act was repealed along with the Group Areas Act.

1996   The new Constitution of South Africa declared it unconstitutional for a person to be subject to prejudice as a result of their race, ethnicity, gender, religion, age or sexual orientation.

"Apartheid was in many senses a shambles. There were many aspects of apartheid policies that never worked. But this was one of those aspects in which unfortunately, apartheid achieved awful successes and an accomplishment which does, I think, pose a considerable challenge to the project of democratisation and the aspirations of a non-racial society."

Deborah POSEL

ADDRESS > High Court Annex, Queen Victoria Street, Cape Town

Roderick Sauls wanted to remind people of the humiliation caused by South Africa's racially charged past without giving offence. He was inspired by the opportunity to create an artwork in the city with which people could interact.

Saul's two benches, constructed from concrete and wood, mimic apartheid-era public benches with the inscription 'whites only' and 'non-whites only'. The text etched into the wooden beams quotes extracts from the Population Registration Act. Sauls hopes his benches, evoking the laws that separated black and white South Africans in all public spaces, will invite people to transgress the labels and reflect on the absurdity of it all.

Bessie HEAD

"If I had to write one day I would just like to say people is people and not damn white, damn black. Perhaps if I was a good enough writer I could still write damn white, damn black and still make people live. Make them real. Make you love them, not because of the colour of their skin but because they are important as human beings."

Bessie HEAD, *New African*, September 1962

01

In 1950, aged 12, Bessie Head, one of Africa's most respected writers, was removed from the woman she believed to be her mother and sent to what was then St Monica's Diocesan Home for Coloured Girls. She spent six years at the Home, where she was encouraged to read and study for the first time. In 1951 she was told that she was the child of an 'insane' white woman and an unknown 'native' man. Her resulting struggle with issues of identity is reflected in her writing – as is a positive influence from this time, that of Home Warden Margaret Cadmore, whose name Head used for the protagonist in her second book, *Maru* .

Text from the Sunday Times memorial plaque

01   As a young woman, Bessie Head made her name as a journalist. She is pictured here during one of the happiest times of her life, when she was writing for *Drum* magazine.

02   *Things I Don't Like* This was the only one of her poems that was ever published.

'THINGS I DON'T LIKE'

"I am Black.

Okay?

Hot sun and the geographical set-up

Made me Black;

And through my skin

A lot of things happen to me

THAT I DON'T LIKE

And I wake each morning

Red murder in my eyes

'Cause some crook's robbed me again,

Taken what little I had right out of my hands

With the whole world standing by

And doing nothing...

Okay?

Oh no.

Today is my day.

Going to get back tit-for-tat,

All you stole.

Going to fight you till you or I

Lie smashed and bleeding dead

And don't care who dies, You or I,

But going to fight –

OKAY?"

Bessie Head

STRUGGLE FOR IDENTITY

Bessie Head is recognised as one of Africa's most important writers. Much of her writing reflects the extreme difficulties she experienced in her own life, particularly with regard to her identity. Bessie Head was born on 6 July 1937 in the Pietermaritzburg mental institution of Fort Napier. Her mother, Bessie Amelia Emery, was hospitalized at the insistence of her own mother, having been diagnosed with schizophrenia. She remained in this institution for the rest of her life. Bessie's father was a black labourer in the area.

According to the racial legislation of the time, Bessie was classified as white and was placed with a white adoptive family. However, her racial identity later became blurred as the white family's lawyer noted: "The child is Coloured, in fact quite black and Native in appearance." The state authorities hastily removed Bessie and placed her under the care of a 'Coloured' adoptive family, George and Nellie Heathcote. Soon after moving in with the Heathcotes, George passed away, leaving Nellie to raise Bessie by herself. Nellie was strict and often abusive. Bessie loved to read, but Nellie believed that reading was a waste of time and only provided Bessie with a single book. Despite Bessie speaking of Nellie with great fondness, the local welfare committee decided to remove Bessie from the Heathcote home when she was twelve. They placed Bessie at St Monica's Diocesan Home for Coloured Girls in Durban.

Bessie spent the next six years of her life at St Monica's, which had a profound impact on her. The school promoted academic excellence for the girls and Bessie was encouraged to read, which she did voraciously. She was so inspired by her new surroundings that she published her first piece, a parable called *The Stepping Stones of Truth*, in the school magazine. In the same year, however, Bessie learnt in the most brutal manner about her true heritage.

A TRAUMATIC INCIDENT

Without her knowledge, Louie Farmer, the authoritarian Warden of the school, applied for a government grant for Bessie. At the age of fourteen, Bessie was taken to the Durban Magistrate's Court in order for the grant to be approved. There she was informed that her mother was an "insane" white woman and her father "an unknown Native stable hand". Six months passed after this traumatic incident before Bessie was allowed to return to the Heathcote home and Nellie finally admitted that the story Bessie had heard in court was true. The news devastated Bessie. She later commented:

> "I have always just been me with no frame of reference to anything beyond myself...I just don't fit in or belong anywhere and I tend to pride myself on not fitting in or belonging."

This brave proclamation masked her feelings of loneliness and rejection. Indeed, this struggle with her identity hounded her throughout her whole life and greatly influenced her writing.

In 1954, Bessie Head's life changed yet again, this time for the better. The dynamic ex-nurse, Margaret Cadmore took over the leadership of St Monica's. According to Bessie, Cadmore brought great changes: "When Miss Cadmore came, we got sheets and knives and forks... We could listen to the radio and dance on Sundays. When Miss Cadmore came, it meant a right-about turn for us." As Bessie was one of the older girls at St Monica, Cadmore gave Bessie her full attention and became her much-needed friend and mentor. Bessie was writing her teacher-training certificate at the time, and was encouraged by Cadmore to develop herself in her various creative pursuits, including sketching and writing. Cadmore also introduced a sense of fun and excitement to Bessie's life. Bessie recalls how Cadmore gave her a pair of stockings "so sheer and lovely I am afraid to wear them". Bessie kept up constant correspondence with Cadmore during her time away. Reflecting the importance of this relationship, 'Margaret Cadmore' was the name given to the protagonist of Bessie's second book, *Maru*.

01   During her happy time at *Drum* magazine in Johannesburg, Bessie Head became increasingly involved in black politics. She was drawn closer to the PAC, and was enamoured with the work of Robert Sobukwe.

02   Bessie Head, pictured here interviewing a fortune teller for *Drum*, was known for her ability to capture the intricacies of her subject's lives, both as a journalist and as a writer.

A SEARCH FOR INNER PEACE

Bessie took up a teaching post in Durban after finishing her training. But the teaching life was not for her. At the age of 21, she decided to leave Durban and move to Cape Town. Cadmore was opposed to this decision and told Bessie that she was being foolhardy. Bessie nonetheless moved to Cape Town and established herself as a reporter. She lived in District Six, a vibrant mixed-race community that was later destroyed by the apartheid government under the pretext that it was in an area set aside for whites. Bessie was the only female writer hired to work for the *Golden City Post* newspaper. It was an eye-opening experience. She came into contact with politically active people for the first time in her life. She also reflected on her identity, hoping that Cape Town would be an "ideal place for my mixed-race soul". But she was disappointed and her search for inner peace continued as this extract from a letter to Margaret Cadmore, written and published in a book on Bessie in 1958, shows:

> "I detest snobbery but maybe I'm a mental snob... I search avidly for anyone really intelligent. With intelligent people one forgets such shameful matters as the colour of one's skin and facial features which seem to matter so much in South Africa. Heavens! I will not ape anybody. I am an individual. No one shall make me ashamed of what I am!"

After a year in Cape Town, Head moved to Johannesburg where she began writing for the hugely influential *Drum* magazine. This was one of the few magazines that wrote about the lives and stories of black people. These photos, on the opposite page, taken by a *Drum* photographer, show her at her happiest, smiling care-free into the camera. She became one of *Drum's* most popular reporters.

Whilst in Johannesburg, Head became politically active. She met Robert Sobukwe, leader of the Pan African Congress (PAC), just before the Sharpeville massacre. In the political turmoil after the shootings, she was arrested on suspicion of being a PAC operative. The police tortured a confession out of her, despite the fact that she knew very little about the organisation. Her testimony did not result in any arrests but she was shattered and tried to commit suicide. After spending time in hospital, Bessie Head returned to Cape Town.

GLIMPSES OF HAPPINESS

Some light entered Bessie's life when she met Harold Head. They were married in September 1961 and had their first and only child Howard a year later. During this time, both Harold and Bessie wrote for the *New African* newspaper, and Bessie continued to develop a keen political consciousness.

Bessie's happiness with her new family was short-lived. By 1964, she had decided to leave her husband, accusing him of womanising. At the same time, she made the decision to leave South Africa, to seek an escape from the political situation. She took up a teaching job in Serowe in the Bechuanaland Protectorate (later Botswana), but she was barred from getting a passport and was forced to leave South Africa on an exit visa. This meant that she could never return to the country of her birth. In 1967, she officially registered as a South African refugee. She remained a refugee for the next fifteen years before she became a Botswana citizen. Her refugee status reinforced her feelings of being marginalised and rejected by those around her.

SELF-PORTRAIT

Idealist,
And low down,
Apathetic,
Indifferent earth worm;
Plunging, leaping,
Flickering, wavering,
Stammering, hesitating,
Bold, reckless, impatient;
Static, placid,
Of no certain direction;
Isolated, like driftwood
On the tossing, heaving ocean –
Flung to the top of a high-sounding,
Dazzling wave,
Engulfed in the anonymous depths;
Oh contradiction!
THAT is I.

Handwritten; dated 2 July 1961; signed B.Head

SEROWE

After two years in a refugee camp in Northern Botswana, Bessie Head settled in Serowe. She gave up her teaching career to become a full-time writer. It was in this small village that she wrote the first of many books, *When Rain Clouds Gather*, a book which had grown out of her experience in the refugee camp.

The book was well received but this was a time of immense struggle for Head. Psychologically, she felt as if her personality "was being blown to bits". She did not feel part of the Serowe community which, she believed, viewed her with constant suspicion. Her friend and fellow author, Patrick Cullinan, remarked that she never learned to speak Setswana and, "It was as though she kept her language as a barrier". Head lived in a state of almost constant poverty, and struggled to raise her son. She was plagued by depression and psychotic episodes.

ANGUISH AND DEPRESSION

In 1971, Head suffered another breakdown and spent three months in a mental hospital which she referred to as "the loonie bin". She explained her breakdown to Randolph Vigne, a friend and former publisher of *New African*:

"I was not well. I was tortured beyond endurance. For one brief moment I threw myself on the ground and said: 'God, help me'. Then I made an error. In the same breath I said: 'Which God?' As though subconsciously I had not come to the end of the road yet. That question, the pause and looking over my shoulder, unhinged my mind which was already over-burdened with suffering. I wanted to throw everything overboard in one violent breath, which I did. No one followed what I was saying. It was all an internal torment belonging to me alone. In the confusion I opened up a wide radius of pain for other people."

01

Mental instability became a subject in all Head's subsequent novels. *Maru* was published in 1973. In her best-known novel, *A Question of Power*, published in 1975 she most vividly reflects her own anguish and obsession with identity. She writes:

"First they received you from the mental hospital and sent you to a nursing home. A day later you were returned because you did not look white. They sent you to a Boer family. A week later you were returned. The woman on the committee said: What can we do with this child? Its mother is white."

Bessie Head's books were internationally acclaimed and she became known throughout the literary world. She travelled to speak at literary events in the USA, Germany, Denmark, Holland, Nigeria, Australia and England. But her mental illness led to fractious relations with friends and publishers and she felt increasingly alienated.

Bessie began to depend increasingly on alcohol. Jean Marquard, one of the last people to visit Bessie Head, recalled the sorry state in which Head was living towards the end of her life.

On 17 Apirl 1986, she died in Serowe from liver disease.

01 Bessie Head outside her house in Serowe, a difficult place to live. It was described by one of her interviewers, Jean Marquard, as "perfectly ghastly".

1969   Head published her first novel, *Rain Clouds*, which received favourable reviews abroad. She subsequently published: *Maru* (1971), *A Question of Power* (1973), *The Collector of Treasures* (1977), *Serowe: Village of Rain and Wind* (1981) and *A Bewitched Crossroad* (1984).

1986   Bessie began to suffer from intense loneliness and depression, especially after her estranged husband instituted divorce proceedings in 1985. She also fell out with her son. She developed a strong dependency on alcohol, and on the 17th of April, died in Serowe from liver disease.

"From the confusions of her daily living, she would withdraw to her desk and typewriter and there she would almost take on a new personality. While she sat there, she seemed to have her life under control. Her fears, anxieties and physical needs were pushed to one side, as she collected her ideas and concentrated her thoughts on what she was writing. It was here that the disparities in her complex personality were quietened for a while. It was here the realist and the diviner achieved a brief common purpose."

Patrick VAN RENSBURG, *eulogy delivered at Bessie Head's funeral, 1986*

ARTIST > JANE DU RAND

ADDRESS > Werda Hoerskool (formerly St Monica's Diocesan Home for Coloured Girls), 90 Parkside Road, Hillary , Durban, KwaZulu-Natal

I feel that the life of Bessie head was one of contrasts, of polar differences which she battled to come to terms with, of different identities and a feeling of never really belonging to any place or community.

I have tried to portray this in the proposed memorial which tries to represent these differences; strength and fragility, permanence and transience, and at the same time to make it something quite beautiful, peaceful and lasting.

3 REPRESSION AND RESISTANCE

1952 - 1961

This section reveals how far people were prepared to go to resist apartheid. The sacrifices they made were enormous, sometimes costing them their lives. The stories are linked by the courage that people displayed in facing the might of the apartheid state.

26 June 1952 — Raymond Mhlaba launched the ANC's Defiance Campaign by entering the 'Europeans Only' section of the New Brighton railway station in Port Elizabeth.

1950s — George Pemba undertook his first national tour after receiving a Bantu Welfare Trust loan. It was a period of growth for Pemba, who returned to Port Elizabeth and decided to run a spaza shop to support his painting. He exhibited a number of times in Port Elizabeth by the end of the 1950s.

1952 — The Defiance Campaign transformed the ANC into a mass organisation. Membership rocketed from 7 000 to 100 000. In the same year, Albert Luthuli was elected as President of the ANC.

1952 — The Abolition of Passes and Co-ordination of Documents Act made the pass laws much stricter. All black men over the age of sixteen had to produce a reference book if ordered to do so. About 500 000 blacks were arrested every year in the 1960s and 1970s for not producing a pass with the correct permissions.

1952 — A Native Laws Amendment Act turned all town and cities into 'white' areas. Black people could not remain for more than 72 hours unless they had special rights.

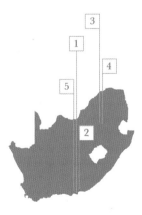

SAHA/*SUNDAY TIMES* MEMORIAL SITES:

>> ·

1 — Raymond MHLABA
Red Location Museum, New Brighton, Port Elizabeth

2 — George PEMBA
28 Ferguson Road, New Brighton, Port Elizabeth

1953   The newly re-elected National Party passed the Bantu Education Act which destroyed mission education and introduced a syllabus designed to keep black students "in their place as labourers".

1955   The government succeeded in removing blacks from the previously freehold township of Sophiatown.

1955   The ANC, the SA Indian Congress and the Congress of Democrats met in Kliptown, Soweto to adopt the Freedom Charter which spelled out a vision for a democratic post-apartheid SA. The Charter began with these famous words: "South Africa belongs to all who live in it, black and white…"

3

March 1956   Duma Nokwe was denied access to the previously all-white common room of the Johannesburg Bar.

4

9 August 1956   Lilian Ngoyi, along with Helen Joseph, Sophie Williams and Rahima Moosa, led 20 000 women in a march to Pretoria to protest against the extension of pass-laws to women.

1956   The Security Police arrested 156 political activists on charges of high treason. The Treason Trial lasted for five years until the state's case was thrown out of court for lack of evidence against the accused.

1956   HF Verwoerd, widely referred to as the architect of apartheid, came to power after the death of Prime Minister JG Strijdom.

21 March 1960   Police opened fire on peaceful protestors in Sharpeville who had gathered to protest against the pass-laws. 69 were killed and 180 injured.

1960   In the aftermath of the Sharpeville Massacre, the government declared a State of Emergency and banned the ANC and PAC. Many activists fled into exile, including Oliver Tambo, who was ordered by the ANC to establish an external mission.

1961   Both the ANC and PAC abandoned peaceful means of protest and formed armed wings. Albert Luthuli became the first South African to win the Nobel Peace Prize.

5

1961   The first of Athol Fugard's "mature" plays, *Blood Knot*, debuted. It focused on the oppressiveness of racism in SA.

December 1961   Nelson Mandela made a shock appearance at the All-In Africa Conference, delivering his last public speech before his life imprisonment on Robben Island.

---

3   Duma NOKWE
High Court, Pritchard Street, Johannesburg

4   Lilian NGOYI
9870 Nkungu Street, Mzimphlophe, Soweto, Johannesburg

5   Athol FUGARD
St George's Park Tearoom, Port Elizabeth

Raymond MHLABA

"I led the very first group and we entered the 'Europeans only' section of the New Brighton station. By half past six we were already in police vans on our way to jail. It turned out that my party was the very first to defy unjust laws in the whole of South Africa. Little did we know that we were making history."

Raymond MHLABA

In the early hours of June 26, 1952, after praying through the night, Raymond Mhlaba led 30 volunteers to defy apartheid by entering the 'Europeans Only' section of New Brighton railway station, Port Elizabeth, the first act in a nationwide defiance campaign in response to the passage of a slew of apartheid legislation. They were swiftly arrested, and Mhlaba served a month's hard labour. As one of the Rivonia treason trialists a decade later, Oom Ray, as Mhlaba was affectionately known, was sentenced to life imprisonment. He served 26 years, and went on to become the first Premier of the new Eastern Cape.

Text from the Sunday Times memorial plaque

01 Raymond Mhlaba in 1994. Mandela had just appointed him the first Premier of the Eastern Cape.

02 Raymond Mhlaba's act of defiance on 26 June 1952 launched the Defiance Campaign in the Eastern Cape. The widespread support for the campaign was evident in the thousands of well-wishers who attended Mhlaba's trial.

DEFIANCE OF "UNJUST LAWS"

Daily Dispatch

Some Non-European Volunteers Sentenced in P.E.

PORT ELIZABETH, Thursday.

Thirty non-Europeans who were the first Port Elizabeth volunteers in the "unjust laws campaign," launched on June 26 by non-European organisations, appeared in the Port Elizabeth Magistrate's Court today.

They were charged with contravening the apartheid regulations by entering the New Brighton Railway Station at the entrance reserved for Europeans.

All pleaded not guilty.

The separate trial of each man was begun and in each case formal evidence of two witnesses was taken. After sentencing the first two men, the magistrate, Mr. M. R. Hartogh, sent the others back to the cells and told them he would give them time to consider whether or not they wished to alter their pleas.

All refused to change their pleas and were brought before the court, one at a time. Those sentenced refused the option of a fine.

The Public Prosecutor, Mr. D. W. Geldenhuys, said he had been instructed by the Solicitor-General to ask for a severe sentence.

LEADER OF GROUP

The first man to be sentenced was Mpakamise Mhlaba, described by the magistrate as the leader of the group. He was sentenced to a fine of £10, or three months' imprisonment, half the sentence being suspended for six months.

In evidence Mhlaba said he deliberately entered the station by the European entrance. He said he was defying an "unjust law which was against God's rule."

Before continuing with the next case Mr. Hartogh said it would not help them if they all pleaded not guilty and then admitted their guilt in the witness box.

When another of the accused persons said during the hearing that he intended to continue using the European entrance, Mr. Hartogh said: "It is not going to help you to adopt a defiant attitude. It seems hat Mhlaba regards himself as your leader.

"If you do not want to think for yourselves and want to follow him, and others like him, you will find yourselves in serious trouble."

The magistrate sentenced 16 of the Natives to a fine of £6 or 30 days' imprisonment. Half the sentence was suspended in each case for six months.

The hearing against the others is continuing.

While the 30 passive resisters were being tried a crowd of about 4,000 non-Europeans gathered behind the court buildings, singing hymns and praying for those who had been arrested. They were ushered by men wearing African National Congress arm bands.

A TITAN IS BORN

Raymond Mhlaba, known affectionately as 'Oom Ray', was one of the key figures in South Africa's struggle against apartheid. He was born in Fort Beaufort in the Eastern Cape, one of the strongholds built by the British in the 1820s to repel the Xhosa during the frontier wars. The War of the Axe or Seventh Frontier War started right in the centre of the town. Mhlaba's early childhood was difficult. His parents, Mxokozeli 'Ginger' and Dinah Mhlaba, struggled financially and suffered from a series of tragedies. Mhlaba was one of eight children but only three survived infancy. Mhlaba's father, who worked as a policeman, returned home once a month to settle the credit at a general dealer.

Mhlaba's strongest influences in his early life were his mother and his grandfather. Mhlaba spoke of his mother as a "proud, confident and attractive woman...stubborn yet intelligent, independent and assertive". She instilled in him a deep respect for the church. His grandfather was steeped in Xhosa oral tradition and told Mhlaba stories of the Maqoma, who had struggled for nearly a century against white domination. From a young age, Mhlaba imbibed the importance of the fight for freedom. As Mhlaba later recalled:

"One of the memorable lessons I learnt from my grandfather was the value of fighting for my respect and dignity...Little did I know that as *isizukulwana*, the ensuing generation of Maqona, I would continue the struggle against white domination."

At the age of nine, Raymond Mhlaba was enrolled at Mazoka, the local mission school. He learnt basic literacy while still carrying out his domestic chores of ploughing the fields and tending livestock. After completing primary school, Mhlaba was sent to the famous Healdtown Mission Secondary School. Founded in 1853 as a Methodist mission school, Healdtown became a bastion of black education. Nelson Mandela was a Healdtown boy as were Robert Sobukwe, Govan Mbeki and Robert Mugabe. It was a tumultuous time for Mhlaba, as he was inducted into the world of political activism through the school-based organisation, Mayibuye Students Association.

>> . . . .

1920
12 February
Raymond Mhlaba was born in the Eastern Cape. He attended the famous Healdtown Mission Secondary School.

1942
Mhlaba moved to PE to find a job, and spent the next years working in a laundry. He joined the Non-European Laundry Workers Union. The following year, he joined the Communist Party of South Africa (CPSA) and married his first wife, Joyce Meke. In 1944, Mhlaba joined the African National Congress.

THE UNIVERSITY OF LIFE

Mhlaba's years at Healdtown came to an abrupt end, however, when his father retired from the police force and could no longer pay for his son's tuition. Mhlaba left home and joined his father in Port Elizabeth (PE), a rapidly growing industrial centre. Mhlaba found work at Nannucci Dry-Cleaning and Launderers, where he worked for years removing stains with an ammonia solution. Soon after arriving in Port Elizabeth, Mhlaba found love and married Joyce Meke.

04

Living in Port Elizabeth proved to be a major turning point in Mhlaba's life. Soon after taking up the job at the laundry, a group of politically active Coloured women convinced him to join the Non-European Laundry Workers Union. Mhlaba later recalled:

"They regarded me as an enlightened and educated person, fresh from school. After little persuasion, I joined the Laundry Workers Union unofficially, without signing papers or a contract. This happened within a week of commencing work."

Mhlaba frequently attended union meetings held in Queen Street in the centre of PE and was schooled in trade unionism, its aims and objectives, advantages and disadvantages. Mhlaba grew hugely committed to the union and became a recruiter. He reflected in his memoirs how, "Many of us certainly were not graduated from the conventional universities. Rather, we were graduates from the university of life."

Mhlaba befriended another unionist, Clifford Dladla. Dladla gave him a booklet, written by the Communist Party of South Africa (CPSA) entitled, *Why Are You Paid Low Wages?* Mhlaba decided to attend a CPSA meeting. He was intrigued by the free interchange of ideas between the CPSA's white and black members:

"What struck me was to see a white person discussing issues openly with an African as an equal. What was even more peculiar was to see an African telling a white comrade that a point the latter made was 'nonsense'...It was a shock for me to learn that no one was superior to another in the meeting."

01   Mhlaba's parents, Mxokozeli 'Ginger' and Dinah Mhlaba. Mxokozeli came from a poor family and went to work on the mines to raise money to pay for *lobola*. Dinah's parents were initially reluctant to accept Mxokozeli's offer of marriage, but finally relented.

02   Mhlaba married Joyce Meke in 1943, a year after moving to PE. She was also from Fort Beaufort. They had three children together before her tragic death in a car accident in 1960.

03   Bukeka Mhlaba was Mhlaba's first-born daughter. She trained to be a nurse.

04   Mhlaba was a young and efficient organiser of mass resistance.

1947   Mhlaba was elected Chairman of the New Brighton branch of the ANC.

1952
26 June   Mhlaba, with 29 others, walked into the whites-only section of a PE railway station. He was immediately arrested, but was released quickly.

A DASHING FIGURE

Mhlaba signed up to the party and showed much the same enthusiasm for party work as he did for his union activity. By 1946, he had been nominated as a district secretary. He also officially joined the ANC and set to work helping to organize a rent boycott the following year. His attractiveness and charisma ensured his rapid rise through the ranks of the ANC. He was, as Nelson Mandela recalls, not ashamed to display a vain streak: "I must say that if there is one area where that ingrained modesty deserts my old comrade, it is in his judgements about his appearance...young Raymond had a way with the opposite sex because 'girls are attracted to handsome and tall men, as I consider myself to be.'"

Around the time that Mhlaba was elected Chairman of the ANC's New Brighton branch, he participated in a strike of the LWU and was "fired from my job for my involvement in the workers' struggle". He became a waiter and a "public bar boy" until finding a full-time job as a clerk in a steel company. One day, after arriving late for work because the bus driver was late, he was severely reprimanded. He organised a month-long bus boycott. For the first time, black drivers sat behind the wheels of buses in New Brighton.

DEFIANCE

The ANC's Defiance Campaign changed Mhlaba's life. The ANC conceived of this non-violent form of resistance after a sitting of the "most shameful session" of the all-white South African Parliament in 1951. In a single sitting, some 75 pieces of racist legislation were placed on the statute book. In response, the ANC planned the Defiance Campaign to coincide with the 300th anniversary celebrations of Jan van Riebeeck's arrival in the Cape. On 6 April, the ANC held large public meetings in Johannesburg, Cape Town, Durban and PE where over 55 000 delegates pledged to defy the unjust laws. Mhlaba worked tirelessly to promote the campaign and attract volunteers. He was shadowed by police informers and was amused to discover that his own speeches were being recorded.

Two and a half months into the organisation of the campaign, Mhlaba spent the night praying with a group of thirty volunteers. Early in the morning of 26 June 1952, he stepped into the New Brighton train station accompanied by his comrades. They planned to walk into the 'Europeans only' section of the train station and purchase a ticket in a deliberate attempt to break one of apartheid's many race laws. Mhlaba describes this tense and difficult time:

01

Call for Volunteers in "Defiance Campaign"

Chienile 23/6/52

Durban, Sunday.

CHIEF A. J. Luthuli, president of the Natal African Congress, called for volunteers today for the "Defiance Campaign" planned jointly by the African National Congress and the South African Indian Congress, to begin on June 26.

01   The ANC Defiance Campaign was the most successfull of all its programmes to date. Thousands of volunteers supported the campaign.

02   After defiers were arrested they received huge community support. In the Eastern Cape where church activism was established, the suppot often had religious overtones.

03   These head shots of the leaders of *Umkhonto we Sizwe*, were released by the government after the men were caught red-handed at their headquarters at Liliesleaf farm. Mhlaba is top-right, next to his long-time friend and comrade, Govan Mbeki. Top Row left to right: Nelson Mandela, Walter Sisulu, Govan Mbeki, Raymond Mhlaba. Bottom Row: Andrew Mlangeni, Ahmed Kathrada, Dennis Goldberg.

02

The Friend, Bloemfontein, Thurs., July 24, 1952   7

Natives Sing and Pray Outside Court House

Disobedience Campaigners Get Thumb-Up Salute

EAST LONDON, Wednesday.

ABOUT 250 SINGING and praying Natives gathered outside the Magistrate's Court here this morning while 85 of their fellow "civil disobedience" campaigners appeared on charges of not being in possession of night passes. The 85 were arrested last night after 11 p.m.

The crowd gradually swelled and police officials arrived on the scene shortly after 10 a.m. The District Commandant of Police, Major A. L. Prinsloo, addressed the crowd.

1961   Mhlaba was central in the ANC's decision to launch the armed struggle. He went to China to receive military training and was then appointed Commander-in-Chief of the ANC's new military wing, *Umkhonto we Sizwe* (MK).

1963   Mhlaba was arrested during a raid on Liliesleaf Farm, and put on trial during the infamous Rivonia Trial. He was found guilty and given a life sentence. He served it on Robben Island along with Nelson Mandela and other Rivonia trialists.

"We prayed the whole night at the civic centre in New Brighton. From the civic centre we left for the New Brighton station in the early hours on the morning of June 26. By five o'clock that morning we found sergeants, not even ordinary policemen, waiting for us. All the people from Red Location came to witness this event. The sergeant in charge asked me how to deal with the crowd after watching volunteers. I assured him that our people were well aware of the procedure of the campaign. I addressed the people and told them to go home or to work after watching the volunteers defying unjust laws. Those who wanted to join the volunteers were to go and register for the Defiance Campaign in our ANC offices. People of Port Elizabeth gave me the name *Vulindlela* (Open the way), as I opened the way for the others to defy an unjust system."

Mhlaba was arrested along with the other volunteers. They were sentenced to thirty days in prison. All agreed to serve the time instead of paying a fine. When they were brought before the court, they refused to sit in the 'Natives only' sections, much to the consternation of the presiding magistrate.

03

TREASON

The Defiance Campaign raised the profile of the ANC tremendously. Paid membership of the party sky-rocketed from 7 000 to 100 000, and the number of ANC branches multiplied from 14 to 87. The Eastern Cape was the most important province in the campaign; 5 941 out of 8 326 arrests nationwide took place there and 2007 volunteers, a full quarter of all those arrested during the campaign, were arrested in PE. They filled the city's brand new jail and police reinforcements had to be sent to PE from all over the country. Mhlaba was one of the many leaders who were banned.

Around this time, the ANC began to doubt the ability of peaceful resistance to bring about change. After hours of heated debate, the ANC adopted the strategy of armed struggle. On 16 December 1961, the party launched its armed wing, *Umkhonto we Sizwe*, also known as MK or Spear of the Nation. Nelson Mandela was its first Commander-in-Chief. Mhlaba traveled to China in 1961 to receive basic military training.

When Mandela was arrested in 1962, Mhlaba stepped into this key leadership position. From abroad, Mhlaba recruited and trained military operatives. He travelled to Czechoslovakia and Algeria to learn more about military tactics.

In July 1963, Mhlaba returned to the country but his time as a free person was short-lived. On 11 July 1963, the police raided the MK headquarters at Liliesleaf Farm in Rivonia. They arrested Raymond Mhlaba, Govan Mbeki, Ahmed Kathrada and Walter Sisulu, and put them on trial for treason.

After a year-long trial, Mhlaba and his 'co-conspirators' were found guilty of treason. Many feared they were to receive a death sentence. To their great relief they were sentenced to life in prison on Robben Island.

1982   Mhlaba was transferred to Pollsmoor Prison. He married his second wife, Dideka Heliso, here in 1986. Mhlaba was released from prison in October 1989, after which he had three children with Heliso.

1994   Mhlaba served as Premier of the Eastern Cape after South Africa's first democratic elections. In 1997, he was appointed High Commissioner to Uganda and then a year later to Rwanda. Mhlaba held this position until his retirement in 2001.

A FREE MAN

In 1989, after 25 years in prison, Mhlaba was finally released to begin life as a free man. For the next 16 years, he lived a full life. Reunited with his wife, daughters, sons and grandchildren, Mhlaba had a further three children in his old age with his beloved wife, Dideka. At last, Mhlaba was able to live the normal family life that apartheid had denied him.

He continued to work actively in politics. In 1994, at the age of 74, Mhlaba was appointed Premier of the Eastern Cape. He held this position until 1997, after which he served as the High Commissioner to Uganda and Rwanda.

His death, in February 2005, was greeted with widespread grief throughout the country. 'Oom Ray' was remembered as a 'titan' and a 'visionary'. But it was also a time for celebration. Although Mhlaba had suffered years of imprisonment, he lived long enough to see the free country he had worked towards. As Thabo Mbeki so eloquently stated at Oom Ray's funeral:

"Indeed, we too should exult and ring the bells of victory to celebrate the life Oom Ray gave to our people so that we could secure our liberation. We should exult and ring the bells of victory that he lived long enough to see
our country freed from the curse of white minority rule."

01 While on Robben Island, Mhlaba and Govan Mbeki were particularly close. They taught new arrivals about the history of the ANC and provided a crash course in political economy. In 1994, Govan Mbeki (left), Raymond Mhlaba (middle) and Robben Island prisoner Ahmed Kathrada (right) shared a laugh.

02 Mhlaba after his appointment as the first Premier of a democratic Eastern Cape.

03 Mhlaba married his second wife, Dideka Heliso, at Pollsmoor Prison in 1986. They were only given the right to marry after persistent appeals to the government. Nelson Mandela was a witness to the ceremony in the prison Commandant's office.

2005
20 February
Mhlaba died of complications arising from advanced liver cancer.

"Oom Ray and the other titans of his generation took it upon themselves to organise and educate our people to become the makers of history. They unleashed the enormous energies of the masses of the people, creating a mighty force which not even the armed might of the brutal apartheid state could vanquish."

Thabo MBEKI, *eulogy delivered at Raymond Mhlaba's Funeral*

ARTIST > MXOLISI 'DOLLA' SAPETA AND ANDREW LINDSAY

ADDRESS > Red Location Museum, New Brighton, Port Elizabeth

Andrew Lindsay developed the large floor mosaic depicting scenes from the 1952 Defiance Campaign from a concept put forward by PE artist, Mxolisi Sapeta.

"I wanted to keep it simple," Lindsay says. The use of black and white evokes a sense of the past, while the use of colour brings in light and hope, as well as emphasizing the feelings of the time. The footprints are not evenly spaced. They are placed at irregular intervals to create a sense of a negotiated walk. Lindsay explains: "It would not have been an easy walk for Raymond Mhlaba and his group."

George PEMBA

"I was always able to put myself in the place of
another person, and this ability helped me a
great deal in building up my art."

George PEMBA

01

In 1952, George Pemba resigned
from his hated job as a rent collector
to become a full-time artist. Although
encouraged to do so by fellow pioneer
artist Gerard Sekoto and by his
own successful exhibitions, Pemba
did not believe he would be able to
"live by art". Working in the garage
of his house in New Brighton, Port
Elizabeth, where he lived for more
than 40 years, he felt himself to be
in what he called "the wilderness",
although his talent was obvious to
those exposed to it. In 1931, one
of Pemba's portrait subjects, a man
named Ncgobo, told him, "But I
never thought you could draw souls!"

Text from the Sunday Times memorial plaque

01 George Pemba's neighbours often saw him
painting in the garage or backyard of his home
that served as his studio for most of his career.
When Pemba wasn't painting, he was helping his
wife run their *spaza* shop, Gabby's Store, from the
front of the house.

02 This watercolour painting, entitled *Portrait of Ting
Ting*, was painted by Pemba in 1944. *Collection of
the King George VI Art Gallery, Port Elizabeth.*

PEMBA

A BUDDING ARTIST

George Pemba had virtually no formal art training and spent most of his life unrecognised for his art. Yet today he is one of South Africa's best-known artists. From as young as he can remember, Pemba's father, Titus, encouraged creativity in the household. George's older brother, Jimmy, painted on the walls in chalk while George painted murals on every available surface. When a white school inspector labelled George "the idiot of Korsten" because of his stammer and because he didn't pay attention in class, Titus got very angry with the inspector. To make his son feel better, he bought George his first set of water paints, paper and brushes. Titus also took George's painting to show his employers at Cuthbert's Shoes. They were so impressed with the youngster's art that they sent him photos and commissioned George to turn these into watercolour paintings from the silver screen.

Pemba earned his first money from painting when, having saved up for tickets to what was then known as the bioscope, in Bethelsdorp, he sold the portraits of film stars that he drew.

Tragically, Titus was killed in a motorcycle accident just before two of Pemba's portraits were exhibited at the Feathermarket Hall in Port Elizabeth in 1928. They were received enthusiastically by the public. Pemba was just 16 years old.

After Titus's death, Pemba's mother Rebecca was forced to move the family to New Brighton township, which was closer to Port Elizabeth than Korsten and offered better work opportunities. Rebecca became a washerwoman and walked more than 40 kilometres to do laundry to support her family.

Pemba focused on his studies so that he could help his mother financially. His diligence paid off and he received a scholarship to attend Lovedale Training College in 1931. It was here that Pemba's artistic talents were first spotted, albeit in a rather unusual way. Pemba was admitted to Victoria Hospital for a burst appendix and whiled away the hours in his hospital bed by sketching and painting the doctors, nurses and patients. One of his subjects, Ngcobo, so loved his portrait that he remarked to

Pemba, "But I never thought you could draw souls," and took the work to show Ethel Smythe, an art teacher at Fort Hare University. Smythe gave Pemba a five-week crash course in watercolour painting. At the same time, Pemba befriended Reverend Shepherd, the principal of Lovedale, who became his mentor and secured him many painting commissions for Lovedale's locally produced textbooks.

From 1935, Pemba taught at a school in King William's Town. Shepherd continued to mentor Pemba. In 1937, Shepherd arranged for Pemba to try out for the Bantu Welfare Trust scholarship, which he won. Pemba spent the next four months studying art under Professor Winter-Moore at Rhodes University. He was registered as an external student to get around the fact that black people were not allowed to study at Rhodes University. Winter-Moore entered Pemba's work into the May Esther Bedford Art Competition, the first art exhibition for black South Africans. Pemba won first prize and Sekoto was runner up.

01

ART AMONG THE BANTU

MAY ESTHER BEDFORD COMPETITION

The results of the May Esther Bedford competition (art section) are as follow:—

First prize (£20): Mr. G. Pember, Kingwilliamstown.

Second prize (£5): Mr. G. Sekoto, Khaiso Secondary School, Pietersburg.

There were six entrants and although this number is small it is by no means surprising when it is borne in mind that the development of art among the Bantu does not receive much encouragement even in Bantu schools.

>> . . . .

1912   George Pemba was born in New Korsten on the outskirts of Port Elizabeth. In 1928, after his father was killed in a motorcycle accident, he moved to New Brighton township in Port Elizabeth. The township became a key inspiration in his early work.

1931   Pemba trained at Lovedale Teacher Training College and worked as a teacher for the next seven years.

BECOMING A DAD

In the same year as winning the competition, Pemba married his second wife, Nombeka Mnidi. They had five children, and lived happily together for 47 years. Pemba's new family responsibilities forced him to leave teaching to take better-paid jobs, first as a messenger in the Native Commissioner's Court in Port Elizabeth and later, as a rent collector in New Brighton. Pemba hated this work. But as he told Barry Feinberg, who wrote about his life, "I had no idea that people could live by art. I did it more for my own entertainment."

MEETING SEKOTO AND MOHL

Despite not becoming a full-time artist, Pemba took commissions on the side. He painted the portrait of a woman he referred to as a "wealthy lady" who encouraged him to take a two-week art course in Cape Town. In 1941, he set off to study at the workshop of the artist Maurice van Essche who had been trained by Henri Matisse. He did not like the course and left early but it was here that he met his contemporaries, Gerard Sekoto and John Koenakeefe Mohl, one of the few black art teachers. They were impressed by Pemba's work. Sekoto persuaded Pemba to move beyond portraiture and to try to capture the vibrancy of African township life. In his diaries, Pemba wrote how Sekoto also "recommended that I revert to oil paintings because water colours were an English medium. South Africans prefer solid paint and effective colour…He also encouraged me to go independent…". Mohl reinforced Sekoto's opinion that Pemba should become a full-time artist.

01 After receiving his first formal training in art at Rhodes University, his professor convinced Pemba to enter a local art competition. Pemba beat his fellow artist, Gerard Sekoto.

02 Pemba married his second wife, Nombeka Mnidi, in 1939. They had five children.

03 George Pemba most often painted portraits, for which he became famous. As J De Jager, a prominent Pemba scholar, noted: "He has a sensitive attunement to the human face, and in portraiture he is concerned with more than mere representation of a true likeness. He is also concerned with what he can reveal about the inner state and character of his subjects."

04 This letter to his mentor, Reverend Shepherd of Lovedale College, shows that because of financial constraints, Pemba considered his painting more of a hobby than a viable career.

1938 Pemba resigned from his job as a teacher to take a better paying job at the Native Commissioner's Court. A year later, he married Nombeko Eunice Mnidi. To support their family, they opened a spaza shop at their house in New Brighton.

1941 Pemba met fellow artists Gerard Sekoto and John Mohl during a trip to Cape Town. They convinced Pemba to paint in oils and to focus on his art full-time.

PAINTING THE 'SOUL OF A NATION'

It took three years from the time of meeting Sekoto and Mohl before Pemba felt he could take more time for his art. At the age of 34, he applied to the Bantu Welfare Trust for money to tour South Africa and learn more about her people as he explains in these extracts from his diary published in a book on Pemba by Sarah Hudlestone:

"It was during the year 1944 that I wrote to Dr Kerr of Fort Hare applying for a loan. This loan was intended to enable me to see the beautiful plains and mountains of my own land, as I felt I could no longer tolerate being shut up in an office. I longed to see the Zulus, from whence the Xhosa originated, and the Basothos, the original people. By the way, I belong to Ngquosini tribe, the river people, who fled Moshoeshoe, and joined the Xhosa many years ago.

My letter to the Bantu Welfare Trust was quite a work of art...I stressed the point that I was proud of being a Bantu artist, of painting the soul of my nation, which I loved from the depth of my heart.

I achieved what I wanted. They granted me 25 pounds plus the loan of 50 pounds. This would not allow me to travel in luxury, but I did not intend doing so. On the contrary, I wanted to live like a tribesman, to share the conditions prevailing amongst the classes of Natives with whom I would have to deal, but to be for a short time someone else. I was always able to put myself in the place of another person, and this ability helped me a great deal in building up my art. I think that one must be like this if one wants to create truthfully."

Pemba was "full of expectations" to see "South Africa's largest city" but was deeply disappointed with Johannesburg, where he felt that he could not fulfill his quest to depict African people in their own milieu. In his diaries, he observed,

"I think there is nothing connecting them with the town in which they live. There is not the love of the homeland, no pride of tradition. There is only the ardent wish to make money, to gamble, to be thrilled at the thought of getting rich."

He went on to Durban and Umtata, but it was in Basutoland that he believes he did his best portraits:

"I certainly was very keen to paint such extraordinary scenery [in Basotholand] and also to become acquainted with the people living in these surroundings...I was able to paint Basotho in their primitive apparel. These pictures were among the best I painted on my journey through South Africa. I felt inspired by the spirit of the past and my strength grew with the task which I had in front of me; to capture the essence of native South Africa."

Pemba held two successful exhibitions in 1945. The *PE Herald* called him the "best seller" at the annual exhibition of the Society of Arts and Crafts in Port Elizabeth and Pemba himself wrote that his work "sold like hot cakes". His paintings were sold out after a few hours at an exhibition for black artists at the Durban International Club.

A SIGNIFICANT YEAR

1948 was a significant year in Pemba's life. He held his first solo exhibition in Port Elizabeth. It was also the year that he considered leaving the country, as did many of his peers, after the Nationalist Party came to power. He was persuaded to stay by his neighbour Raymond Mhlaba, featured in a previous story in this book. Mhlaba further encouraged Pemba to participate in the ANC's Defiance Campaign which he spearheaded. He also persuaded Pemba to do illustrations for the *Isizwe* newspaper, launched by ANC activists to provide political news to the Port Elizabeth community.

1944   Pemba won a Bantu Welfare Trust grant to travel through South Africa to witness the life and experiences of ordinary people. He showed his paintings the following year at the Eastern Province Society of Arts and Culture.

1957   Pemba only exhibited twice the following decade: once at the Mutual Arcade in Port Elizabeth (1957) and then at the Queenstown Art Society Annual Exhibition (1958).

Ndingu Mthanjiswa ka Tixo—
I Bunguza liyeza

A LEAP OF FAITH

Against this political backdrop, Pemba experienced more keenly his frustrations with his job in the government administration. In 1952, he gathered the courage to quit. He succeeded in getting a licence to open a *spaza* shop with his wife Nombeka. At the time, *spaza* shops were important meeting places in township life. They functioned as dealers of credit and presented an opportunity for black people to boycott the expensive white-owned general dealers. Most importantly for Pemba, the shop allowed him to dedicate more time to his art.

With a steady income from his *spaza* shop, Pemba began to flourish creatively. In addition to his paintings, which he exhibited three times in the late 1940s and throughout the 1950s, Pemba became an avid playwright and completed two plays. The first, *Ntsikana: the Xhosa Prophet*, was staged in New Brighton to mixed response. In 1968, he staged his second play, *The Story of Nonqawuse*. This play focused on the life of the famous Nonqawuse, whose prophecies in the Eastern Cape in the 19th century led to the infamous cattle-killing epidemic. This play debuted to a much better response and was received, as he later recalled, to "enthusiastic acclaim".

Over the next twenty years, Pemba refined his painting style. He moved away from an academic and formal style to a more expressionistic one. He gave himself license to play with his material, rather than forcing himself to represent things exactly as they appeared. He also simplified his approach, and focused on simple forms and bold colours. Later in his life, Pemba adopted a more hurried, looser sketching style. The work from the latter period of his life is now recognized as emblematic of his approach, and is often the most highly regarded.

01 In *Isizwe's* first issue, Pemba depicted then Prime Minister HF Verwoerd in tribal dress – a reference to Verwoerd's obsession with ethnicity and separate development.

02 Pemba in his *spaza* shop, 'Gabby's Store', which was a meeting place for young and old alike. Raymond Mhlaba, who lived next door to the Pemba's, tried to support the black-owned establishment as much as possible.

1968 Pemba completed his first play, *Ntsikana*, which was performed at the New Brighton hall to much acclaim. The play centred on the story of a fictional Xhosa prophet.

1979 Fifty-one years after his first exhibition, Pemba was finally recognized for his contribution to the art world. He was granted three honorary degrees from various institutions.

FIGHTING HIS DEMONS

Pemba's life was filled with many challenges. Alcohol was a demon that haunted him for many years. In his diaries he says that,

> "The history of my drinking started [with me being persuaded] into a Coloured bar where I had a glass of beer. I passed for Coloured because of my fair complexion and being fluent in Afrikaans…[Later] I was part of an 'elite' class in which inebriation was the order of the day. I was at the top of the world in my drunken stupor."

The church saved him from drinking himself to death, as was the fate of so many others around him. He reflects on his battle with alcoholism and how he recovered: "I felt addiction to liquor was a disease…the church gave me the confidence which I lacked and in a short time, I was completely cured. " Later he tellingly wrote in his diary about the key to being a successful artist, "Draw from life and imagination. Try to interpret your daily life and surroundings. Keep away from strong drink and distractions."

On 17 November1968, his brother Jimmy died and Pemba felt that "he could not paint at all…I was in the wilderness." His brother's death was followed by the departure of a relative to join *Umkhonto we Sizwe*, the armed wing of the ANC. George and Nombeka were left with 20 children in their care. Pemba feared that he would have to give up painting to support his new extended family. He was saved by an unexpected envelope of money that arrived in the post in 1969. It was from the International Defence and Aid Fund, a British organisation that supported victims of apartheid. For the first time, Pemba had enough money to feed his family and buy art supplies.

Pemba's artistic growth received belated attention. Although he was always appreciated by the black intelligentsia, Pemba finally came into his own in the 1970's. In 1979, he received his first honorary degree from the University of Fort Hare. This was followed by honorary degrees from the University of Zululand (1986) and the University of Bophuthatswana (1987).

RECOGNITION AT LAST

In the early 1990s, as apartheid crumbled, Pemba's work was admitted into the mainstream art world. The response was enthusiastic. In 1991 and '92, he held his first exhibition at the Everard Read Gallery in Johannesburg. Most of the works on show were obtained from a German art dealer who had bought all of Pemba's paintings from his studio. He had paid R4 000 for 178 pictures. Pemba commented that each painting was now on sale for more than the total for which he had sold his entire collection!

In response to the popularity of the Everard Read Galley exhibition, Pemba held a massive retrospective exhibition at the National Gallery of South Africa. Almost sixty years after he published his first illustration for the Lovedale Press, Pemba was finally recognized as one of South Africa's most important, influential and engaging modern artists. In notes for a speech dated 25 June 1991, Pemba thanked his supporters but added with characteristic good humour:

> "I also have to thank myself for holding on to the hope that one day the sun will also shine on me."

01 Pemba basking in the glow of belated glory at the 1996 launch of Sarah Hudlestone's monograph on his work, *Against All Odds*. Hudlestone's monograph was published to support Pemba's 1996 exhibition at the National Gallery.

1996 Pemba received full recognition from the South African mainstream art world with a retrospective exhibition at the National Gallery of South Africa.	**2001** George Pemba died.

2004 Pemba posthumously received the Order of the *Ikhamanga* (gold), a prestigious award by the South African presidency for distinguished achievement in arts and culture.

"With Pemba's death the era of the pioneers comes to an end. He blazed a trail through the art establishment in South Africa, laying claim to a place for black artists, but at the same time refusing to compromise his political and moral principles. His works are now in the major museums in South Africa and he has taken his place as one of the leading figures in not only the history of South African art, but of African art in the 20th century."

'Bobo' PEMBA, *Pemba's grandson and Trustee of the George Pemba Art Foundation*

ARTIST > ANDREW NHLANGWINI

ADDRESS > 28 Ferguson Road, New Brighton, Port Elizabeth

Port Elizabeth-based painter and art lecturer, Dandheni Andrew Nhlangwini feels a deep resonance with George Pemba's work and leapt at the chance to take on this project. "Since my student days, I admired his courage and his work - he recorded his people's life through visual images," Nhlangwini says. "He suffered as an artist, but he decided to stay here in South Africa, where he documented the history of township life."

Nhlangwini's artwork is both a tribute to Pemba and a means of bringing the memory of the artist into the public domain. The site of the artwork is the home Pemba lived and worked in for 40 years - 28 Ferguson Road, New Brighton. Today, it is the base of the George Pemba Art Foundation. It is situated on the main road running into New Brighton, visible to all who pass by.

Duma NOKWE

"Racialism of whatever kind is an abomination."

Duma NOKWE

On 9 March 1956, Duma Nokwe became South Africa's first black advocate at the Johannesburg Bar, beating his rival, Nelson Mandela, to the honour. The Minister of Native Affairs, Hendrik Verwoerd, turned down Nokwe's application to have offices, known as chambers, in His Majesty's Building where the white advocates were housed. Fellow advocate George Bizos illegally shared his chambers with Nokwe from 1956 to 1962.

Text from the Sunday Times memorial plaque

01   Duma Nokwe in his advocate's robes. He was the first black South African advocate to wear these robes in court.

02   Nokwe's degree certificate was submitted as an appendix to his application for admittance to the roll of South African advocates.

A N N E X U R E   "A"

UNIVERSITAS WITWATERSRANDENSIS JOANNISBURGI

SCIENTIA ET LABORE

HOC SCRIPTO NOS UNIVERSITATIS WITWATERSRANDENSIS

JOANNISBURGI VICE - CANCELLARIUS RECTOR,

FACULTATIS LEGIS DECANUS ET REGISTRARIUS

TESTATUM VOLUMUS

........PHILEMON..PEARCE..DUMA..NOKWE..........

GRADUM LEGUM BACCALAUREI

consecutum esse

.R..HAHLO......Facultatis Decanus .W.G.SUTTON... Vice
                                            Cancellarius
                                                et
.V.Herholdt.... Registrarius   .... Rector

Joannisburgi,

anno...MCML.V...mensis.DECEMBRI die..XV.

BECOMING AN ADVOCATE

Duma Nokwe was an only child, born into a working-class family in the township of Evaton, halfway between Sebokeng and Vanderbijlpark in what is now Gauteng. Little is known of Nokwe's early life.

Nokwe attended St Peter's Secondary School, a famous school in Rosentenville, Johannesburg, that produced many future black professionals and intellectuals. Nokwe was taught there by Oliver Tambo, with whom he later shared the leadership of the ANC.

After school, Nokwe enrolled at the University of Fort Hare to study a Bachelor of Science degree. Nokwe was immediately drawn into the heady world of politics in the Eastern Cape. He joined the ANC Youth League and quickly rose up through the ranks, becoming the organiser of the branch. This branch played a leading role in formulating the ANC Youth League's programme of action, which was used to create the famous Freedom Charter issued seven years later.

Nokwe received his Bachelor of Science degree in 1949. Like many other black professionals at the time, he followed his degree with a teacher's diploma. Teaching was one of the few professional avenues for blacks. Nokwe took up a teaching post in Krugersdorp near Johannesburg. There he met and married his fellow teacher, Vuyiswa, better known as Tiny. They had two children together.

In 1952, Nokwe and his wife took part in the ANC's Defiance Campaign. Together, they entered a Germiston location without a travel pass, and were arrested. The consequences were devastating. Both were barred from teaching ever again. The Transvaal Education Department would not even allow their students to organise a farewell party for them.

The next year, Nokwe went on an overseas tour with Walter Sisulu. Amongst other countries, they visited the People's Republic of China and the Union of Soviet Socialist Republics (USSR). Nokwe was impressed by the communist political ideal of those countries that the wealth of the country should be shared by all citizens.

01

There were serious arguments at that time in the ANC about the best way forward for South Africa. Nokwe argued that South Africa should adopt communism once apartheid was overthrown. Furthermore, he believed that the ANC should be working with other organisations to bring down apartheid.

On his return to South Africa, and possibly influenced by his comrades Nelson Mandela and Oliver Tambo, Nokwe enrolled at the University of the Witwatersrand (Wits) to study law. He simultaneously pursued his political career and was elected Secretary of the ANC Youth League, a position that he held until 1958. This was not an easy role to fill as in 1954, Nokwe was named under

>> . . . .

1927
13 May

Duma Nokwe was born in Evaton, in the then Transvaal. He attended the famous St Peter's Secondary School in Johannesburg.

1949

Duma Nokwe graduated with a Bachelor of Science degree from the University of Fort Hare. A year later, Nokwe trained as a teacher and took up his first teaching post in Krugersdrop. It was at this time that he met and married a fellow teacher Vuyiswa, nicknamed Tiny.

the Suppression of Communism Act along with many of his comrades. He was banned from attending large political meetings or engaging in any political activity, and from being with more than three people at a time. This banning order lasted a full five years.

OBSTACLES

In 1955, Nokwe became the first black South African advocate. This was a remarkable achievement considering how many obstacles he had to overcome. Entrance to Wits University was severely limited for black students. By 1963, only four blacks had ever graduated from the law faculty. The fees were extremely high and many of Nokwe's fellow black students were forced to drop out because they could not afford it. Nokwe was banned during his studies and was constantly harassed.

After graduating, Nokwe faced a whole new set of hurdles. Because he was still a banned person, he could not travel to take up any cases outside of Johannesburg without permission. When he was allowed to appear in court in Bethlehem in 1956, the judges humiliated Nokwe. They asked him to take a seat at tables specially set aside for non-European advocates and attorneys. Nokwe's objection to this indignity fell upon deaf ears. As one of the 160 advocates in Johannesburg, and the first black South African ever to be admitted to the Bar, Nokwe faced a great indignity amongst his own colleagues upon his admission. The future Prime Minister, BJ Vorster, an advocate and member of the Bar, together with 20 of his colleagues, furiously opposed the sharing of chambers, the common room and the library with a black South African.

They argued that in terms of the Group Areas Act, the area in downtown Johannesburg where the chambers were located was set aside for white business only. Nokwe's presence was, in their estimation, a transgression of one of the most important laws of the day.

While Nokwe was told he couldn't operate from town, another Supreme Court ruling stated that an advocate's chambers had to be in reach of the court in central Johannesburg. If Nokwe's chambers were in what was known as a 'native location', he would not have been able to work as an advocate at all!

01 Nokwe married Tiny in 1950. Both were teachers and were politically active.

02 Nokwe outside the Johannesburg High Court.

1952   Nokwe took part in the Defiance Campaign, as a result of which he and his wife Tiny were barred from teaching ever again. Nokwe read law at the University of the Witwatersrand.

1953   Nokwe was elected Secretary of the ANC Youth League (ANCYL). A year later, he was banned for five years under the Suppression of Communism Act.

1955   Nokwe graduated from Wits. The following year, he was admitted to the Johannesburg Bar but was banned from using the whites-only common room.

LACK OF A CUP OF TEA

The situation caused a furor in the Bar. The majority of the advocates supported Nokwe's admission and petitioned the Minister of Native Affairs, Hendrik Verwoerd, to allow Nokwe to be granted access to chambers. They were however, unsuccessful. Writing through his private secretary, Verwoerd argued, in this letter on the right, that allowing Nokwe access to chambers and the common room would violate government policy.

In response to Verwoerd, the Johannesburg Bar constituted a special sub-committee to make further presentations against the Minister. Advocate BJ Vorster tried his best to derail their plans as these minutes of the sub-committee meeting, featured on the facing page demonstrate.

Nokwe was deeply upset by these deliberations. He consulted his ANC colleagues who persuaded him not to persist in requesting permission to use the common room. Walter Sisulu argued strategically: "Are we to lose an opportunity to break the (racial) barrier for lack of a cup of tea?"

The matter of Nokwe's chambers was more complicated. Issie Maisels, the leader of the Defence in the Treason Trial, and George Bizos hatched a plan. They staged a discussion so that Bizos could offer to share his chambers.

ARRESTED FOR TREASON

This ploy worked but some three months after his name went up on the door, Duma was arrested on a charge of treason and could only practice law when the trial was adjourned. "His name remained on the door of our shared chambers but his practice was erratic", explains George Bizos. "He could only work on cases when the preparatory examination and trial were adjourned. Our office was regularly used for meetings after working hours. Those prohibited from attending gatherings felt safer at the advocates' chambers."

By 1960, the number of accused standing on charges of treason had been whittled down to 30, of which Nokwe was one. When the government declared a State of Emergency (SOE) after the Sharpeville massacre in 1960, Nokwe was ironically afforded new opportunities to hone his legal skills.

COPY.

N.A.456.

OFFICE OF THE MINISTER OF NATIVE AFFAIRS,
Room 290 (East Wing),
~~Room 290 (East Wing),~~
Union Buildings,
PRETORIA.

P.1/2A.

August 29th 1956.

Dear Sir,

 On behalf of the Honourable the Minister of Native Affairs I wish to acknowledge receipt of your letter of August 16th, 1956 in connection with the decision that P.P.D.Nokwe cannot be granted permission to occupy chambers in a European urban area, but can, if he so wishes, find suitable accommodation within a proclaimed native residential area where provision is made for shops, offices, etc. for native occupation.

 The Minister has considered the arguments advanced by you and the request to receive a deputation. Since the decision was based on the legal position which has existed for some considerable time, and is in full accord with Government policy there can be no departure from the stand taken, and consequently an interview will serve no good purpose.

 It is noted that your claim that the Government should sacrifice State Policy on this matter, and be prepared to create a precedent for granting such exemptions in spite of the clear intention of the Native Urban Areas Act and the Group Areas Act, rests upon your apparent determination not to vary certain rules of the Bar as stated in paragraph 5 of your letter or the policy of your society as in paragraph 10, and furthermore rests upon the implication that personal inconvenience to a restricted number of persons (your paragraphs 7 and 8) must be given preference over what is judged to be in the best interests of the community as a whole.

 Such rules and policy of a Society can, however, be more easily altered than the laws and policy of the State.

Yours faithfully,

(Sgd). J.Fred.Barnard.

PRIVATE SECRETARY.

02

1956 Nokwe was arrested and charged with treason. He played a central role in the Treason Trail and, for a short period, led the defence of the accused with Nelson Mandela.

1958 While the Treason Trial was still ongoing, Nokwe was appointed Secretary General of the ANC. He was only 30. He held this position until 1969.

MINUTES OF A SPECIAL GENERAL MEETING OF
THE BAR HELD IN THE COMMON ROOM ON
THURSDAY 13TH SEPTEMBER 1956 AT 4.15 P.M.

PRESENT: I.A. MAISELS, Q.C. (In the Chair)
and members as per the attached list.

The CHAIRMAN opened the meeting and outlined the events which had taken place with regard to NOKWE.

The CHAIRMAN stated that the issues now before the meeting were:-

1. The use by non-Europeans of the Library.
2. The use by non-Europeans of the Common Room.
3. The publication of the correspondence between the Bar Council and the Minister of Native Affairs.
4. The issue of a statement setting out the views of the Bar on the Minister's action.

THE BAR COUNCIL proposed:

1. That non-European members be permitted the use of the library.
2. That the correspondence be published with a statement setting out the views of the Bar.
3. That no action be taken at present on the question of the Common Room.

Interview with Prime Minister - Carried. 6 against of these, van Loggerenberg and Vorster recorded that their reason for voting against was that they supported the Minister's decision.

IT WAS AGREED to hold a ballot on the attitudes of members towards:-

1. Accommodation of Nokwe in a native Residential Area.
2. Accommodation of Nokwe in a "mixed area".
3. Accommodation of Nokwe in His Majesty's Buildings.

A vote was taken on Nokwe being allowed to use the LIBRARY the result being that, with the exception of one member, the meeting approved that Nokwe be permitted the continued use of the Library.

IT WAS AGREED that pending an interview with the Prime Minister no statement should be issued to the press for publication.

THE MEETING TERMINATED AT 6 P.M.

READ & CONFIRMED: ....

CHAIRMAN: ....

SECRETARY: ....

As a result of the emergency restrictions, the accused in the Treason Trial were unable to consult with their lawyers.

Nokwe orchestrated the defence proceedings together with Nelson Mandela. Their strategy was simple: delay the case until the SOE was called off. They decided that the accused would cross-examine each other, a ploy, as Mandela recalled, that would keep them at trial "until the millennium". Luckily for the accused, the SOE was lifted in September and the original defence team was able to return to court. By March 1961, the Treason Trial had collapsed with the judge stating that the government could not prove its case. Nokwe, along with the other accused, was released from prison after nearly five years of standing trial. But it was only a temporary reprieve.

01 This letter from Verwoerd presents the objections of 21 advocates against Nokwe being granted access to the Bar, stating that he could not take chambers in a 'European Urban Area'.

02 Duma Nokwe sharing a quick meal with his co-accused Robert Resha during the Treason Trial. Both men fled into exile after the Treason Trial.

03 Most members of the Johannesburg Bar saw no problem in admitting Nokwe to chambers as a full member.

1961 March The Treason Trial collapsed, and Nokwe was released. However, he was arrested later the same month under the Unlawful Organizations Act. Nokwe was able to successfully appeal the arrest.

1963 Nokwe was instructed by the ANC leaders to go into exile. He joined the ANC External Mission.

A MASSIVE BLOW

At the end of March 1961, Duma Nokwe was arrested once again, this time under the Unlawful Organizations Act. Drawing on his impressive legal skills, Nokwe was able to contest the arrest, and won his case. Regardless, it was becoming increasingly apparent that it was dangerous for Nokwe to remain in the country.

In 1963, Nokwe was ordered by the ANC High Command to leave South Africa. The organisation could not afford to lose such a valuable member at a time when Mandela, Mbeki, Mhlaba and others had just been arrested at Rivonia. Nokwe obliged and moved with his family to the ANC External Mission in Lusaka.

In exile, Nokwe worked tirelessly in the Foreign Affairs Department of the ANC. In 1975, his persistence was rewarded when he was made the ANC Director of International Affairs, tasked with meeting foreign diplomats and presenting the public face of the ANC. Nokwe's health suffered in exile. For six years, between 1969 and 1975, he was too ill to work for the ANC in any capacity. In 1978, he finally succumbed. For many of the diplomats with whom he was in frequent contact, his death came as a shock. Tributes to Nokwe poured in from around the world. He was survived by his parents, his wife Tiny, and their two children.

01 As the ANC's Director of International Affairs, Nokwe was the public face of the organization. Here he holds hands with delegates from around the world at the International Conference against Racism in the German Democratic Republic in 1968. The text in the background can be roughly translated as 'no racism or neo-colonialism for the freeing of South Africa.'

02 Nokwe's death was a massive blow for the ANC in exile.

1969 Nokwe began suffering from a severe illness, and relinquished his post as Secretary General of the ANC.	**1975** After recovering from six years of illness, Nokwe was appointed Deputy Secretary-General and Director of International Affairs of the ANC.	**1978** 12 January Duma Nokwe passed away in Lusaka after a further bout of illness at the age of 50. He was survived by his wife and their two daughters.

"The armed wing of the African National Congress has lost a leading soldier. Fortunately not before he had painstakingly sharpened the spear which is now harassing the fascist murderers at home. *TSAMAYA SINHLE DUMA. AMANDLA NGAWETHU!* DEATH TO IMPERIALISM!"

Umkhonto we Sizwe pays tribute to Duma NOKWE on hearing of his death.

. . . .

ARTIST > LEWIS LEVIN

. . . .

ADDRESS > High Court, Pritchard Street, Johannesburg

"I thought the best homage I could give to a figure as significant as Duma Nokwe was a portrait," says Lewis Levin. "The idea was almost to produce a photographic image that is a ghost. When we die we become ghosts. A ghost is a beautiful name for an invisible person...We live among ghosts."

Levin says he looked at a photograph of Nokwe and was moved by the white of his eyes, the light on his forehead, his open mouth, his quiet dignity: "All of those things spoke to me." The frame around the portrait resembles a doorway, "the door that Nokwe couldn't go through physically".

Lilian NGOYI

"Strydom, stop and think for you have aroused the wrath
of the women of South Africa and that wrath might put you
and your evil deeds out of action sooner than you expect."

Lilian NGOYI

01

"Vorster, you strike a woman, you strike a rock."
It was with these words that 20 000 women
warned the apartheid state that its oppressive
policies would not be tolerated without a fight.
Leading this fight was Lilian Masediba Ngoyi,
the fiery President of the ANC Women's League.
On 9 August 1956, Ngoyi, along with Helen
Joseph, Rahima Moosa and Sophie Williams,
led a march of 20 000 women to the Union
Buildings in Pretoria to deliver armfuls of
petitions against the extension of pass-laws to
women. When they were turned away by an
apartheid functionary, Ngoyi watched as the
assembled crowd warned Vorster in a way that
defined much of the anti-apartheid struggle - in
song. Ngoyi, however, came to bear much of the
brunt for the warning. In 1961, she was banned
and confined to her home in Orlando West,
Soweto. Barring a reprieve of three years in the
mid-1970s, Ngoyi lived under house arrest until
her death in 1980.

Text from the Sunday Times memorial plaque

01   After Lilian Ngoyi was banned in 1961, she
      spent much time at home writing letters to
      friends and family at home and abroad.

02   When Ngoyi's ban was lifted for a brief time,
      in 1973, she travelled the country. In this
      letter, written to Belinda Allen, her American
      friend living in Switzerland and working for
      Amnesty International, Ngoyi expressed her
      joy at being free.

AEROGRAM
PER LUGPOS
BY AIR MAIL
PAR AVION
AEROGRAMME

AAN
TO Mrs B. Donald Allan
P.O. Box 5902
Beirut
Lebanon

[lower-left handwritten continuation]
... July, I hired a taxi to take me to Groutville to the grave of Chief Albert Luthuli. I'm sure you read about him he was our Leader. When he died I could not attend his funeral according to our Custom. I do not need a wreath, and ofcourse I could not afford one. Our car stalled for about 3 hours & it was getting dark I was able to through to the spot on behalf of all those who did not have the priviledge. And on behalf of those sentenced to life imprisonment. I will make a day to see his widow. Next week, I'll go back home to arrange for Cape Town if allowed will try & see the life sentenced colleagues. You can answer to Johannesburg you know my address. There is too much activity. I'm rushing to go to the snake park. Much love to Donald & the Children   Lilian

[right-hand page]
24 - 7 - 73

My Dearest Belinda & Donald

I immediately booked a second class coach to Durban, and within a day I was on a train bound for Durban. A wonderful coincidence when your parcel arrived also another from a friend in London yours amounted to R40 and the friend Another. so I was alright for Durban, 430 miles from Johannesburg as I write, I've been swimming in the sea. Now as I'm having my launch thought of writing to you and thanking you. May the love of God which is above all knowledge be with you Now and for ever. I never thought I would ever come here. I'm looking at the sea waves, the ships, the multitude of people and I say yes 11 years thanks you were not renewed. I sat by the window noticing the wonderful changes, the guard of our train says tickets tickets Ladies. we were three Black Women. How nice to our ears to be addressed ladies. Then the next man comes in. Bedding, & Supes. I proudly said yes because of you, & your Family. As we were at a certain place called black rocky. ofcourse let me tell you Durban is full of Hills. at the places you notice the Hill is full of mud houses, and can notice a few women carrying water pots on their heads you wonder where they do their shopping. immediately you get to the next Hill you notice very nice white buildings almost every house a garage. then you get depressed. So it because of the Colour of our skins Lord? Then as you enter Pietermaritzburg you notice a place called the Valley of thousands Hills. Oh! nature can provide beauty. I felt now this is where I would suggest a University of our children should be erected one without discrimination of Colour race or creed. I arrived at Durban to find no friends to meet me, as usual my telegram was delayed. Never the less I got to their place safely. Durban is noted for producing Sugar the place is Marvellous. The Sunday the ...

A FEARLESS LEADER

Lilian Masediba Ngoyi was born in 1911 just outside Pretoria. The only female in a family of five boys, Lilian's early life was marked by struggle and poverty. Her father was a mineworker, while her mother took in washing to make ends meet. Lilian experienced an incident of racism when she was young that she never forgot. Ngoyi's mother, Anne, sent Lilian to deliver a clean batch of laundry to the home of a white woman. To Lilian's dismay, the white woman refused to tether her vicious dog and wouldn't let Ngoyi cross the threshold of the house. Her grandfather, a Pedi chief turned pastor, said it was only prayer that could save them from the oppression of apartheid, but Lilian, forced to leave school in Grade 8 to earn a living, soon learned that prayer was not enough.

In 1945, when Ngoyi was 33, her life changed completely. Like many other black women in those times, Ngoyi moved to Johannesburg in search of better-paid work. She lived in a series of breeze-block compounds in Soweto, known as 'the shelters'. Ngoyi found work as a machinist at a garment factory. She joined the Garment Workers Union (GWU) led by the firebrand unionist, Solly Sachs. This was one of the few unions where black women worked for the same wages and under the same conditions as their white counterparts. Lilian quickly developed a reputation for being fearless and was elected shop-steward to represent her factory. Lilian's friend and fellow political activist, Amina Cachalia, remembers meeting her for the first time:

> "I realised that here was a great lady, a woman of substance in a way, and she is going to go a long way, and be our leader. That is the impression that a lot of us had at the time of Lilian when we first met her."

In 1952, Sachs was banned under the Suppression of Communism Act. He defied a government order to resign from the union, and addressed a protest gathering in contravention of his banning order. Lilian was in the thick of the demonstration - an experience she would later describe as formative.

Spurred on by her experience, Ngoyi joined the ANC and the ANC Women's League and signed on for the Defiance Campaign. She invited her own arrest by walking into a whites-only post office and sending the following telegram to Prime Minister Malan:

> "Dr Malan, will you please withdraw your bills? South Africa has been a peaceful country. If not, remember what happened to Hitler in Germany and Mussolini in Italy."

Ngoyi was arrested but was soon released. She started to make her mark politically with her speeches and remarkable presence. She worked her way through the ranks of the ANC and the ANC Women's League, and was recognised as a fearless fighter. Towards the end of 1952, she was elected President of the ANC Women's League and, two years later, she became the first woman to serve on the ANC's National Executive Committee. She chastised the men, using public platforms to goad them into action. As her close comrade, Sophie Williams, recalled:

> "She challenged them a lot…She would stretch herself up and make her eyes big and say, 'Where are you hiding? You are the men. Are you hiding behind a woman's skirt?'"

The author, Es'kia Mphahlele, wrote of her force and beauty:

> "She can toss an audience on her little finger, get men grunting with shame and a feeling of smallness, and infuse everyone with renewed courage."

1911 Lilian Masediba Ngoyi was born on the 25th of September near Pretoria. She was the only girl in a family of six children.

1944 Ngoyi moved to Johannesburg in search of work.

1945 Ngoyi found work at a garment factory and joined the Garment Workers Union (GWU). She was elected as a shop-steward for her factory.

THE BURDEN OF LIFE

While Lilian was making her mark politically, she was at the same time a single mother and the family's sole breadwinner. Her life was a far cry from the relatively carefree days of her early 20's when she took up competitive ballroom dancing and met and married her husband, a van driver called John Ngoyi, while she trained to become a nurse a the City Deep mine hospital. Their only daughter Edith was born, and shortly afterwards her husband died of complications arising from tuberculosis. Lilian then took on the added responsibility of adopting her dying aunt's new-born child. Memory Mphahlele lived with Edith, Lilian and her grandmother in a small four-roomed house in Orlando West in Soweto for most of her childhood. Memory's most striking memory of her childhood was of the "police coming in to fetch my mum to go to jail."

Indeed, by the time Lilian was in her early 40's, her life was consumed by politics. After the Defiance Campaign ended in 1954, a group of women leaders met in Port Elizabeth to discuss the launch of a national, multi-racial women's organisation to promote women's rights. They looked at incorporating women from organisations outside of the political spectrum, like *stokvels*, church groups and domestic workers. Lilian became President of the newly-created Federation of South African Women (FEDSAW).

NEW PERSPECTIVES

In her new role, she was chosen to represent South Africa's women, together with Dora Tamane, at the World Congress of Women in Switzerland in 1954. She tried slipping unobtrusively out of the country without a passport, at first aboard a Union Castle ship and, when that didn't succeed, by air.

When white passengers complained about Lilian and Dora's presence, the pilot announced that he wasn't having any apartheid on his plane and continued the journey. Her trip to London and then on to Switzerland, Uganda, Germany, Italy, the USSR and China changed her life.

02

01 Ngoyi's fiery speech-making style and physical beauty made a major impact on those around her.

1953 Ngoyi was arrested after taking part in a demonstration against the banning of GWU leader, Solly Sachs. She joined the ANC and the ANC Women's League. She took part in the Defiance Campaign and provoked arrest by using a whites-only post office.

1954 Ngoyi was elected President of the Federation of South African Women (FEDSAW). She was also elected to the ANC National Executive Committee (NEC).

'YOU HAVE STRUCK A ROCK'

JG Strijdom's election as Prime Minister in 1954 gave Lilian the opportunity to flex her muscle. Strijdom rigorously pursued the policy of apartheid and in 1955 - shortly after the Congress of the People adopted the Freedom Charter - Strijdom hit back. He announced that passes would soon be required by black women, who would not be allowed in urban areas without a pass and would have to abide by a strict curfew. Strijdom's announcement provoked a storm of reaction and FEDSAW decided to fight against this issue.

On the 9th of August, after months of organisation, 20 000 women marched to the Union Buildings in Pretoria to protest against the pass laws for African women. Amina Cachalia, heavily pregnant with her first child, was the first to arrive at the Union Buildings on that freezing cold morning in 1956:

"I walked up to the amphitheatre and just sat there and waited and waited...until I saw these women coming from all sides of the Union Buildings, walking, singing and carrying blankets. It was freezing cold but...my day brightened when I saw the women coming from all around."

Amina Cachalia was joined at the helm of the march by Lilian Ngoyi, Helen Joseph, Rahima Moosa, and Sophie Williams. Williams picks up the story:

"This was the first time in the history of South Africa that black women took over the citadel of apartheid ... We regarded Lilian as the natural leader. She said 'now it's time to go and knock on the door of Strijdom'. And it was Lilian who knocked and said, 'We've come to see Strijdom', to a clerk that opened the door. He said, 'Mr Strijdom is not here'. And Lilian said,

01 From left: Rahima Moosa, Lilian Ngoyi, Helen Joseph and Sophie Williams, delivering armfuls of petitions to the government.

02 Sophie Williams, Helen Joseph, Lilian Ngoyi and Rahima Moosa were furious when Strijdom refused to see them.

'He ought to have been here, because he knew we were coming. We wrote him a letter. We've brought these petititons.'"

The five angry women leaders placed the petitions in the arms of the clerk. Lilian turned to the thousands of women who had travelled long distances and said, "Strijdom has run away, he is not in his office." The throng of women chanted in unison:

"*Strijdom, Wathint Abafazi, Wathint Imboko, Uzokufa. Wena Strijdom*, you are messing with the women. You touch the women, you strike a rock. You are going to die."

Phyllis Naidoo remembers how: "Lilian led everybody in singing, and she was a beautiful women hey, and she said 'Power', and you could see it oozing, and she was afraid of nobody. Nobody could frighten Lilian."

THE GOVERNMENT STRIKES BACK

In a stroke of organisational genius, FEDSAW signed up most of the 20 000 women at their conference after the march. But their jubilation was short-lived. In December 1956, the authorities charged 156 people, including Ngoyi, with treason. The petitions the women had deposited at Strijdom's door were used as evidence in the trial that followed. For the third time in her life, Ngoyi was taken into custody and was held at Pretoria Central Prison. She served five months in jail, including 71 days in solitary confinement.

03

H.O. REF. NO. 3/50/166

17/33/4/1/26

838-8346

MAGISTRATE,
JOHANNESBURG.

26th April, 1965.

To LILIAN MASEDIBA NGOYI,
9870b, White City,
Orlando,
JOHANNESBURG.

2/1/497

Greetings,

1. PERMISSION is hereby granted for you to absent yourself from Orlando Location on one day per week, on Mondays, or on the following day should Monday fall on a public holiday, between the hours of 8 a.m. and 2 p.m., for the purpose of proceeding to the central city area of Johannesburg to make purchases essential to your business.

   You are required to report to the Orlando Police before departure and on return to Orlando on each occasion.

2. A separate application should be made on each occasion you wish to interview your attorney.

Greetings,

I. DEKENAH

03 This letter granted Ngoyi permission to visit town one day per week to buy supplies.

A CRUEL PUNISHMENT

Although Lilian was eventually cleared of all charges of treason in 1960, she was soon re-arrested in the wake of the Sharpeville massacre. Ngoyi was detained without trial for a further 19 days. These prison episodes were very traumatic. Conditions for black women prisoners were shocking, far worse than those for white women prisoners, as the veteran anti-apartheid leader, Albertina Sisulu, explains:

> "In solitary confinement you are there, sitting on the mat, with lice in the blanket, running up and down. There for months on end, with nobody to talk to. Taken out for exercise for 30 minutes. The food that was there, my dear, you wouldn't eat."

After being released, Ngoyi faced a new and cruel form of punishment that had been introduced by the apartheid government in the early 1960s. She was served with a five-year banning order, which was renewed in 1967 for a further five years. Ngoyi was prevented from leaving her four-roomed house in Orlando West, or from attending any gathering of more than three people. She became a prisoner in her own home.

Ngoyi struggled to make ends meet. Her banning order limited how and when she could purchase goods to make her living as a dressmaker. She mostly sewed blouses worn by the women in the organisations she belonged to. In 1965, as can be seen in this letter, she was given permission to travel to the town once a week – on a Monday – for six hours to buy supplies. The costs and time spent getting to town were considerable. Ngoyi's good friend and political comrade, Nthato Motlana, comments:

> "The thing that makes me so sad up until this day is when I recall the state that Lilian lived in. She lived in such poverty it breaks my heart. It was so sad that somebody who sacrificed so much could have lived in such dire poverty."

She enjoyed an all too brief three-year reprieve when her ban was not extended in 1972. But she was banned again in 1975 until her death in 1980.

1960 The charges of High Treason against Lilian Ngoyi were dropped. However, she was arrested again in the wake of the Sharpeville massacre, and was held without trial for 19 days.	**1961** Lilian Ngoyi was served with her first banning order, which restricted her to her home in Orlando West in Soweto. She was prevented from attending gatherings of more than three people, and made a meagre living as a seamstress, supporting two children.

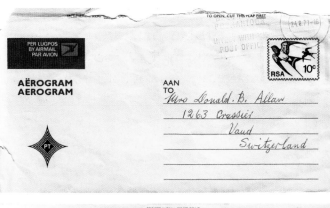

My Dearest Mrs & Mr Allan.   24th August 77

This is to thank you, for your letters of the 15 August which I received promptly. Lately my letters to me takes a month or a little less than a month. It always pleases me very much to read the family was together and that this pleases you in particular. You are a wife to be kept. I admire your sincerity to the children. May courage & peace throne you my love. Your expression of saying your people are in Heaven makes me wonder if one day I shall speak the same language. God Bless you my love. Yes, chickens, cheese, mutton etc are lately the order in my fridge after years of severe starvation. You and my other friends have kept the fire burning, and all the time asking me this question :– Is there anything else we could help, I always felt embarrassed, Because my needs were rather too much to mention. Until one day just after spring cleaning this match box house of mine, As I have already told you that it is cement low the roof cement on the walls, cement on the floor. Now this house is a fridge in Winter and an oven in Summer. This is my story that very day a tall gentleman knocked at my door, I would like to see Mrs Ngoyi, I said come in and I in turn smiled. He said you are talking to ugly now. He then introduced himself, my Dear, and I said yes my needs. I was ashamed a bit, and asked me what being shyly. I explained, I think bed room a bit, I said yes, & went to the kitchen yes, you need a stove, blankets as well. Then I got the most burning issue is my boys school uniform. The special branch men, he said come in lent the store it is only few days old and my store the warmth I a wonderful woman, am a changed woman then I have forgotten about the surroundings of cement, fruits and vegetables then I got a note the rest of my needs will be attended too by Barbra, so she has written to them to give her an address of where she must sent them. I this not marvellous? Am happy it happened this way. Not forgetting that you kept the fire burning in all fields, books etc. A friend in England had asked me to ask my friends in America to try & get me this Jane Pitmans Biography this I did, it was out early July but it is not received yet. Am so worried about all this, the latest in our country is the position is ugly, it is seriously, let me put this way, it is like a volcano which can erupt any minute. As it is now Im just a pack of nerves, I was in bed for two solid weeks. My Blood Pressure was very high. This is what happened, one morning I was picking up papers in my garden, when I suddenly head screams, when I lifted my head up I saw woman at the corner, as a banned once body I stood alof when I looked towards the school opposite our Mgamhlope this is the name of my area 4 Police Trucks and each truck had two Police dogs, chasing children from the lower Primary and biting them, I screamed to the top of my voice helpless, & suddenly I lost conscious I was carried to my bedroom & a doctor summoned. After examing me he said you better try and be calm I got more angry, I said how on earth can I be calm when my children are bitten by Dogs. Oh! Belinda my Dear, we are in rage between ages Hell is loose here. I would not like to see the brutality of Hitler happening in any country, dogs set on them Pray, for Southern Africa, pupils are shot dead almost every day. School are right in the school rooms. right up to the grave yard. School are determined empty. Students are

to oppose Bantu Education even if it cost their lives. Jails are full of our students detentions without trials. some die in detention. Oh! Donald my Dear can you imagine war fought by students and their parents standing and watching? students with stone against guns tear gas and dogs. This is so simply our Government meet the students & scrape Bantu Education. This will go on, a the scars on our children will create even lasting hatred between and blacks. An unfortunate position. when our children will hate each because of colour. When there is a variety of colours, it is beautiful a in other words, apartheid seems to challenge God for having created a black man. Any how do not worry much, about my health I have, improved. Also I wish to thank you for the gift, How is my Diana? I said so have always been a mother to this family.

Greetings & love Lilian

THE SOWETO UPRISING

During her period of house arrest, Lilian Ngoyi lived through one of the most important historical events in South African history – the June 1976 student protests. Watching from her house, she was able to comment on the events on the ground. This letter above, written to Belinda Allen in August 1977, provides a fascinating glimpse of this tumultous time.

01   The state of South Africa and, particularly, Soweto caused Ngoyi great distress. So did raising a family on limited means. Three years after this letter was written, Ngoyi passed away in her home.

LIFE TOOK IT'S TOLL

From the late 1970s, Ngoyi's stressful life took its toll. She started to suffer from health problems and on the 13th of March 1980, Ngoyi died in her home from heart complications. She was 68 years old and her untimely death was only weeks before her banning order was due to be lifted.

Ngoyi's death was greeted with dismay and grief in the community. Her funeral at Avalon cemetery was attended by thousands of mourners who draped her coffin in green, black and gold – the colours of the ANC. Among those gathered were Helen Joseph and Desmond Tutu. Tutu delivered her eulogy and paid a fitting tribute to Ngoyi:

> "For the past 300 years blacks had been oppressed but God heard their cries and sent them leaders such as Nelson Mandela, Govan Mbeki, Walter Sisulu and Mrs Ngoyi."

1972   Lilian Ngoyi's banning order was lifted. She used the opportunity to travel around South Africa meeting comrades.

1975   After her three-year period of freedom, Lilian Ngoyi was again served with banning orders, and was confined in her home until her death.

1980
13 March   Lilian Ngoyi died in her home from heart complications. Her funeral, held in Orlando East, was attended by 2 000 mourners.

"For 18 years this brilliant and beautiful woman spent her time in a tiny house, trying to earn money by doing sewing, and with her great energies totally suppressed."

Hilda BERNSTEIN, *friend and political comrade*

ARTIST > STEPHEN MAQASHELA

ADDRESS > 9870 Nkungu Street, Mzimphlophe, Soweto, Johannesburg

Artist Stephen Maqashela created the sculpture of Lilian Ngoyi's sewing machine, with an ANC blouse lying next to it. He was fascinated by the idea of Ngoyi "earning money through sewing until her death". Maqashela used car parts to represent Ngoyi's industriousness. He used a pick-up truck's differential which he painted bronze to make up the body of the sewing machine, and a car's oil sump which he painted in ANC colours to represent the blouses Ngoyi sewed at her home for ANC Women's League members.

Athol FUGARD

"Theatre is a very powerful agent for change. It created a climate of dialogue when bombs and bullets were replacing words."

Athol FUGARD
The Star Tonight, 19 June 1989

01

On a "wet and windy Port Elizabeth afternoon" in 1950, Athol Fugard – then a teenager – insulted his friend and "surrogate father", Sam Semela, a waiter at the St George's Park Tearoom run by Fugard's mother. Thirty years later, haunted by shame, the now famous playwright wrote his coming-of-age play about that day, *Master Harold and the boys*, which premiered in the US in 1982. While still living in Port Elizabeth, Fugard met John Kani and Winston Ntshona, sparking one of the best-known collaborations in South African theatre and resulting in two of this country's most famous plays, *Sizwe Bansi is Dead* and *The Island*.

Text from the Sunday Times memorial plaque

01   Athol Fugard, with his ever-present pipe, sits in front of St George's Park Tearoom in Port Elizabeth in 1985. Fugard's mother ran the tearoom during his childhood and one of his best-known plays, *Master Harold and the Boys*, is set here.

02   Fugard and his future wife chose to perform this play as their first at the new Space theatre in Cape Town. The poster caused such an uproar that some shopkeepers refused to put it up in their stores.

Athol Fugard / STATEMENTS AFTER AN ARREST UNDER THE IMMORALITY ACT

with Yvonne Bryceland, Athol Fugard, Percy Sieff and Christopher Prophet

Directed by Athol Fugard

booking at Hans Kramer

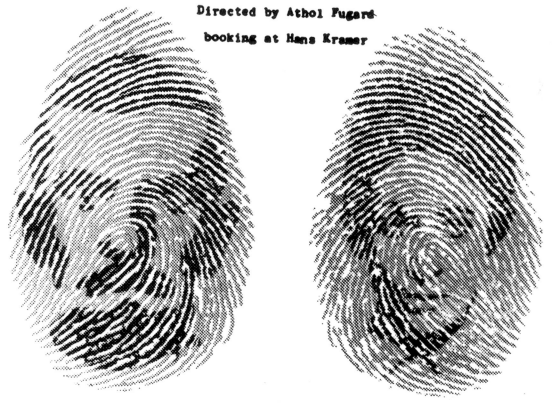

THE SPACE / DIE RUIMTE

"FLESH AND BLOOD, SEA, WIND AND SKY"

As a youngster, Harold Athol Lannigan Fugard persuaded everyone into calling him Athol. Today, he is one of South Africa's most famous literary figures. Fugard has written dozens of acclaimed plays, acting in and directing many of them. His novel, *Tsotsi*, was made into an Oscar-winning film in 2007, although interestingly, the conclusion of the novel was changed for the screenplay. While his themes are universal, his writing is profoundly local and is rooted in both his times and places.

The "ugly little city" of Port Elizabeth (PE) and its former black township of New Brighton, features prominently in his work. In his autobiographical *Notebooks 1960-1977*, Fugard describes "the ingredients" of Port Elizabeth as, "…flesh and blood, sea, wind and sky; dirty little streets; faces under street lamps late at night; never rich and most times poor, poor enough for too much hope…". The character in Fugard's play *The Coat*, addressed this question to the white audiences of the time: "New Brighton. I wonder what that means to outsiders like you…That world where your servants go at the end of the day, that ugly scab of *pondokkies* and squalor that spoils the approach to PE".

Fugard's relationship with PE began when his family moved there in 1935 in an effort to improve their financial circumstances. Fugard's father, who was of Irish stock, had become crippled and could not make a decent living as a jazz musician. Fugard's mother, Elizabeth, who was Afrikaans speaking, earned the family's keep by running the St George's Park Tearoom for 30 years. The tearoom was Elizabeth's "pride and joy". For Fugard, it was "a place where we all came together to tie and untie that rosary of knots that is every family's unique history".

01 Fugard with Sheila Meiring and their daughter, Lisa.

02 Fugard in 1961, the year that *Blood Knot* premiered to critical acclaim at home and abroad. He recalls that the play "launched my career".

A MOMENT OF SHAME

It was here that Fugard befriended one of the waiters, Sam Semela. In *Notebooks*, Fugard writes that Semela was "The most significant – the only friend of my boyhood years." The shame that overwhelmed Fugard when he spat in his friend's face one day during a fight lies at the centre of his play *Master Harold and the Boys*.

It was not long after this incident that Fugard left PE to take up a scholarship to study philosophy at the University of Cape Town. After two years, Fugard dropped out, worrying that the restrictive academic environment would affect his writing. He hitchhiked through Africa instead. In the Sudan, he joined the crew of a tramp-steamer which travelled between Japan, India and the South Pacific. Fugard was often the only white ordinary crew-member and shared his quarters with black seamen. He reflects that this experience cured him of whatever "colour prejudice" he might have had.

When Fugard returned to PE in 1955, he found it traumatic to encounter the new levels of racial segregation that had been imposed by the apartheid government. After working for a year as a regional reporter, he moved to Cape Town. Here he met and fell in love with Sheila Meiring, who was an actress and later a writer. Her book, *The Castaways*, won the Olive Schreiner Prize and was adapted for television by the BBC. They were married in September 1956 and had a daughter, Lisa, who is a writer and has acted in Fugard's plays. Fugard speaks of the importance of the women in his life:

> "My relationships with women have always been the decisive and sustaining ones…I believe my writing reflects this. Whenever there is a woman present…hers is always the dominant and affirmative voice."

Fugard expressed worry about Lisa growing up in apartheid South Africa: "They have now finally succeeded in making a foul, corrupt, diseased world for her to grow up in."

1932 11 June	Harold Athol Lannigan Fugard was born in Middelburg in the heart of the Cape Province's Great Karoo. Fugard's parents owned and ran a general cash store. In 1941, Fugard's father was crippled. Fugard's mother supported the family by running the St George's Park Tearoom in Port Elizabeth.	**1955** After travelling for years through Africa to gain life experience, Fugard returned to South Africa and got a job as a regional reporter in PE. He was soon transferred to work in Cape Town, where he met and married the actor Sheila Meiring. They formed an actors' workshop, performing plays directed by Meiring.

FINDING HIS VOICE

It was through Meiring that Fugard developed a taste for the theatre. Together, they formed an actors' workshop, and staged a series of one-act plays in Cape Town, with Meiring directing.

In 1958, Fugard and Meiring moved to Johannesburg to find work. He took a job as a clerk in the Fordsburg Native Commissioner's Court where black people were tried for 'pass offences'. He remembered this as "the ugliest thing I've ever been part of". Although he hated the job, he gained insight into how the machinery of a racist society worked.

During this period, the Fugards visited Sophiatown, Johannesburg's famous mixed-race western suburb. There they met writers who would become synonymous with the time and the place; Bloke Modisane, Can Themba, Lewis Nkosi, Nat Nakasa, Casey Motsisi, and the musicians Kippie Moketsi and Mackay Davashe. Fugard formed his first drama group with his new friends and wrote his first plays for them. But he says that it was with *The Blood Knot*, written after the Sharpeville massacre, that he "found his voice".

The Blood Knot explores the sometimes violent feelings of jealousy and resentment between two Coloured brothers – one of whom is light-skinned and can pass for white, the other of whom is dark-skinned and cannot. The play explores "the blood knot that ties every human being to another human being…that cannot be untied" and is a stinging critique of apartheid's race classification laws.

Fugard and Zakes Mokae appeared in the lead roles of *The Blood Knot* in 1961 in an old abandoned factory, Dorkay House, in Johannesburg. Audiences streamed in to watch Mokae and Fugard playing brothers.

1958 Fugard became a clerk at the Fordsburg Native Commissioner's Court in Johannesburg. The following year, he began his career as a playwright with debut performances in Johannesburg of two plays, *Good Friday* and *Nongogo*.

1961 Fugard and his wife moved back to PE where their daughter, Lisa, was born. He completed his first mature play, *The Blood Knot*, which was performed to critical acclaim. The following year, Fugard requested that British playwrights boycott plays performed in segregated theatres. The boycott lasted over a decade.

A REMARKABLE PLAY

Stark tragedy of a Coloured man

By OLIVER WALKER

IN "THE BLOOD KNOT" Athol Fugard has written a very remarkable new play. It is remarkable not only for its content, but also because he, the author (like some of the "new wave" playwrights of London) acted one of the two roles on Sunday night at a private showing with a power and conviction that held the audience enthralled for some three hours.

The favourable reviews led to Fugard taking the play on tour to the United Kingdom. It was received there with critical acclaim and, in 1967, the play was adapted into a movie and broadcast by the BBC. As a result of the screening of the film, and the negative publicity it created for the apartheid government, Fugard's passport was withdrawn until 1970.

Fugard's letter to the great writer, Nat Nakasa, pictured below, shows the extent to which the creative community defied apartheid by working together across the colour line. It also shows how Fugard constantly tried to push the boundaries of South African theatre.

Dear Nat,

Under the circumstances — unless I wanted to be a real bastard — there is nothing for me to say except: Go ahead and print. In truth I am delighted that an excerpt from the play is to appear in The Classic. Your magazine has my most fervent moral support. I would however have appreciated a earlier notice of your intentions. Which section of the play do you intend printing? Could you drop me a line and let me know? I'm very interested.

Could you also forward me a copy of the last and new issue of The Classic? None of the book shops down here — including the C.N.A — stocked your last issue. I know this for a fact because Sheila tried very hard to get a copy locally but without success. You should really do some thing about this. I'm sure you'd sell copies locally.

Sheila will definitely respond to your request for a contribution. She is just on the point of finishing a second and I think better novel. So expect some thing from her in the course of the next few weeks.

The enclosed cutting will tell you some thing of my activity down here. I spend my days writing but at night I work with the New Brighton group mentioned in the cut.

We are now planning our next production Wayzeck by George Buchner. This is going to be it! If I can realise the images forming in my mind we will present some thing unlike anything S.A. has ever seen. I'm using a Jazz 'combo' in this production — in fact it will most probably be more of a musical than a straight play.

Do keep in touch Nat. I think P.E. is ready for some thing — and should figure in the pages of The Classic.

To repeat — go ahead and print your excerpt(s) from my new play.

Athol.

01 Athol Fugard's *Blood Knot* premiered in 1961 and effectively launched Fugard's career. This review in *The Star, 5 September 1961*, praised the work.

02 This letter was written from Athol Fugard to writer Nat Nakasa.

1963 Fugard helped establish The Serpent Players, so named because their first performance took place in a disused snake pit. It marked the start of a longstanding collaboration with the actors John Kani and Winston Ntshona.

1967 *The Blood Knot* was televised on BBC after which the government seized and retained Fugard's passport until 1970. One of Fugard's most famous plays, *Boesman en Lena*, premiered and was turned into a movie. This was the start of a productive screen acting career for Fugard.

THE SERPENT PLAYERS

Fugard's career took off after *The Blood Knot*. In 1963, he returned to PE where he was approached to form a theatre group by five inexperienced actors: Norman Ntshinga, Welcome Duru, Fats Bookholane, Mike Ngxolo and Mabel Magada. Three of the men were labourers, while Mabel was a domestic worker. Initially reluctant, Fugard agreed and the group began meeting at his home in the suburb of Schoenmakerskop. They met secretly, because black people were not allowed in a white suburb at night. Their staged adaptations of classic plays such as *Antigone* and *The Mandrake* were all clandestine. In search of a more public venue, Fugard hired the old PE museum, which had recently been vacated. As a rehearsal space, he made use of a disused snake pit, which had been used for shows with performing snakes. The venue for their rehearsals gave the group its name, The Serpent Players. The police often raided the rehearsals. One of the Serpent Players, Sipho Mguqula, was sent to Robben Island for 20 years for his political activities. He was replaced by the young up-and-coming actor, John Kani. The collaboration between Kani and Fugard lasted for 30 years.

The Serpent Players redefined theatre in South Africa. They were joined by Winston Ntshona who, like Kani, became one of Fugard's closest workmates.

SOUTH AFRICAN CLASSICS

Together the group workshopped *Sizwe Banzi is Dead*, *Boesman en Lena* and *The Island*. These plays became South African classics. Fugard remembers that when *Sizwe Banzi is Dead* was first performed, members of the township audience got really worried and tried to stop Sizwe from taking a dead man's pass that would allow him to stay in the city.

"After watching the first few seconds of the operation in stunned silence – a voice shouted out from the audience: 'Don't do it brother. You'll land in trouble. They'll catch you!' Another voice responded immediately: 'To hell with it. Go ahead and try. They haven't caught me yet.' That was the cue for the most amazing and spontaneous debate I have ever heard."

03 Fugard with the cast of *My Children! My Africa!* From left to right: Rapulana Seiphemo, Kathy-Jo Ross, Athol Fugard and John Kani.

04 *Boesman en Lena* was one of Fugard's most famous and influential plays. The play depicts two individuals, Boesman and Lena, undertaking a punishing trek from one shantytown to another. Subsequent to its debut in 1969, it was made into two feature films. Fugard, pictured here, played Boesman in its first outing, while the play went on to be made into a film with James Earl Jones, Angela Bassett and Danny Glover.

1971 Fugard moved back to Cape Town. He and his wife created the Space fringe theatre, one of the only non-segregated theatres in South Africa. Five years later, Fugard returned to Johannesburg to work at the newly-opened Market Theatre. By the end of the 1970s, theatre was officially desegregated.

2005 Fugard co-wrote the script for a feature film of his 1980 novel, *Tsotsi*. It won the American Academy Award for best foreign feature, the first South African film to receive this award.

INTERNATIONAL RECOGNITION

Spurred on by the success of The Serpent Players, Fugard extended his acting repertoire. Many of his plays were televised in the UK, and Fugard often acted in the lead. His considerable talents also landed him the role of Jan Smuts in the feature film *Gandhi* in 1982. He toured extensively throughout Europe, the UK and America. Fugard's plays were acclaimed abroad and won prestigious awards; the Tony Award for Best Play, the New York Drama Critics Circle Awards (1981 and 1988) and the Writers Guild Award for Outstanding Achievement.

01   Fugard playing Jan Smuts in the 1982 movie *Gandhi*.

02   Fugard starred in the televised version of *The Guest*, a biography of Eugene Marais, one of the greatest Afrikaans poets.

03   Athol Fugard in the 1992 production of *A Place with Pigs*. The play looked at the life of Soviet deserter, Pavel Ivanovich, who hid for 44 years behind a pigsty. For Fugard, the play was also a parable of how he struggled to overcome his own addiction to alcohol. As he later told an audience at New York University: "I made a pigsty out of a bottle of Jack Daniel's whiskey."

In 1980, Fugard published his first novel, *Tsotsi*. He wrote it in 1961, but never sought a publisher. It was rediscovered by two students searching through Fugard's papers and they convinced him to publish it. *Tsotsi* (slang for criminal or gangster) was the story of Tsotsi, a young gang leader in Soweto. One night, he attacks a woman carrying a box. When she runs away, he is left with the box which turns out to contain a baby. This experience leads to a period of deep introspection and, ultimately, redemption.

Fugard worked with South African filmmaker Gavin Hood to rewrite *Tsotsi* as a movie. The movie premiered in 2006, when it won the Oscar Award for Best Foreign Film. The award has further cemented Fugard as one of South Africa's favourite sons and foremost creative figures.

Fugard and his family now live in America, where he continues to write plays. His daughter Lisa is a writer.

2008   Fugard lives with his wife and daughter in the United States, where he continues to write plays.

"The passion for the truth. Three men locked the door and elaborated on a tiny idea inspired by a photograph of a man in a white suit with a cigarette and lit pipe in a little African studio...out of that came the most telling story of the South African people under the apartheid regime. Out of that also came a new genre of theatre for South Africa that was later known as protest theatre, which became the voice of South Africa. I remember those moments with incredible fondness."

John KANI describing working with Athol Fugard and Wintson Ntshona, interview with Robert Woodruff, American Repertory Theatre

. . . .

ARTIST > MARK WILBY

. . . .

ADDRESS > St George's Park Tearoom, Port Elizabeth

Fugard's friend, Mark Wilby, was certain that the last thing the esteemed writer would want was a monument: "Monuments are generally mute or propagandistic - neither of which apply to Fugard. So, I view this project not so much as an honouring, but as an opportunity to explore what it is that Fugard does," he says.

In his memorial, Wilby references the moment in the *Master Harold and the Boys* when young Harold recalls flying a kite made for him by his friend and father-figure, Sam Semela. Hally shouts: "The miracle happened! I was running, waiting for it to crash to the ground, but instead suddenly there was something alive behind me, at the end of the string, tugging as if it wanted to be free." But, Wilby says, young Harold's memories are not without complication, and it is these "incidents of shame" forged into the dramatic tension of the play that also see Wilby's kite now snagged on a lamppost.

4 THE NEW GENERATION

1960 - 1980s

This section focuses on the new generation of young people who took on the challenge of resisting political control. They used politics, music, poetry and sport to express themselves and to transcend the barriers that apartheid imposed.

1963   The General Laws Amendment Act allowed the government to detain any political activist for 90 days without access to a lawyer. This was the first of a series of harsh laws designed to crush resistance.

July 1963   The Security Police captured some of the key leaders of the ANC at their secret headquarters at the farm, Liliesleaf, in Rivonia and seized their plan for armed struggle. Eight comrades, including Nelson Mandela and Raymond Mhlaba stood trial for high treason. They narrowly escaped the death sentence in the Rivonia Trial and were instead sentenced to life in prison.

1

19 July 1965   Ingrid Jonker committed suicide by walking into the sea in Gordon's Bay, Cape Town.

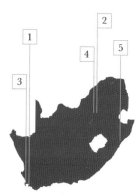

1966   Prime Minister HF Verwoerd was assassinated. BJ Vorster, the previous Minister of Justice became Prime Minister. In 1969, Vorster created the infamous Bureau for State Security (BOSS).

2

23 August 1968   John Vorster Square, the largest ever police station in SA, was officially opened.

SAHA/*SUNDAY TIMES* MEMORIAL SITES:

>> ●

1 Ingrid JONKER
Beach Road, Gordon's Bay

2 John VORSTER Square
Corner Henry Nxumalo and Loveday Streets, Johannesburg

3 Basil D'OLIVEIRA
Newlands, Campground Road, Cape Town

<table>
<tr>
<td>

3

August - September
1968

The English cricket tour of SA was cancelled after BJ Vorster banned the Coloured ex-South African cricketer, Basil D'Oliveira, from playing for England in South Africa.

1969

The charismatic leader of the South African Students Organisation (SASO), Steve Bantu Biko, articulated the hugely inspiring philosophy of black consciousness (BC). Black people were encouraged to reclaim their dignity and fight their own mental oppression.

1971

The Homeland Citizenship Act stripped black people of their South African citizenship and reclassified them as citizens of ethnically defined Bantustans or homelands. This was the beginning of a string of forced removals. Over 1 million "surplus" black people were forcibly relocated to their assigned homelands.

4

16 June **1976**

Tsietsi Mashinini led the schools protest against Bantu Education and the use of Afrikaans as a medium of instruction. The police opened fire on the throng of kids marching through Soweto. Student protests spread throughout the country. A new generation of freedom fighters was born.

</td>
<td>

1983

The United Democratic Front (UDF) brought together an impressive range of anti-apartheid organisations in a united front against apartheid.

1985

The Congress of South African Trade Unions (COSATU) connected South Africa's progressive trade unions in an umbrella body. COSATU had a massive support base.

1986

COSATU organised a massive work boycott that saw 1.5 million workers stay away from work on May Day. The government was forced to repeal key apartheid legislation, including the Prohibition of Mixed Marriages Act and sections of the Immorality Act. The hated pass laws were finally abolished.

5

1986

Brenda Fassie's hit song, *Weekend Special*, debuted in the US Billboard Hot Black Singles Chart and cemented her place as one of South Africa's freshest music exports. It also highlighted the birth of a new commercial township culture.

6

March **1988**

Ladysmith Black Mambazo, a choral music group from Kwa-Zulu Natal, won the Grammy Award for Best Traditional Folk Recording.

</td>
</tr>
</table>

4 Tsietsi MASHININI

Opposite Morris Isaacson School, Mputhi Street, Central Western Jabavu, Soweto, Johannesburg

5 Brenda FASSIE

Bassline, Newtown Precinct, Johannesburg

6 Ladysmith BLACK MAMBAZO

KwaMashu Hall, F Section, KwaMashu, KwaZulu-Natal

Ingrid JONKER

"I saw the mother as every mother in the world. I saw her as myself. I saw Simone as the baby. I could not sleep. I thought of what the child might have been had he been allowed to live. I thought what could be reached, what could be gained by death? The child wanted no part in the circumstances in which our country is grasped...He only wanted to play in the sun at Nyanga... (The poem) grew out of my sense of bereavement."

Ingrid JONKER, *talking about her poem, The Child.*

01

In 1963 Ingrid Jonker's poem, *The Child*, about a child who was shot dead by soldiers at Nyanga, was published. Two years later, at the age of 31, her ongoing battle with depression and anxiety caught up with her and she took her own life. Gordon's Bay is where Jonker spent much of her childhood and where she was happiest. Almost 30 years later, President Nelson Mandela reminded the country of this poet's insight and prescience when he read *The Child* during his inaugural address to South Africa's first democratic Parliament, on May 24, 1994: "...*the child grown to a man treks through all Africa; the child grown into a giant journeys through the whole world; without a pass.*"

Text from the Sunday Times memorial plaque

01 Ingrid Jonker was a strikingly beautiful woman, and an immensely talented poet.

02 Ingrid Jonker wrote her most famous poem, *Die Kind*, in response to the Sharpeville massacre. This translation appeared in *Drum* magazine in May 1963.

THE CHILD
that died at Nyanga

The child is not dead
The child lifts his fist against his mother
Who shouts Africa; shout the breath
Of freedom and blood
In the locations of the cordoned heart
The child lifts his hand against his father
In the march of the generations
Who are shouting Africa; shout the breath
Of righteousness and blood
In the streets of his embattled pride

The child is not dead
Not at Langa nor at Nyanga
Not at Orlando nor at Sharpeville
Not at the police station in Philippi
Where he lies with a bullet through his head

The child is the shadow of the soldiers
On guard with their rifles Saracens and batons
The child is present at all assemblies and legislation
The child peers through the windows of houses and into the hearts of mothers
This child who just longed to play in the sun at Nyanga is everywhere
The child grown into a man treks on through all Africa
The child grown into a giant journeys through the whole world

Without a pass.

Translation from Afrikaans by Jack Cope

JONKER

HEARTBROKEN CHILD

Ingrid Jonker was born in her grandparents' house in
the Northern Cape. Only a few months previously, her
mother separated from her husband, Dr Abraham Jonker,
who claimed that she had been unfaithful and that Ingrid
was not his child.

Jonker lived with her grandmother, mother and
sister, Anna, in Gordon's Bay. She remembered her
surroundings fondly and that she played a lot with her
sister on the beach. But at an emotional level, Jonker's
early life was deeply traumatic. Her mother suffered
from recurrent nervous breakdowns and was frequently
hospitalised. Dr Jonker continued to claim that Ingrid
was not his daughter. He was always distant towards
her and gave her only two presents during her entire
childhood: a red spinning top and a bible. Around
the age of seven, she began to understand her father's
attitude towards her. As Anna recalled:

"Ingrid and I played on the carpet and Granny
and Mommy sat there looking at us. Ingrid
looked up, and I heard Mommy say: 'How can
he say that Ingrid is not his child…she has
the same broken look in her eyes.' Ingrid was
about six or seven years old at the time. She
never forgot the words, and never spoke about
it, but she must have started to realise why she
was always Granny's little 'heartbroken child'.

When Ingrid was thirteen years old, her mother died of
cancer. She and her sister were forced to move into the
home of their father, Dr Jonker. This was traumatic for
the sisters. Ingrid was deeply upset at having to leave her
grandmother. Their father was a strict authoritarian, and
refused to engage with her poetry, which she had already
begun to write. Their life became dull and regimented, as
Anna later recalled:

>> •

1933
19 September — Ingrid Jonker was born in her grandparents'
house in the Northern Cape.

1946 — Jonker's mother died. She moved with her sister Anna to
Cape Town and they were enrolled at the Wynberg Girls High
School. She started publishing poems in the school magazine.

> "At home nobody mentioned her poetry. We had to adapt to an ordered life, totally different from what we had known before. There was a chill that came over us in our adolescent years…"

Ingrid continued to write poetry. She attended the Wynberg Girls High School, where many of her teachers recognized her talent and encouraged her to write. Jonker published a series of poems in the local school magazine.

Jonker left home immediately after matriculating. She moved to Cape Town and worked in the offices of various publishers for four years. During this time, she compiled *Ontvlugting* (Escape), which was published in 1956 to instant critical acclaim. It contained many of her earlier writings.

MORE TRAUMA AND HARDSHIPS

For the first time, Jonker came into contact with other poets and writers. One of these, Piet Venter, made a huge impression on her. By December 1956, the two had married and within a year, Jonker gave birth to her only child, Simone.

Jonker's marriage to Piet Venter did not last long and she moved back to Cape Town after just a year together in Johannesburg. She began a relationship with the writer, Jack Cope. When Jonker fell pregnant, they decided that she should have an abortion, which was then illegal.

While enduring these personal hardships, Jonker came into conflict with her father. Dr Jonker had recently been appointed National Party (NP) representative in charge of the parliamentary sub-committee on censorship. While Jonker believed in total creative freedom - *Die Kind* was published just as Dr Jonker was appointed to his position - Dr Jonker proclaimed: "The politicians run the country, why can't they rule art as well?"

Jonker signed a petition along with 129 other writers and 55 painters and sculptors against the passing of the draconian Publications and Entertainments Act. Her action against censorship and her father made headline news. Her father claimed in parliament that Ingrid was not his real daughter, a public declaration that hurt her deeply. During this time, Jonker was admitted to Valkenberg Psychiatric Hospital for severe depression. She continued to express her opposition to censorship and wrote to the author Laurens van der Post:

> "We are and have been fighting for expression in our country and we, as writers, shall never come to terms with the enemy."

01 By the age of 13, Jonker had compiled her first volume of poetry, *Na die Somer*. She is pictured here, in her teens, reading in her father's library.

02 *Ontvlugting* drew much of its poetic inspiration from Jonker's need to escape from her father's grey world. Here she reads the copy she just received from the publishers.

03 Ingrid Jonker and her daughter, Simone.

1956 Jonker became part of Cape Town's creative scene, and met key Afrikaans writers and artists. In December, she married Piet Venter, a poet. A year later, Jonker gave birth to Simone.

1959 Jonker and her family moved into a house in Emmarentia, Johannesburg. The following year, Jonker separated from her husband and moved back to Cape Town, taking Simone with her.

Dad was "ridiculous," says Ingrid Jonker

SUNDAY TIMES CORRESPONDENT

CAPE TOWN, Saturday.

MISS INGRID JONKER today described as "ridiculous" the description of the Afrikaans writers who signed the anti-censorship petition as "nobodies" by her father, Dr. Abraham Jonker, Nationalist M.P., when he addressed the Cape Parliamentary Debating Society this week.

He said that with few exceptions those who had signed the petition protesting against the Publications and Entertainments Act were minor authors who had never been heard of before.

Miss Ingrid Jonker is one of the 130 writers and 55 painters and sculptors who signed the petition of protest which was handed to the Minister of the Interior, Senator Jan de Klerk.

She told me that most of the Afrikaans writers who had signed the petition were among "the best literary brains in the country."

"Of course, no one can call Uys Krige a nobody," said Miss Jonker. "He has published more than 30 books.

"Other eminent Afrikaans signatories are D. Opperman, Anna Louw and W. A. de Klerk, to mention only a few," said Miss Jonker. "Who are these eminent writers who have not signed the petition? The two mentioned by my father, Malherbe and Boshoff, have not written anything for 20 years."

A COMPASSIONATE POET

Regardless of the turmoil in her life, Jonker continued writing. While her early writing reflects the trauma of her childhood, her more mature work expresses compassion and sensitivity to the plight of the poor. However, she did not see herself as political. Speaking of *Die Kind*, she told a *Drum* reporter:

"It grew out of my own experience and sense of bereavement. It rests on a foundation of all philosophy, a certain belief in life eternal, a belief that nothing is ever wholly lost. I am surprised when people call it political. I am warmed when others read it and thank me for it..."

In 1963, she published her second volume of poetry, *Rook en Oker* (Smoke and Ochre). It received instant critical acclaim, and won the prestigious *Pers Boekhandels* prize the following year. Her father refused Jonker's offer to bring him a signed copy of the book and told her to post it. He added that he had no wish to be seen with her in public:

"After what you have done to me in your interviews with the *Sunday Times* and other papers over the past year I am not inclined to meet you in a café or any other public place.

If you have something to discuss with me you know where I live. All that's needed is for you to phone and enquire whether a time is suitable. In the afternoons on the weekend I usually go fishing."

With love
From Dad
Abraham H. Jonker

Jonker used her prize money to travel to Europe. At that time, she was in a fraught relationship with the well-known writer, Andre Brink. But she struggled to settle and, after a fall out with Brink, she returned to South Africa.

1961   Jonker's father became Chairman of the parliamentary sub-committee on censorship. Jonker openly rejected his approach to censorship.

1963   Jonker's second volume of poetry, *Rook en Oker* (Smoke and Ochre), was published to critical acclaim. It won the prestigious *Pers Boekhandels* prize.

SUICIDE

After Jonker's return, her life began to unravel. Her split from Andre Brink sent her spiralling into depression. She was treated for anxiety, but the treatment made little difference. On 28 April 1965, she wrote a letter, effectively a suicide note, to Jack Cope. In the letter, she told Cope: "The truth is, I can no longer go on living like this."

At the age of 31, in the early hours of 19 July, Jonker finally succumbed to her depression. She walked into the sea at Three Anchor Bay. She was carried along by the waves, and drowned. Earlier that day, she had walked the promenade with a friend. Feeling depressed, she had later gone to the Sea Point police station where she spoke to a sergeant who walked her to her flat close by. He was the last person to see her alive.

Jonker's suicide was a great shock to her friends and colleagues. More shocking, however, was her father's response. Dr Jonker phoned Jack Cope to tell him that he was organising a religious ceremony. Cope told Ingrid's father that if a religious ceremony was to take place, then her friends should read tributes and poems in her honour. Dr Jonker accused Jack and Jonker's other writer friends of attempting to make a "political issue" out of her funeral. He threatened them with legal action if they spoke at the graveside.

Ingrid's sister, Anne, refused to attend the funeral. Many of Jonker's friends attended but stood at a distance while the ceremony took place. At Dr Jonker's request, two Special Branch policemen were there. One of them remarked: "I have never read the poetry of Ingrid Jonker." The Dutch Reform Minister who conducted the service referred to Jonker as a 'young housewife'.

01   While Jonker's father argued for imposing strict censorship laws on the arts, Jonker signed a petition opposing any form of censorship.

02   Jonker receiving the *Pers Boekhandels* prize for her second volume of poetry.

03   Jonker's father is pictured here, holding his hand over her grave.

04   Jack Cope, devastated by Jonker's death, is led away from her funeral by a friend.

'HER VOICE WILL BE HEARD'

A few days later, Jonker's closest friends held a private ceremony. Uys Krige, the famous Afrikaans writer, delivered the following eulogy:

> "Ingrid had something of her own, peculiarly her own, her own distance, individuality and personality. And it is this individual tone, this personal voice that marks the true poet. Her very best poems are, in my considered judgment, among the finest written in South Africa since the war. She ends one of them, *Korreltjie Sand*, with these words I am quoting her in my literal, inadequate translation:

> 'Carpenter build me a coffin,
> Prepare myself for the nothing,
> Grain, little grain, is my word,
> Little grain of nothing my death.'

> Yes, the poet in her quiet, almost shy way, is right, quite right. In a sense her death is a little grain of nothing. For with her words she has exorcised death. Her voice will be heard by us for a long, long time beyond her grave." *Sunday Times*, 25 July 1965

Jonker's only child, Simone, moved back to Johannesburg to live with her father, Piet Venter. When Venter picked Simone up from the airport, he was shocked to find out that she had not been told of her mother's death. Venter broke the news to her, explaining that her mother had gone for a swim in the sea and had drowned.

01   Poem from Jonker's second volume of poetry, *Rook en Oker*. Translated from the original Afrikaans by William Stewart.

LADYBIRD
(A memory about my mother)

Shining ochre
And a light bursts
Out of the sea.
In the backyard
Somewhere between the washing
A tree laden with pomegranates
Your laugh and the morning
Unexpectedly and small
Like a ladybird
Dropped on my hand

Jonker, I. Rook en Oker.
Translated from the original Afrikaans by William Stewart

1965
22 July   Jonker's estranged father hijacked the arrangements for his daughter's funeral. He forbade her friends from paying proper tribute to her.

1965   Three days later, Jan Rabie and friends arranged a second funeral.

136 : 137

"She was both a poet and a South African. She was both an Afrikaner and an African. She was both an artist and a human being. In the midst of despair, she celebrated hope. Confronted by death, she asserted the beauty of life."

Nelson MANDELA,

inaugural address to parliament, 24 May 1994, after reading Jonker's poem, Die Kind, in full

. . . .

ARTIST > TYRONE APPOLLIS

. . . .

ADDRESS > Beach Road, Gordon's Bay

Tyrone Appollis' artwork is based on Ingrid Jonker's *Die Kind*. Appollis used the image of a tricycle as the concept for this piece, inspired by a line from the poem: "…this child who just wanted to play in the sun…". He included several lines from Jonker's poem in a childlike handwriting on the four sides of the plinth for the sculpture.

"This child who just wanted to play in the sun"
"The child peers through the windows of houses and into the hearts of mothers"
"The child grown into a giant journeys through the whole world"
"The child is not dead"

John VORSTER SQUARE

"John Vorster Square was the pinnacle of torture chambers."

Jackie SEROKE, former detainee

Between October 27, 1971 and January 30, 1990, seven people died here while being held indefinitely under apartheid's detention laws. An eighth man died in hospital a week after being interrogated by the security branch on the infamous tenth floor. The lift went only to the ninth floor. Political prisoners were walked up a final flight of stairs to reach the tenth. An undetermined number of detainees were tortured. The station was named after Prime Minister BJ Vorster. In September 1997, John Vorster Square was renamed and transformed into Johannesburg Central Police Station. The bronze bust of Vorster was removed to the police museum.

Text from the Sunday Times memorial plaque

01 John Vorster Square was designed by the firm Harris, Fels, Janks and Nussbaum.

02 Chris van Wyk wrote this now famous poem entitled *In Detention*, as a dark satire of the ridiculous excuses made by the police about those who died at John Vorster Square.

IN DETENTION

He fell from the ninth floor

He hanged himself

He slipped on a piece of soap while washing

He fell from the ninth floor

He hanged himself while washing

He fell from the ninth floor

He hung from the ninth floor

He slipped on the ninth floor while washing

He fell from a piece of soap while slipping

He hung from the ninth floor

He washed from the ninth floor while slipping

He hung from a piece of soap while washing

Chris Van Wyk

A 'STATE-OF-THE-ART' POLICE STATION

On a chilly day in late August 1968, Prime Minister Balthazar John Vorster opened John Vorster Square (JVS) Police Station. Vorster heralded the squat 10-storey blue structure that overlooked the motorway in downtown Johannesburg, as a "state-of-the-art modern police station because it housed all major divisions of the police under one roof". He also boasted that the shining new precinct was "the largest police station in Africa".

01   This frowning bust of John Vorster, was proudly displayed on the cover of the South African Police (SAP) magazine in 1977. After the fall of apartheid, the bust was removed from the entrance to the building. It was recently found by SAHA researchers lying forlornly under a stairwell at the South African Police head office in Pretoria.

02   Prime Minister BJ Vorster with his wife, Tienie.

The building was christened with the Prime Minister's name and a large bronze bust of him was placed in the foyer. Vorster had been elected Prime Minister two years previously, following Hendrick Verwoerd's assassination. He was a natural successor because of his extreme right-wing pedigree. As the former Minister of Justice, he had overseen the institution of harsh security laws designed to deal with the growing opposition to apartheid. Following the Sharpeville Massacre in 1960, Minister of Justice, BJ Vorster warned that, "…the breakdown of law and order in South Africa will not be tolerated under any circumstances whatsoever."

DETENTION WITHOUT TRIAL

Vorster ensured that the Security Branch of the police acquired formidable powers. He introduced 'detention without trial' as the apartheid government's central weapon to combat political opposition. First the law allowed for 90 days detention in solitary confinement for the purposes of interrogation. Then it was amended to allow for 180-day detention without trial. Eventually, the formidable Terrorism Act of 1963 allowed for indefinite detention for purposes of interrogation. Detainees were permitted visits by a magistrate but were not permitted access to the courts or visits with legal representatives. Vorster signalled his tough approach when, in 1962, he asked in parliament: "Perhaps it is not inappropriate to remind honourable members that the great American lawyer, Wigmore, asked on one occasion, 'Why the sudden concern for criminals?' My question is, 'Why the sudden concern for communists in South Africa?'"

1961   Prime Minister HF Verwoerd appointed BJ Vorster as the Minister of Justice in the aftermath of the Sharpeville Massacre. Vorster was a *verkrampte* - a hard-line Afrikaner nationalist.

1963   The government passed the General Law Amendment Act which allowed the state to detain suspects for 90 days without access to courts or legal representation. These 90-day periods were renewable on an indefinite basis. This law became the lynchpin of the apartheid government's security policy.

MEN WITH NO SOULS

The Security Branch developed a reputation for extreme viciousness and inhumanity in its methods of interrogation, particularly at John Vorster Square. The offices of the notorious Security Branch were on the 9th and 10th floors of the building. The detainees' cells were on lower floors. They were specifically designed for solitary confinement. They were painted dark grey and the floors were black. In one corner was a foam mattress, in the other a toilet. Thick fiberglass covered the windows and bars. In the centre of the high ceiling was a single light bulb that was never switched off. For the hundreds of anti-apartheid activists who were detained in the cells, John Vorster Square was hell.

"Whenever you were there, you knew you were between death and life." *Tsanki Leagkotla, former detainee*

"The Security Police had a cruel calmness of people with no souls." *Molefe Pheto, former detainee*

A STATE OF TOTAL DEPENDENCE

From the 1960s, all members of the Security Branch (SB) were sent on courses to receive special training in torture techniques. They were known to be especially cruel at John Vorster Square because this station was considered a key posting, close to the police head office in Johannesburg:

> "The pressure was tremendous. You must remember that we were in a war and the scoreboard is there to show if we are doing our work. Fighting a revolutionary war is much more difficult than fighting ordinary criminals. You are fighting sometimes against the best brains. You have to be one step ahead of these people. In retrospect it's unfortunate that these things happened."
>
> *Hennie Heymans, former Security Policeman*

Detainees described the interrogation rooms on the 10th floor as "painfully neat". "Those offices upstairs were more kind of 'normal'. Sun came in. They had carpets and desks. But they were more menacing. Once you were in those interrogation rooms, there was absolutely no protection," recalls former detainee, Barbara Hogan.

Nighttime was often when "the nasty stuff was done". Sleep deprivation formed the basis of all interrogation and there was a squad of interrogators working round the clock to reduce detainees to a state of total dependence. The following accounts by former detainees show the brutality of the torture:

> "I was slapped and kicked. That was better than when they covered my head with a black hood and electrocuted me. That was quite scary. They did that about once every second day. But even then when I went through that type of torture I just thought that there was nothing more I could do, what would it help?" *Penelope Baby Twaya, former detainee*

> "It was winter. They would take my clothes off and make me stand there and go get a bucket of ice water, with ice inside and pour it on top of me and open a fan all the time and I wouldn't be able to speak or to say anything." *Jabu Ngwenya, former detainee*

Between 1960 and 1990, over 80 000 South Africans were detained, including 10 000 women and 15 000 children and youths under the age of 18. The number of people in detention reached its peak after the government declared a State of Emergency in June 1986. 25 000 people were detained over a period of 12 months.

Seventy political detainees died between 1960 and 1990. Between 1970 and 1990, eight people died while being detained without trial within John Vorster Square. Their stories are on the pages that follow.

1968 23 August	BJ Vorster became Prime Minister. One of his first official duties was to open John Vorster Square Police Station. The 9th and 10th floors were occupied by the notorious Security Branch.	**1971** 27 October	Ahmed Timol 'fell' to his death from the 10th floor of JVS becoming the 12th person to die in detention in South Africa. The police claimed that Timol had committed suicide. An official inquest confirmed their claim even though the state pathologist noted that Timol's body showed signs of being severely beaten.

AHMED TIMOL'S 'SUICIDE'

Ahmed Timol was the first person to die in detention in John Vorster Square. Ahmed was 30 years old when he died. He was born in 1941 in the Eastern Transvaal (now Mpumalanga). His father was close to Yusuf Dadoo and other founders of the Indian Congress. Ahmed became a teacher. At the end of the 1960s, he went on a training trip to the Lenin School in Moscow with Thabo Mbeki. Ahmed was a member of the Communist Party of South Africa (SACP) and he went back to South Africa to persuade people to join the SACP, which was a banned organisation. Almost two years after he got back, the police arrested him in Coronationville, Johannesburg, at a roadblock. He was carrying banned literature.

His family was told that he had committed suicide while in detention in John Vorster Square. But they did not believe this. The pathologist at the post-mortem examination of his body noted that he had bruises and bleeding beneath the skin. The injuries were between four and seven days old. In other words, it looked as if they had been inflicted while Ahmed was in detention – before he 'jumped'.

The Security Police used to tell detainees that "Indians can't fly" and referred to John Vorster Square as 'Timol Heights'. Timol's death was the 22nd death in detention in South Africa.

Timol's nephew, Imtiaz Cajee, has remained convinced that Timol was murdered: "To me and the rest of the Timol family it's very clear that my uncle was severely tortured and ultimately he was murdered. There's absolutely no doubt, he was murdered."

Ahmed's family hoped that the policemen involved in his death would come forward at the Truth and Reconciliation Committee (TRC) hearings to tell the truth about how he died. But they did not.

01   Ahmed Timol with his mother. Timol was the first person to die in detention at John Vorster Square.

02   Timol's coffin was carried through the streets of Johannesburg during a mass funeral.

1976	In the wake of the June 1976 Soweto uprising, the Internal Security Amendment Act gave the police further powers to detain suspects without trial.

1976 December	On 7 December, Wellington Tshazibane was found hanged in cell 311 of John Vorster Square after being arrested for alleged complicity in an explosion at the Carlton Centre. An official investigation exonerated the police of any wrongdoing.

Dr NEIL AGGETT
dedicated unionist

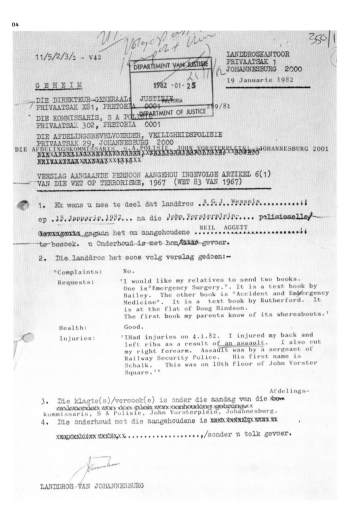

AGGETT'S 'SUICIDE'

Neil Aggett was a doctor. He worked in hospitals in Umtata, Tembisa and at Baragwanath in Soweto. He learned Zulu so that he could communicate better with his patients and colleagues.

Aggett supported the rights of workers and became an organiser for the African Food and Canning Workers' Union and helped establish the South African Allied Workers' Union. He played a central role in organising a boycott of Fattis and Monis products to make the bosses recognise the workers' right to belong to a trade union. The government saw his ability to organise workers as a threat and said that he was a communist.

He was arrested with other members of the anti-apartheid movement at the end of 1981 and taken to Pretoria Central and then to John Vorster Square. Early the next year, the police announced that he had been found hanged in his cell. Aggett had hanged himself with a scarf knitted for him by a friend after being extensively tortured by the Security Police.

A high profile court case led by Advocate George Bizos showed how Aggett's 80-hour interrogation the weekend before his death had led to his emotional collapse. Nevertheless, the police were again cleared, as they claimed that Aggett had suicidal tendencies.

03 This is one of the few surviving photographs of Neil Aggett. Aggett's was the 52nd death in detention in South Africa and the first death in detention of a white person since 1963.

04 During the inquest into Aggett's death, the state claimed that he had suicidal tendencies. Aggett's family argued that he was pushed to suicide by being repeatedly tortured. This affidavit from two weeks before his death recorded Aggett's complaints that he had been beaten.

1977
20 January

Elmon Malele, arrested on 10 January 1977, died of a brain haemorrhage at the Princess Nursing Home in Johannesburg. He had been taken there after he allegedly lost his balance after standing for six hours and hitting his head on the corner of a table. An inquest found that Malele's death was due to natural causes.

1977
15 February

Barely a month after Elmon Malele's brain haemorrhage, Matthews Mabelane 'fell to his death' from the 10th floor of John Vorster Square. The police claimed that he had climbed out of the window and lost his balance. Mabelane was the 39th person to die in South Africa's prisons.

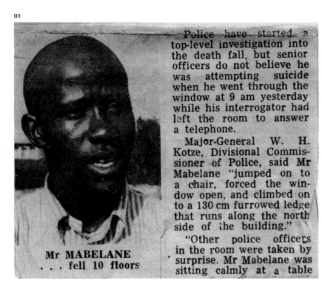

01

Police have started a top-level investigation into the death fall, but senior officers do not believe he was attempting suicide when he went through the window at 9 am yesterday while his interrogator had left the room to answer a telephone.

Major-General W. H. Kotze, Divisional Commissioner of Police, said Mr Mabelane "jumped on to a chair, forced the window open, and climbed on to a 130 cm furrowed ledge that runs along the north side of the building."

"Other police officers in the room were taken by surprise. Mr Mabelane was sitting calmly at a table

Mr MABELANE
... fell 10 floors

MATTHEWS MABELANE

Matthews Mabelane was born in 1955. He was arrested in Meadowlands in Soweto in 1977. The police said he was on his way to Botswana for military training. He was taken to John Vorster Square. A couple of weeks later, the police said that he had died while trying to escape out of the window. At an inquest, the magistrate ruled that his death was an accident. He died aged 22 years old.

Findings in terms of section 16 of the Act:

(a) Identity of the deceased person: Matthews Mabelane, Bantu Male, 22 years unknown.

(b) Date of death: 15.2.77

(c) Cause or likely cause of death: MULTIPLE INJURIES – Sustained by the deceased while questioned by police jumping through a window and walking along a ledge on the outside of the building at the 10th floor loosing his balance and falling to the ground below – Accidental.

A.G. 1/4/3/1/216/77 /JJ

G.P.-S.45811—1975-76—200 000 (M-S)

J 56

No. 287 1977

INQUEST: ACT 58 OF 1959
GEREGTELIKE DOODSONDERSOEK: WET 58 VAN 1959

Holden at JOHANNESBURG in the district of JOHANNESBURG
Gehou te in die distrik

by W.P. Dormehl esquire, Magistrate for the said district
voor mnr. Landdros van genoemde distrik en
as assessor(s) on the 14th day
with as assessor(e) op die 30th dag
of April , 19 77 into the circumstances attending the death of the person mentioned below.
van Mei aangaande die omstandighede in verband met die dood van ondergenoemde persoon.

Findings in terms of section 16 of the Act:
Bevindings ingevolge artikel 16 van die Wet:

(a) Identity of the deceased person. MATHEWS MABELANE
Identiteit van die oorledene
Bantu male 22 Years Unknown
(State full name, race, sex, age and occupation/Meld volle naam, ras, geslag, ouderdom en beroep.)

(b) Date of death 15.2.77
Datum van sterfgeval

(c) Cause or likely cause of death. MULTIPLE INJURIES - Sustained the deceased whilst
Oorsaak of waarskynlike oorsaak van dood
questioned by the police jumping through a window and walking along
a ledge on the outside of the building at the 10th floor loosing
his balance and falling to the ground below – Accidental.

(d) Whether the death was brought about by any act or omission involving or amounting to an offence on the part of any
Of die dood veroorsaak is deur 'n handeling of versuim, wat 'n misdryf aan die kant van iemand insluit of uitmaak
person No

Date 14.4.1977 30.5.77. W.P. Dormehl
Datum Magistrate/Landdros

NOTE.—Section 16 (3) of the Act provides that if the Magistrate is unable to record any of the findings set out above
OPMERKING.—Artikel 16 (3) van die Wet bepaal dat indien die Landdros nie in staat is om enige van die bevindings
he shall record that fact.
hierbo vermeld aan te teken nie, hy dié feit moet boekstaaf.

THE ATTORNEY-GENERAL,
DIE PROKUREUR-GENERAAL,

PRETORIA
In terms of section 17 (1) of the Inquests Act, 1959 (Act 58 of 1959), I submit herewith the record of proceedings.
Ingevolge artikel 17 (1) van die Wet op Geregtelike Doodsondersoeke, 1959 (Wet 58 van 1959), word die notule van
verrigting hiermee voorgelê.

Date 14.4.77 W.P. Dormehl
Datum Magistrate/Landdros

The record is returned herewith for filing. My reference number is
Die stukke gaan hiermee terug vir liassering. My verwysingsnommer is

Date Chief Clerk to the Attorney-General
Datum Hoofklerk van die Prokureur-generaal

01 A newspaper article with the only surviving photo of Matthews Mabelane, *Sunday Times*, 4 December 1988.

02 The magistrate who investigated Mabelane's death on 15 February 1977 found that the Security Branch was not to blame and that he had jumped out of the window whilst trying to escape.

1982 Dr Neil Aggett was found hanged in his cell.
5 February

1982 Ernest Dipale was found hanged in his cell. Dipale, who was
8 July only 21 at the time of his death, had been subject to severe assault and torture, including the use of electric shocks.

Foto 1

Foto 2

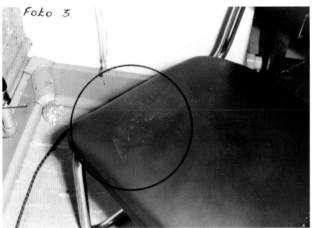

Foto 3.

Foto 8

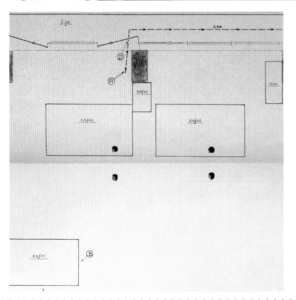

03   The police put together the following report of how Mabelane tried to escape from John Vorster Square. The hand-drawn map shows the route that Mabelane took, while the photos show how he stepped on a chair to exit the building. The final photo is the car on which Mabelane landed when he 'fell' from the 10th floor of the building.

1988
5 June

Stanza Bopape died 'unexpectedly' of a heart attack. Concerned how another death in detention would reflect on the police, they claimed that Bopape had escaped from custody. It was only during the Truth and Reconciliation Commission hearings in1997 that the police finally admitted that Bopape had died in detention.

1990
30 January

Only two days before Nelson Mandela was released from jail, 20-year-old Clayton Sithole was found hanged in his cell. Prior to his death, Sithole allegedly provided damning evidence of criminal conduct against Winnie Mandela and her daughter, Zinzi. Sithole was, in fact, the father of one of Nelson Mandela's grandchildren.

ERNEST DIPALE'S 'SUICIDE'

Ernest Moabi Dipale was born in 1960 and came from a politically active family.

Ernest was arrested and detained at the same time as Neil Aggett in November 1981. He made a statement to a magistrate, in which he complained of assault and torture by electric shock. Nothing came of his complaints. He was eventually released after three-and-a-half months. He was detained again on 5 August 1982 and held at John Vorster Square, where he was found hanged with a strip of prison blanket shortly after midnight on 8 August.

THE GHOSTS REMAIN

Seventy-five deaths in detention were officially recorded in the Truth and Reconciliation Commission's report. In spite of clear evidence that the police were torturing detainees, not a single policeman had been found responsible for the death of a person in detention. Those involved in these abuses have refused to talk to this day.

Following the release of Nelson Mandela in 1990, widespread changes were made to the security laws in the country. Detention without trial was outlawed. In 1991, the Security Branch merged with the Criminal Investigation Division into a unit known as 'Crime Combating and Investigation'.

In 1997, John Vorster Square was renamed Johannesburg Central Police Station and now functions to fight crime in Johannesburg. The bust of BJ Vorster was removed from the foyer. Despite these changes, the bleak interior and the dank smell remain just the same. The ghosts of its former occupants are far from banished.

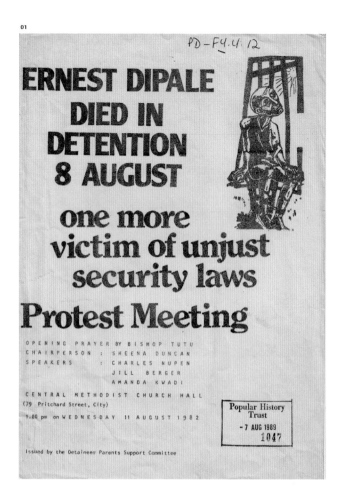

ERNEST DIPALE DIED IN DETENTION 8 AUGUST

one more victim of unjust security laws

Protest Meeting

OPENING PRAYER BY BISHOP TUTU
CHAIRPERSON : SHEENA DUNCAN
SPEAKERS : CHARLES NUPEN
JILL BERGER
AMANDA KWADI

CENTRAL METHODIST CHURCH HALL
(79 Pritchard Street, City)
1.00 pm on WEDNESDAY 11 AUGUST 1982

Popular History Trust
- 7 AUG 1989
1047

Issued by the Detainees Parents Support Committee

01   This poster, depicting Dipale's death, urged people to attend a mass meeting to protest against the security laws and the rising number of deaths in detention.

1997   John Vorster Square was officially renamed Johannesburg Central Police Station. The bust of John Vorster was removed from the entrance to the building.

"It's probably the iconic institution of the apartheid years, of the years of torture, of the reign of the Security Police, of the reign of the mad forces."

Barbara Hogan

● ●

ARTIST > KAGISO PAT MAUTLOA

● ●

ADDRESS > Johannesburg Central Police Station (John Vorster Square's new name), corner Henry Nxumalo and Loveday Streets, Johannesburg

The *Sunday Times* Heritage Project chose John Vorster Square as a site for one of its street memorials so as to honour the thousands who suffered in detention and to pay homage to eight people who died whilst imprisoned here. Artist Kagiso Pat Mautloa says that his installation symbolises resilience. The word *simakade* (forever standing) has been etched into the plinth in several South African languages.

Basil D'OLIVEIRA

"In 1966, I achieved something I shall be proud of till my dying day — I played for England, the country that gave me a chance denied to me by the land of my birth."

Basil D'OLIVEIRA

On August 28 1968, the England selectors met at Lord's cricket ground to choose a side for the 1968/69 tour to South Africa. Among the in-form batsmen almost certain of selection was the black Cape Town-born Basil D'Oliveira who, excluded from first class cricket in his own country, had moved to the United Kingdom in 1960. D'Oliveira was not picked and there was an outcry in Britain and jubilation amongst apartheid's supporters. When he later joined the side, the South African Government was outraged and the tour was cancelled, triggering events that sealed South Africa's sporting isolation for the next 25 years.

Text from the Sunday Times memorial plaque

01   Basil D'Oliveira served as a huge inspiration for many young South Africans. He became the symbol of how non-white sportsmen could overcome the obstacles of apartheid.

02   When Basil D'Oliveira was selected to be part of the England team to tour South Africa, Prime Minister John Vorster tried to bribe D'Oliveira to pull out of the tour.

Offer to Basil: R80000

Star 23/4

The Star Bureau

LONDON. — Basil D'Oliveira has spoken for the first time of his innermost feelings when he was "approached to make himself unavailable" for the 1968 tour of South Africa.

In a 45-minute B.B.C. talk with Ian Wooldridge and Dick Knight the Cape Coloured England cricketer also told why he wanted "desperately" to visit South Africa as a member of the M.C.C., and what he felt about the future.

The interview, which will be broadcast only from British Forces broadcasting stations abroad, probably next week, was played over in London yesterday for pressmen.

D'Oliveira said he was offered a large sum which he could have, then and there, or scattered over a number of years.

that you are a second-class citizen.

"You know this: You're there and you are going to be kept there. And then you come away and you prove all this wrong. You prove the whole blooming thing wrong.

"You prove to yourself and to everyone else that you can play and mix and behave the same as any other man. And this is the great thing."

Speaking of his motive in wanting to tour South Africa, he said: "I wanted to go there, mix in that community with the England side and come away leaving a doubt in the minds of the people I met.

"My behaviour was going to

CRICKET OBSESSED

Basil D'Oliveira - fondly known as 'Dolly' - was born on the 4th of October 1931 in the Bo-Kaap in Cape Town. He came from a sporting family of some repute. His father, himself a keen cricketer, played for the local cricket club, St Augustines, and won a series of trophies and awards.

As a youngster, Basil was an excellent soccer player, but cricket was his great passion. He played wherever he could, most often on the streets of the Bo-Kaap where cricket-obsessed youths formed teams, boundaried by the streets they lived on. D'Oliveira was the captain of the Upper Bloem Street team. Playing the local rivals, the Buitengracht Rovers, D'Oliveira had his first taste of cricketing glory as he recalled in the June 1960 edition of *Drum* magazine:

"We needed four runs to win and I was batting, last man in. I gave my khaki shorts a last hitch, took centre in front of the old paraffin *blik* (tin) that was the wicket and gripped firmly the plank that was the bat.

Frankie Brache, (whose sister Naomi was later to marry D'Oliveira), was bowling. He hurled down a fast one. It hit a sympathetic cobblestone and blitzed straight at me. I swung hard and connected. Up it went, soaring over the telephone wires for a six. My heart went with that ball in a bounding thrill of exultation."

Dolly also recalls: "We were never coached. We used to practice in the streets of Signal Hill, where some of us would be hauled off to jail by the police if we were caught playing on the road…Although we Coloureds had little to do with white people, I eventually wanted to find out more about their style of play and facilities. Whenever possible, I'd go to Newlands, Cape Town's famous stadium, to watch the great white players in test matches.

I could only afford to go for one day – I'd clean my father's pigeon loft to earn my shilling for admission and walk the seven miles to the ground. I'd sit in the segregated part of the ground, blissfully unconcerned that I couldn't sit beside a white man but terribly envious at the skills on display."

REAL DEDICATION

At the age of 17, D'Oliveira took the step up to formal cricket competition. He joined his father's club, St Augustine's. Playing for the club was an act of immense dedication, as he later recalled:

"I played for my father's club, St Augustine's, on a vast open space a few miles from both the sea and Cape Town. Looking back on it, the conditions we played under were a tribute to our fanatical love for cricket: about 25 teams shared the same open space and we had to tend the matting wickets ourselves.

On the morning of the match I'd walk about ten miles from my home to help prepare the wicket. We'd roll it, water it so it would cake hard on top, nail the matting down on the caked mud and then place boulders and stones on it to keep it down while we changed for the match."

D'Oliveira made an immediate impact on the Western Cape sporting scene. Soon after joining St Augustine's, he was selected for the Western Province Board Cricket Team. In 1956, D'Oliveira achieved his first national honour. He was selected to captain the first black South African team to tour against an all-black Rhodesian team. Two years later he again captained the black South African side for a whirlwind tour of East Africa. He was immensely popular with the fans; even more so after he powered a dazzling 96 runs in his first innings against the Kenyan team.

By the time he was 27, he had scored 80 centuries in the black leagues but could never test his skill at the highest level because the national Springbok side was for whites only.

>> . . . .

1931
4 October

Basil D'Oliveira was born into a talented sporting family in Cape Town. In 1948, at the age of 17, he joined St Augustine's Cricket Club, where his father played. His great performance led to his selection for the Western Province Board Cricket Team.

1957

D'Oliveira captained the first black South African side to tour Rhodesia. Two years later, he retained his captaincy for the team's tour to East Africa.

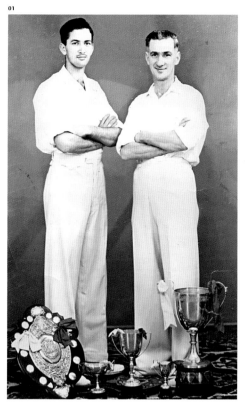

AN EXCITING OPPORTUNITY

In 1960, D'Oliveira received news that would change his life. John Arlott, an English writer-broadcaster, approached him and suggested that he ply his trade in England. Arlott had convinced the English Lancashire League team, Middleton, to give Dolly a chance. D'Oliveira jumped at the offer and moved with his wife Naomi, to England.

Living in England was difficult at first. D'Oliveira had no experience of the unique conditions there and suffered from his lack of professional coaching in South Africa. As he later recalled:

"I was an absolute disaster in those early weeks at Middleton. After just a few days in the nets, I realized I knew nothing about this game. I'd been used to hitting the ball as far as possible and expecting a fast bowler to try to knock my block off. I'd never seen the ball swing through the air before and the ball kept 'stopping' so I was through with my shot far too early with the ball going straight up in the air. I was a novice and what's more, everyone knew it."

01   Basil D'Oliveira and his father with the various trophies and awards that they both won playing for St Augustine's Cricket Club in Cape Town. Basil was barely out of his teens.

02   In addition to cricket, D'Oliveira was a premier league soccer player. He played right wing for the South African Coloured Soccer Team against the South African Indian Soccer Team in 1958.

03   Basil D'Oliveira won South African colours for cricket, but only for the non-white team. He is pictured here in 1958 with his wife, Naomi, wearing a Springbok blazer.

1960   John Arlott, BBC commentator, convinced D'Oliveira to leave South Africa and join the Central Lancashire League Club, Middleton. After four years in England, D'Oliveira achieved his dream and joined an English County Team, Worcestershire.

1966
16 June   D'Oliveira made his test debut for England against the West Indies. A year later, he was awarded one of the highest cricket honours, and was named one of Wisden's five 'Cricketers of the Year'.

DAZZLING PERFORMANCES

D'Oliveira had a stroke of luck. Eric Price, an English left-arm bowler, took him under his wing. He explained to D'Oliveira how to play in the English conditions, and gave him advice with his bowling. D'Oliveira quickly adjusted his game. By the end of the 1960 season, he had scored more than 1 000 runs and taken 70 wickets with his trundling medium pace bowling: a better return than the West Indian great, Sir Garfield Sobers. On his return to Cape Town, he was driven in an open car through the streets and the mayor held a civic reception in his honour.

Back in England, D'Oliveira was awarded a contract with Worcester, a county team. County cricket was in the top league in England. When Worcester won the county championship in 1964, Dolly was one of only two batsmen to score over 1 500 runs. It seemed inevitable that he would be selected to play for England. He had become a British citizen and in 1966, he was selected to play for his adopted country against the touring West Indian team. D'Oliveira became a fixture in the English cricket team. In the 1966 season, he dazzled with his powerful hitting and became renowned for his medium-paced bowling. The following season, *Wisden*, the bible of international cricket, listed D'Oliveira as one of the top five 'cricketers of the year'. Prior to the upcoming tour to South Africa in September 1968, D'Oliveira scored a match-saving 158 in the final test of a hotly contested series against Australia.

But when the English squad to tour South Africa was announced, D'Oliveira had been dropped. As the date of the announcement had drawn closer, a South African businessman, Tienie Oosthuizen, had met with Dolly and offered him a car, a house, an allowance of 40 000 pounds and a ten-year contract to coach black South Africans if he agreed to say that he wasn't available to play in the game in South Africa. Dolly refused.

Rumours abounded that the team's selectors had come under pressure from their own government, as well as the government of South Africa, in making the decision to drop Dolly. South Africa's Prime Minister, BJ Vorster, it was suspected, had worked furiously behind the scenes to prevent D'Olivera from touring the country.

1968
17 August

The Marylebone Cricket Club left D'Oliveira out of its line-up for the upcoming tour of South Africa. The decision was internationally slated, as D'Oliveira had recently scored a career-best of 158 runs for England against Australia. The following month, he was included in the MCC team to tour South Africa after an injury to Tom Cartwright.

16 | SUNDAY TIMES, JOHANNESBURG, SEPTEMBER 22, 1968

Sunday Times

THE PAPER FOR THE PEOPLE

D'OLIVEIRA

THE belated selection of Basil D'Oliveira provided both Mr. Vorster and Mr. Schoeman with reasons for arguing that the M.C.C. deferred to political pressure.

They may well be correct; but all the evidence suggests that if D'Oliveira had been picked in the first instance, for purely cricketing reasons, there would have still been an objection to him.

From the word go, as we report today, Mr. Vorster was not prepared to allow D'Oliveira to tour South Africa with the M.C.C.; and it may be asked why he did not say so all along.

There is a reasonable explanation for his silence.

His earlier utterances on the subject were cloudy and cryptic, and could mean almost anything one wanted them to mean. This is understandable, since Mr. Vorster did not require to commit himself, in advance, to a ban on D'Oliveira if D'Oliveira was not going to be selected. Why jump your fences before you get to them?

In a sense, the Prime Minister was taking a gamble, in the hope that the whole thing would sort itself out with the omission of D'Oliveira. The gamble has not come off. D'Oliveira is chosen and it seems to us that the motives of the M.C.C. are irrelevant.

It makes little difference whether they chose D'Oliveira because they bowed to political pressure, or for purely cricketing reasons. The end result is the same. D'Oliveira is in the team — and his presence in it is simply not acceptable in the country of his birth, where he is normally not allowed the privileges he would necessarily enjoy as an M.C.C. cricketer.

Our policies on racial issues are very clear and definite on this point; and it may be of interest to see just where they have led us.

The inclusion of one Coloured man in a touring team, it seems, would bring a multitude of embarrassments, on a scale apparently sufficient to unsettle the entire nation.

Apart from the broad propositions that D'Oliveira would constitute a "thin end of the wedge" and that his presence in White group areas conflicts with fundamental principles and with our traditional way of life, he would be a potentially provocative source of incidents—from all sides.

White people might easily be resentful on social occasions and might do things they later regretted: and non-Whites could possibly prove even more "difficult" on cricketing occasions. Thus, out of a simple thing like the visit of one non-White cricketer, our whole country could be stirred up into troubles which all of us would sooner avoid.

Well, we are avoiding them. Everything is now tidy and neat; honour has been satisfied; the Prime Minister is being acclaimed for his statesmanship; and the M.C.C. tour is off.

Some people will say that South African cricket is going to be the chief sufferer. A sufferer, yes, but not the chief one. The main victim is South Africa herself. Our refusal to accept D'Oliveira as a member of the M.C.C. team does us little credit. It is easy enough to fob the thing off as being in accordance with our traditional way of life. What needs examination is the effect some of those "traditions" are having on our judgment.

Mr. Vorster has lost an opportunity. It would have done us all a lot of good to experience a cricket tour with a D'Oliveira in it.

The British journalist, Michael Parkinson wrote in the London *Sunday Times:*

> "The dropping of Basil D'Oliveira from the team to tour SA has stirred such undercurrents throughout the world that no-one but the impossibly naïve can any longer think that politics and sport do not mix, never mind believe it."

When one of the British players allegedly injured himself, the England selectors relented, and included D'Oliveira in the team. But Vorster was having none of it. He blocked D'Oliveira from coming to South Africa to play. Speaking to an applauding National Party (NP) congress in Bloemfontein, Vorster made his feelings clear:

> "We are not prepared to accept a team thrust upon us by people whose interests are not the game, but to gain certain political objectives which they do not even attempt to hide."

The South African Sports Minister, Frank Waring, summed up the NP's fear: "If whites and non-whites start competing against each other, there will be such viciousness as has never been seen before."

The British public exploded with indignation. England cancelled the tour of South Africa.

01   Here, Basil D'Oliveira is training youngsters at Durban's Sastri College in May 1966, whilst visiting SA during a break from cricket in England.

02   D'Oliveira was handed his first test cap for the country. He is pictured here shaking hands with a young Queen Elizabeth on the opening day of the first test against the West Indies.

03   Basil D'Oliveira was given a hearty send-off by family and friends when he travelled to England to pursue his cricketing career in June 1960.

04   The decision to block D'Oliveira's entry into South Africa was criticized in both England and South Africa. In this editorial in the *Sunday Times* on 22 September, 1968, the decision is slammed for its pettiness and for the long-term effect it was to have on South African sport.

1963   South Africa's Prime Minister, BJ Vorster, blocked Basil D'Oliveira's entry into the country to play for England. After a massive uproar in England, the tour was cancelled. It was soon after this that SA was banned from international sporting competitions. SA teams did not compete in the international arena again until 1990.

1969   D'Oliveira was awarded the Order of the British Empire (OBE) for his achievements in sport. Three years later, he played his last test match for England. He retired with a batting average of over 40.

THE SPORTS BOYCOTT

Vorster's decision to ban D'Oliveira had massive ramifications. The sports boycott against South Africa gathered pace and South Africa was soon banned from completing in any cricket matches against international teams. Soon no South African sports team was welcome in the international arena. South Africa was excluded from the 1968 Tokyo Olympics and was expelled from the Olympic Movement in 1970.

South Africa proceeded to introduce a range of bureaucratic devices to bestow 'honourary' white status on black sportsmen and women that allowed them to compete in some SA competitions. In his autobiography, D'Oliveira wrote:

> "These laws which degrade non-whites should be repealed...A black man can't be a white man during a day's sport and then revert to being a black man."

For D'Oliveira, the racial furor was a momentary hiccup. He continued to play for England until his final test in 1972. He ended with a remarkable 5 centuries and 15 half centuries at an average of 40.06 runs per match. He also took 47 wickets, with his best bowling of 5 for 62.

D'Oliveira was showered with honours. In 1969, he was made an Officer of the British Empire. In 2005, he was made a Commander of the British Empire.

Basil D'Oliveira continues to live in England. His son, Damian, has also devoted himself to cricket. Damian played 234 first-class test matches for the county of his father, Worcestershire, up until 1995. He currently works as the academy director for young cricketers at the club.

01   When Basil D'Oliveira heard the news that the tour of South Africa had been cancelled, he was devastated, *The Star*, 29 August 1968.

01

THE MOMENT OF HEARTBREAK

Jan 29.8.

From Our Bureau

London, Thursday.

BASIL D'OLIVEIRA was completely broken when he heard the news yesterday of his omission. He had just come off the field after scoring 128 for Worcestershire against Sussex and was listening to the radio in the dressing room with other members of the Worcestershire team. When the 15 names were announced Tom Graveney took him into a room near by and they talked alone.

D'Oliveira said little before breaking down. He tried to compose himself sufficiently just to say that he had no statement to make apart from being bitterly disappointed.

But he could not control his feelings and had to ask a friend to make the statement on his behalf.

When he reached his home after being given permission to leave the ground early, his seven-year-old son, Damian, ran towards the car. He saw his father's face and said: "Never mind, dad, you are still the greatest."

D'Oliveira said after reaching his home: "I need a period of quiet before. I think too deeply about things."

Earlier, at the ground, after the team had been announced, there were shouts of "Shame, where is D'Oliveira," from the crowd.

The South African Non-Racial Open Committee for Olympic Sports (Sanroc) is to hold a meeting at Caxton Hall, Westminster, on September 13 to discuss racial discrimination in sport. There will be special reference to "the responsibility of British sports administrators."

The two thousand spectators at the Worcester ground, where Dolly is a great favourite, received the announcement of his omission over the loudspeakers in complete silence. Like the players they were stunned and baffled that his name was missing from the 15 read out.

Mr. Joe Lister, the Worcestershire secretary, said: "That Basil has not been chosen for the tour of South Africa is quite the most astounding piece of news I have ever heard.

"We have been told all along that the best side available would be chosen and internal politics would not be brought into it. His form in the series has made his omission from the

second, third and fourth tests all the more mystifying and I
● Cont. on Page 3. Column 5.

Moment of heartbreak

● Continued from Page 1.

know he has established the claim to tour second to none.

"It is hard to believe the real reason is his form."

A spokesman for the M.C.C. selectors said they had "an extremely difficult" job in deciding to drop D'Oliveira but the decision was taken "definitely, purely on his cricketing ability."

Mr. Cyril Smith, the Worcestershire chairman, commented: "Many of us are deeply shocked that D'Oliveira is not picked for the tour. It is most regrettable."

Mr. Jim Baker, chairman of the Sussex Cricket Club committee, declared: "I cannot think of any greater injustice than to omit D'Oliveira."

Emblazoned across the front pages of every national newspaper in Britain today are stories of the dropping of the man who earlier this week enabled England to draw the test series against the Australians.

In most reports the suggestion is made that South Africa's race policies and not form were the deciding factor.

2005
11 June
D'Oliveira was honoured as a Commander of the British Empire (CBE).

2008   D'Oliveira still lives in England. He has struggled with Parkinson's Disease for much of his old age.

154 : 155

"Last Wednesday a group of Englishmen picked a cricket team and ended up doing this country a disservice of such magnitude that one could only feel a burning anger at their madness and a cold shame for their folly. The dropping of Basil D'Oliveira from the MCC team to tour SA has stirred such undercurrents throughout the world that no-one but the impossibly naïve can any longer think that politics and sport do not mix, never mind believe it."

Michael PERKINSON
journalist for the London Sunday Times

. . . .

ARTIST > DONOVAN WARD

. . . .

ADDRESS > Newlands, Campground Road, Cape Town

On the whitewashed wall outside Newlands cricket ground, a sheet of oxidising metal with a hole punched through it by a bronzed cricket ball commemorates a shameful incident that shone a spotlight on apartheid's interference in sport. Artist and sculptor Donovan Ward was barely six years old when the event took place, but like many South Africans - and Capetonians in particular - he knows the story of how the National Party government withdrew its invitation to the English touring team because of the inclusion of a black South African, Basil D'Oliveira, in its squad. Ward says, "In the artwork I focused on the role sport can play in breaking down barriers or boundaries and making the seemingly impossible real."

Tsietsi MASHININI

'Students today want to be recognised as human beings...

Tsietsi MASHININI, 1976

01

At 8 a.m. on June, 16 1976 Tsietsi Mashinini interrupted the school assembly to lead the first group of students out of the gates and on the march that started the Soweto uprising. They were protesting the use of Afrikaans in schools. A reward was posted for his capture and one afternoon Security Police checked every student leaving the grounds. Mashinini, who was a prefect at the Morris Isaacson School, escaped detection by dressing up as a girl. After the march he never slept at home again and fled the country two months later.

Text from the Sunday Times memorial plaque

01 Tsietsi Mashinini, pictured here in exile in 1977, was considered one of the most charming and persuasive of South Africa's young generation of political leaders.

02 The day Mashinini went into exile in August 1976, he released one final statement. He attacked the government for its heavy-handed treatment of protestors, but also urged students to return to school to secure their futures.

We the SSRC (Soweto Students Representative Council) condem

1. Police action in Soweto by irresponsibly shooting out students on their way to school or black children playing in the location as it has been reported in the newspapers. We see it as an unofficial declaration of war on black students by our "peace-officers"

2. The statement by Mr Gert Prinsloo that the racist regime will not "succumb to the demands of a handful students". Instead we are the voice of the people and our demands shall be met

3. The response by Jimmy Kruger that he will not accept the B.P.A. as the authentic body representing us. We see no peace and order if our demands are not met

4. The statement by the Prime Minister that the racist regime "will not panic". We do not anticipate panic but expect responsible ACTION from the leaders of this country.

5. The action of elements burning schools we believe that is no black man's action.

6 The brutality experience by students in police hands especially those who have been recently arrested and released.

7. The abuse of power by security officers to refuse relatives to see detainees and demand a just investigation in the suspicious conditions in which Mr Mapetla Mohapi died and we are afraid the same may befall our people

detained in connection with the so called "riots"

* I do Tsietsi Mashinini appeal on students to report back to school and notify the authorities of any injured dead or missing students. We still have our end exams to write and we must have our priorities sorted.

⑧ We lastly condem the detention of B.P.A. members and see it as an unwarranted move by the system. We never meant them to meet Mr Kgr Kruger in detention

Ours is a peace-ful struggle whith only the racist regime can curb by a dialoque with our leaders

Tsietsi Mashinini
(Chairman)

THE KARATE KID

Tsietsi Mashinini is recognised as one of the heroes of South Africa's struggle for democracy for his role in leading the June 1976 Soweto uprising.

Teboho 'Tsietsi' Mashinini was born on 27 January 1957 in Western Jabavu in the sprawling township of Soweto. He was the second son of Ramothibi and Nomkhitha Mashinini. Tsietsi's siblings, Tshepiso and Dee, also fled into exile following the June 1976 uprising. Tsietsi (which means trouble) could be a difficult child, as his biographer, Lynda Schuster, describes:

> "As a youngster, he appeared highly-strung and given to histrionics: when denied something he wanted, Tsietsi cried until he vomited. He would suddenly and inexplicably start to sob, as though he had been hurt. But as Tsietsi grew, he evolved into a charismatic personality who charmed everyone he met."

As an adolescent, Tsietsi excelled at sport, especially softball, tennis and dancing. His major passion, however, was karate which he began to learn while at Morris Isaacson High School. Being a 'karate kid' gave Tsietsi an exotic air in Soweto, as he showed off his moves to the township's roughneck gangsters. At home, however, his karate training caused considerable trouble:

> "Tsietsi was forever frightening Nokhitha [his mother] with sudden karate chops and high-pitched yells. When his siblings begged to learn, Tsietsi taught them turns and kicks, lining them up in the yard for drills. They were thrilled: this was the big brother who deigned to notice them. And they adored him." *Lynda Schuster*

01 Tsietsi is pictured here in New York just after he left South Africa, sporting the style of the American Black Power movement. A former teacher, Bernadette Mosala, recalls that "as a teenager he preferred African-American fashion, he was a hippie. He kept big Afro hair and wore bell-bottom trousers with high shoes."

MORRIS ISAACSON

In 1971, Tsietsi Mashinini was enrolled at Morris Isaacson High School. It was a rigid but rewarding environment. It was known for its academic excellence, as a former teacher, Caiphus Morutse, recalls: "The pupils used to take their studies very seriously... Morris Isaacson was the best when it came to music competitions, examination results and sports. This was the school." Fanyana Mazibuko, a science teacher at the school in the 1970s, recalled later that Morris Isaacson "was a highly disciplined school, almost military in its discipline." But the school was also known as a 'cradle of resistance', no doubt helped by the fact that Onkogopotse Abram Tiro was a teacher there. As a leader of the student's movement, Tiro had been expelled from the University of the North (Turfloop) in 1972 after organsing against apartheid. The Headmaster of Morris Isaacson offered Tiro a history teaching post at his school. Tiro used his history lessons to introduce his pupils to the philosophy of Black Consciousness and encouraged them to question the kind of history they were being taught in the Department of Bantu Education's textbooks. Tiro was instrumental in establishing branches of the South African Student Movement (SASM) in Soweto high schools.

THE GIFT OF THE GAB

It was in this environment that Tsietsi flourished as a political youngster. While at Morris Isaacson, Tsietsi became famous for being an adept and powerful debater with a remarkable grasp of the English language. David Kutumela, a good friend of Tsietsi's recalls:

> "Tsietsi would take a stage. He would be excited. And the atmosphere, the energy around him, would actually excite you when watching Tsietsi talking. He would come up with this English. He would come up with his facts. He would come up with whatever he could bring. Tsietsi was a very powerful speaker who dominated Morris Isaacson, there's no question about that."

>> . . . .

1957
27 Janaury
Tsietsi Mashinini was born in Western Jabavu, Soweto. Six years later, he began his schooling at Amajeli Creche near Pretoria.

1971
Mashinini was enrolled as a student at Morris Isaacson High School. He made an impact on his fellow pupils as a fashionable Soweto hippy and effective debater.

CASANOVA

Tsietsi was also known as a dashing man-about-town. While at Morris Isaacson, he became a freelance reporter for the *Rand Daily Mail* and strutted his stuff in the streets of Soweto. Tsietsi affected the style of American hippies, sporting an afro, bell-bottom trousers and floral shirts. All of this made him desirable, and not just for his ideas, as his former teacher, Mrs Bernadette Mosala, remembers:

> "His social life was very vibrant and short of boredom. Mashinini was loved and adored by girls. He was indeed himself a well-dressed Casanova."

THE STUDENTS TAKE TO THE STREETS

In 1953, the government passed the notorious Bantu Education Act. This law shut down missionary schools which had educated many important leaders such as Nelson Mandela and Oliver Tambo. It also introduced a new curriculum which would ensure that black people remained, in Prime Minister Verwoerd's words, "the hewers of wood and drawers of water".

By the mid-1970s, the education system for black students was in crisis. In 1967, there were 58 pupils to every teacher and throughout the 1970s this ratio only increased. In 1975, R644 was spent on the education of every white child yet just R42 was spent on a black child. Year after year, a flood of students tried to enter an ill-equipped high school system. In 1976, 257 505 pupils enrolled, but there were places for only 38 000. Black students felt more angry and frustrated than ever before.

It was in this highly volatile context that the apartheid government announced the compulsory use of Afrikaans as a medium of instruction from Grade 7 onwards. There was a cry of outrage from teachers and students alike. Officials in the Department of Bantu Education responded with statements such as, "If students are not happy they should stay away from school since attendance is not compulsory for Africans."

Students were furious at the situation and decided to protest. They were spurred on by Mozambique and Angola's new-found independence in 1975. This gave them a sense that their own freedom may be imminent. On 13 June 1976, the Soweto Students Representative Council (SSRC) met in Orlando. It was at this meeting that the 19-year-old leader of the SASM branch at Morris Isaacson, Tsietsi Mashinini, emerged as the foremost student leader. Addressing 400 angry students, he proposed a mass demonstration against the education system and apartheid. This proposal was greeted with cheers of support. His friend Khotso Seathlolo remembers Tsietsi's speech as "the best, shortest, simplest and (most) easy to understand". An Action Committee under Mashinini and Seth Mazibuko set about organising the protest. Students agreed that parents or teachers should not be involved in any way.

| 1976 16 June | Tsietsi led the students in protest against Bantu Education and the introduction of Afrikaans as the medium of instruction. 13 500 students took part in the protest, which rapidly spread to other parts of the country. | 1976 June - August | Tsietsi became the state's number one target. He disguised himself as a woman in order not to be caught. |

BLOODSHED

At 8 a.m. on the cold winter morning of 16 June 1976, the assembly at Morris Isaacson High School was interrupted. Groups of students unfurled banners and shouted, "*Amandla!*". Mashinini led the students in singing songs of defiance as they marched out of the hall. Just before leaving the school gates, Mashinini whispered to his friend, Murphy Morobe: "The main thing is not to provoke the police. We have to keep telling everyone to be disciplined, that we're marching to a particular place and then we'll disperse."

The students from Morris Isaacson were to be joined by protesting students from other schools who had all been instructed to converge at Orlando Stadium and pledge their solidarity in the fight against Afrikaans. Spirits were high as thousands of uniformed students threaded their way through the dusty streets of Soweto carrying banners that they had hidden rolled up in their blazers with slogans such as, "To Hell with Afrikaans" and "This is Our Day". All was peaceful until the growing crowds were confronted by a squad of police vehicles which had rushed to the scene. The officers – who had been kept unaware of the march – leapt out and ordered the students to disperse. With little warning, the officers released their vicious dogs into the crowd and started to shoot rounds of teargas. Nobody knows what happened next. But the students heard loud shots ringing out and realised that the police had opened fire. There was panic and pandemonium as students between the ages of 10 and 20 years old scattered as fast as they could. Six hundred students were killed and about 2 000 were injured during the year of 1976. The official police death toll was 23.

Fired up by news of the shootings, the protest spread and engulfed the whole of Soweto. Protests soon spread to other townships in Johannesburg such as Alexandra and thereafter throughout the country. The street battle against apartheid, led by students and youths, had begun. It would not to stop until 1994.

05

01 As popular protest spread after June 1976, this sort of scene became common throughout the country. This picture shows township youths running from the police (out of the frame) in Alexandra Township.

02 During the 1976 uprisings, government buildings were attacked, including the community beerhalls.

03 The police and military responded with violence against the growing protests. Here, a woman, recently killed, lies next to a military truck.

04 Student protestors are pictured marching in Alexandra with Black Consciousness banners.

05 This poster, seized by the police as evidence of the treasonous activities of Soweto youths, sums up the feelings in the townships: Prime Minster Vorster was the villain (likened to Hitler as seen by the swastikas), Mandela was the hero, and Black Power was the cause to fight for.

06 Protestors used stones and petrol bombs to fight the battle on the streets. Here, a delivery truck is overturned and burnt out by angry protestors. Hundreds of busses and other government vehicles met this fate.

06

07 Here, a school chalk board has been converted from a tool of education into a statement of resistance.

1978 Mashinini met and married Miss Liberia's candidate for the 1977 Miss World Competition, Welma Campbell.

1979 Mashinini was ousted as the leader of the South Africa Youth Revolutionary Council (formerly the SSRC) after outrage at his wedding to Welma Campbell.

THE 'NUMBER ONE' TARGET

As the student uprising spread throughout South Africa, Mashinini's life became increasingly difficult. He moved around Soweto, encouraging students in their protests, but he was now the state's number one target. He was widely recognised as the leader of the student protest and his name was commonly evoked by protestors as heard in this song:

Tsietsi le Vorster	Tsietsi and Vorster
Ba ngola teste	They write a test
Voster ke setlaela	Vorster is stupid
Tsietsi o phasile	Tsietsi has passed

Mashinini used ingenious techniques to evade arrest. In one case, the police raided a school where he was giving a speech. Tsietsi jumped out of the window and put on a labourer's overalls and "cheerfully swung his pick with the other labourers while the police searched the premises for him". It was a frequent trick of Tsietsi's as his former teacher, Fanyana Mazibuku, recalls: "I saw Tsietsi pass between me and the police wearing a balaclava and an overall and he was singing very casually, pushing a wheelbarrow like one of the people who were busy building the laboratory in the school. And he announced that it was tea time and he had to go and have tea in the township. He went through a hole in the fence and off he went."

Tsietsi also often dressed up as a woman: "One night, the police surrounded a house while Tsietsi was there. Tsietsi quickly put on a girl's dress. The police separated the men from the women, searched the men and then left, Tsietsi happily in the company of the laughing women."

Len Maseko, a fellow student and friend of Tsietsi's, adds:

> "Mashinini's daredevil courage imbued him with a mystical aura. And it was not uncommon for him to surface at the unlikeliest flashpoints to poke ridicule at the system and urge pupils on in their *mzabalazo* (fight/struggle)."

EXILE

Tsietsi's life was in danger, regardless of how well he could disguise himself. Drake Koka, a leading figure of the Black Consciousness Movement, warned Tsietsi that he had to leave the country. Tsietsi refused, asking: "What good will I be in exile?". But Drake slowly won him over.

On the 23rd of August, Tsietsi decided to leave. He released one final statement in which he attacked the police and urged students to return to school, study hard and write their final exams. He urged them to have their "priorities sorted". He also conducted an interview with British Television, one of the few surviving interviews with Mashinini. He then met up with Reverend Legotlo, a friend of Koka, who drove Tsietsi across the border into Botswana disguised as a church-goer. From Gaborone, they flew to London via Lusaka. Tsietsi was never to set foot in South Africa again.

When first arriving in exile, Mashinini was treated as a celebrity of the struggle. He toured Africa, moving between countries such as Nigeria, Liberia and Senegal, explaining his political philosophy. Tsietsi made friends with powerful people, asking them for their support in helping him to form a liberation organisation. Lynda Schuster recalls:

> "Tsietsi became the darling of members of the international anti-apartheid movement such as actress Vanessa Redgrave, African American civil rights activist Stokely Carmichael and Miriam Makeba."

But Tsietsi was not popular with everybody. He had deeply upset the ANC, which saw him as a 'third force' that needed to be destroyed. This was a reaction to Tsietsi's outspoken statements just after he went into exile. In March 1977, for example, he claimed that:

> "As far as the students in South Africa are concerned, the ANC and PAC are extinct internally. Externally we are aware they exist. Internally they are doing no work. There may be some underground work which we are not aware of, but as far as the struggle is concerned they are not doing anything."

Intercontinental Press, 14 March 1977

1982 Mashinini separated from Welma Campbell. He struggled after being relieved of his position in the exile student camp, and worries began to emerge about his mental health.

1987 Mashinini finally divorced Welma Campbell after a five-year separation. Campbell took custody of their two children.

ROMANCE

Nevertheless, Tsietsi remained a favourite of the anti-apartheid movement in Africa and became particularly close to Miriam Makeba. The two met in 1977 at FESTAC, a major festival to celebrate African cultural achievements in Nigeria. Tsietsi sought out Makeba, who was singing at the festival, as she later recalled:

> "He had heard about this Miriam Makeba, and so he came to the house I was staying at and said to me, 'I am looking for Miriam Makeba.' I said, 'You are looking at her.' He came with his friends and they sat down. They said they had no money, no clothes, no food. They said they had left, escaped from Morris Isaacson School and had gone to England and then come back here. I sat with them and asked about home." *Miriam Makeba*

Meeting Miriam Makeba changed Tsietsi's life. In 1977, Makeba introduced Tsietsi to one of her backup singers, Welma Campbell. Campbell was a strikingly beautiful and incredibly smart young woman. She was Miss Liberia in 1976. Tsietsi and Welma married in Liberia in 1979.

A DOWNWARD SPIRAL

Tsietsi's marriage in 1979 upset his comrades. The media reported that Tsietsi's wedding was conducted in lavish style in Liberia, although this was never confirmed. His comrades in the South African Youth Revolutionary Council (SAYRCO), previously the Soweto Students Representative Council believed that he lived his life in luxury while they struggled in poverty in exile. Finally, only months after his marriage to Campbell, he was ousted from SAYRCO. Tsietsi, unwelcome in the ANC and PAC, was now without a political home.

01 The day before Tsietsi left South Africa, he gave an interview to the television company, British Thames. Tsietsi is pictured here in a leafy garden belonging to a friend of the TV crew in Hyde Park, Johannesburg. Tsietsi never returned.

02 In exile, Tsietsi remained close to the comrades with whom he had fought side-by-side. Here, he is pictured in an exile safe house holding a black power salute with his friend from Soweto, Khotso Seathlolo.

03 Tsietsi with his wife, Welma Campbell, former Miss Liberia. They had two children.

1990 July Mashinini died in poverty in Guinea under mysterious circumstances. Comrades close to him noted that his body showed signs of being beaten, with his "left eye swollen" and with "marks on his face".

1990 August Mashinini's body was returned to South Africa amidst a huge controversy as numerous political parties attempted to claim him as their own. Disputes raged about who could legitimately memorialize the struggle hero.

TSIETSI BREAKS DOWN

Without a connection to the struggle, Mashinini developed psychological problems. His brother, Lebakeng, received a report from a former comrade about Tsietsi's mental health in the mid-1980s that did not make for good reading:

> "Tsietsi...spends a lot of time in Lagos, always looking for more money. And did you know that he's been ill several times? Oh yes, he required hospitalisation that interrupted his studies for a long time. Mental illness, that's what it was. He had a nervous breakdown and had to be put in a psychiatric institution."

01

P.S. Chief this matter should be given serious and urgent attention.
1. It could happen that here we have a chance to destroy this third force.
2. We must consider whether it would not be wise for us to bring to this conference as many of our cadres who were in the leadership of youth at home to expose those opportunists who are now claiming to lead the youth. In this case we would have to agree to the conference being held and then organise to take it over. We would have to bring some student supporters from home to expose these frauds.
3. I am inclined to think we should allow the conference to take place on condition that our youth attend.
4. I feel if we block it an impression may be created that we have fears of their power.
Matla! Amandla! Cablinga

01   This handwritten note appeared at the bottom of a high-level briefing document handed to Oliver Tambo. It illustrated the ANC's approach to Tsietsi Mashinini was dominated by a need to "destroy" him as he was a 'third force.' The document was found in the ANC archives at the University of Fort Hare.

02   Tsietsi Mashinini's body received a hero's reception in South Africa. His coffin was draped in the flags of the different political parties during his funeral in Soweto in 1990.

AN UNTIMELY DEATH

Tsietsi tried to continue studying despite his ill-health. He enrolled at the Plateua State Polytechnic in Nigeria and, after some hiccups, completed his degree coming near the top of his class. But his relationship with his wife began to crumble. Tsietsi frequently had temper tantrums and was convinced that he was being hunted by apartheid spies. Welma believed that he had multiple personality disorder and separated from him in 1982. They finally divorced in 1987. Welma took custody of their children.

After struggling with mental illness for years, Tsietsi died in poverty in Guinea in July 1990. His body was returned to South Africa the following month and buried at the Avalon Cemetery in Soweto. Many believed that Tsietsi's death was not from natural causes. During Tsietsi's funeral, his close comrade, Khotso Seathlolo, argued:

> "Tsietsi could not have died of natural causes...a young man in his thirties did not die of a nervous breakdown. His left eye...was bleeding. The left eye was swollen and he had marks on his face."

The real cause of Tsietsi's death was never uncovered as his family, already traumatised by their son's death, refused to allow an autopsy. Regardless, Tsietsi returned to South Africa as a hero of the struggle and will always be remembered for his courageous role in the June 1976 uprising.

1990 | On the 4th of August, Tsietsi Mashinini
4 August | was buried at the Avalon Cemetery.

164 : 165

"He didn't do it for the ANC. He didn't do it for Azapo, he didn't do it for the individual. He did it for our liberation."

Eulogy delivered at Mashinini's funeral in Soweto

. . . .

ARTIST > JOHANNES PHOKELA

. . . .

ADDRESS > Opposite Morris Isaacson School, Mputhi Street, Central Western Jabavu, Soweto, Johannesburg

Johannes Phokela was a 10-year-old schoolboy living in Moletsane, Soweto on the momentous day of June 16, 1976. He remembers the protest well: "I was at school, we started coughing and the teacher closed the windows. We were told to lie on the floor. We were kept at school until it was safe… Coming out we saw big smoke. People started burning public businesses, especially those considered to be owned by whites, and drinking places like bottle stores."

Initially Phokela, who describes himself as a painter and a two-dimensional artist, thought of doing a mural. But he rejected the idea as "a little bit old-fashioned and with an old, socialist kind of ethos". He wanted this memorial to have "more to do with hope than anything else". So he decided to create a photographic montage on ceramic tiles. The artwork was placed in the park across the road from Morris Isaacson High School in White City, Jabavu, to mark the place where the march started.

Brenda FASSIE

"I have done more than 25 videos, more than 15 albums, performed in more shows than everybody in this country today, partied harder and funkier than all, while feeding a tribe of relatives as well as throwing myself to the wolves of Jo'burg's smoky nightclub strips. Of course my skin would tell my stories. So, I don't look like Naomi Campell. So what? Man, I will survive, oh, I'll survive!"

The Sunday Independent, 8 Nov 1998

01

Brenda Fassie, known as the 'Madonna of the Townships', was one of Africa's biggest home-grown stars. She was South Africa's top-selling local artist and her record company EMI called her "a once-in-a-generation artist, a true idol". But for most people, she was *MaBrrr* or simply Brenda, a phenomenon like no other. As Brenda once said while talking to fans on *Umhlobo Wenene* FM, "I will always be this way."

Text from the Sunday Times memorial plaque

01 The *Sunday Times* described Fassie as having a "raw, animal magnetism that made her irresistible to men and women".

02 *Weekend Special* was Brenda and *The Big Dudes* first hit album. It made Brenda Fassie a household name in South Africa and spawned a string of hitsingles.

THE 'SONGBIRD OF LANGA'

Brenda Fassie was one of South Africa's most famous musical exports, recognised as a supreme pop star from Langa to Lagos. Brenda, or 'Mbrrr' as she was later known, was born in 1964 in the township of Langa in Cape Town. She was the youngest of nine children born to Makokosi Fassie, who made her living as a pianist. Brenda's early life was marked by tragedy: her father died when she was only two years old. But her mother played an integral role in her early musical life. Brenda's mother worked as a busker employing Brenda as her accompaniment to sing to tourists.

When she was four years old, Brenda joined the *Tiny Tots*, a child group formed by her mother. The group dazzled township residents, especially when Brenda sang her favourite song, *Elaqaba*, a click-filled Xhosa song about Africans who refused to adopt Christianity during colonial times, that would have challenged even Miriam Makeba's agile tongue. At school she dominated in the singing stakes, as her childhood friend, Monwabisi Fesi, recalls:

> "Fassie used to lead the singing in school assemblies from the time she was at primary school. She was known all over the township [Langa] in terms of her singing and social behaviour. She always liked attention."

This Day, 11 May 2004

News of Brenda's unique and powerful voice spread to Johannesburg. In 1978, the talent-scout and producer, Kaloi Lebona, received a call from a fellow musician, Al Etto, raving about Brenda's talent. Lebona was intrigued and travelled to Langa. There he met Brenda and sparks flew, as Lebona recalls:

> "I met Brenda and her family at their home in Makana Square…I was obviously bowled over by Brenda's singing…I spoke to her mother and said 'I would like to take your daughter under my wing. I will treat her like my own daughter.'"

BRENDA'S BIG BREAK

In 1979, at the tender age of 14, Brenda joined Lebona in Soweto carrying with her a young girl's dreams of pursuing a musical career. Lebona tried to make sure that Brenda continued her schooling but Brenda chaffed at the routine and ran away from both Phefeni Secondary School and from Lebona.

Instead, Brenda joined the group *Joy* which had, the previous year, become the first all-black band to have a number one hit in South Africa. Brenda was asked to fill in for one of the group's singers, Anneline Malebo, who was pregnant at the time. Although she lost her place when Malebo returned, she had made her mark. A group called *Blondie and Papa* was looking for a singer to open its tour to Zimbabwe in 1982. They called Brenda and asked her to join the tour.

On tour, Brenda made a major impact on her fellow musicians, as Melvyn Matthews, the song-writing guru who wrote *Weekend Special*, recalls:

> "I went and fetched her, and she did the tour with us to Zimbabwe, and I found her to be a workaholic. She used to WORK, you know. But then she was also the type of person who embraced the glamour as much as she embraced the job."

01 Brenda was nothing if not playful. Here, she can be seen peaking through the legs of fellow musician Themba Kubheka at the Jabulani Festival in Soweto in March 1984.

02 Brenda Fassie posing with the immaculately dressed *Big Dudes* in the mid-1980s. Brenda scored her first international hit, *Weekend Special*, which she recorded with *The Big Dudes* in 1983. The writer of the song, Melvyn Matthews, recalls: "Initially the song was not for Brenda, but after hearing her voice, I thought she was better suited for it. I couldn't have chosen a better person. She really rocked."

03 Brenda formed *The Big Dudes* with members of her former group, *Joy*. Here, Blondie, of *Blondie and the Papas*, congratulates her on a platinum album.

>> •

1968
3 November

Brenda Nokuzola Fassie was born in Cape Town's Langa township. She was named after the famed American country singer, Brenda Lee.

1968

Fassie started her musical career by performing in a local group, *The Tiny Tots*. Koloi Lebona, a Johannesburg-based talent scout, convinced Fassie's family to allow her to move to Johannesburg.

A SMASH-HIT

So impressed were her fellow musicians that, the following year, Brenda convinced members of *Blondie and Papa's* backing band, *The Family*, to leave to form a new group. *The Big Dudes* was born.

Brenda's career went from strength to strength. In 1983, Melvyn Matthews approached the band:

> "I went to the rehearsal room at EMI where the band was practicing. So I went into the room, and I said, 'guys, I have two massive songs.' This was…*Weekend Special*, which was originally called, *Weekend Call* – I'm Your *Weekend Special* because the song was about the phone call that she got every weekend from her boyfriend."

The band was bowled over by the song and recorded it immediately. On release, it became a smash-hit. The record sold over 200 000 copies in South Africa and abroad. *Weekend Special* was the first local act to make it into the US Billboard's Top 100. It also made it on to the dance charts in the UK, and did well in other places too. It became the fastest-selling single of its time. Brenda was only 18. She fast became a mega-star.

PURE TOWNSHIP

Fassie's stature and stardom grew throughout the 1980s. She came to represent the new face of township youth culture in the same way that Orlando Pirates symbolised the Soweto of the sixties. Her songs, such as *Zola Budd*, about a taxi driver who refused to pick her up, resonated with the lives of township residents in the latter days of apartheid. Her 'bubblegum' pop music was also a political statement, as *This Day* later wrote:

> "Why should we pretend that there was a strict dividing line between those who sang freedom songs and toyi-toyed at mass rallies, and those who got down to *Weekend Special* and *Too Late for Mama* in packed nightclubs all over the country? The truth is that we were most times the same people, and that Fassie helped us to cross over without apology to one group or the other. Her music was pure township, and township during the eighties was political by definition."

1980　Brenda Fassie had her big break. She filled in for, the lead singer of the group *Joy*. After her contract with *Joy* expired, she joined a popular group of the time, *Blondie and Papa*, performing a solo act to open their shows on tour.

1983　Fassie founded her own group, *The Big Dudes*, made up of many of the members of *Joy*. The group recorded Fassie's first single, *Weekend Special*, which became an immediate smash hit in South Africa.

MOTHERHOOD AND MARRIAGE

This was also a period of major personal changes for Brenda. In 1985, she gave birth to her only child, Bongani, whose father was *Big Dude* musician Dumisani Ngobeni. But, two years later, she parted from *The Big Dudes* and joined the renowned producer Sello 'Chico' Twala. Together, they produced a string of hits into the early 1990s, including one of Brenda's most famous songs, *Black President*, about the future of South Africa after apartheid, which featured on the best-selling album, *Too Late for Mama*. Twala later recalled how talented she was: "In a minute, she had picked up the melody and started singing with her own lyrics *nogal*. Such talented people don't come easy. She was gold." Brenda was consistently hailed for the beauty of her voice, its melody, and her sense of rhythm and timing. She was compared to the great blues queens like Billie Holliday.

In 1989, Brenda Fassie married a millionaire's son from Durban, Nhlanhla Mbambo. It was no ordinary wedding. They held three ceremonies in Cape Town, Johannesburg and Durban. At the church service in Cape Town, it took Brenda 30 minutes to walk from her black Cadillac with tinted windows to the altar through the throng of fans and photographers who jostled to snap photos of her in one of her several outlandish designer wedding dresses. The priest said, "Never have I experienced anything like this. I may be bruised, battered and bewildered, but it was wonderful." The last ceremony in Durban was held in the KwaMashu Stadium and was witnessed by 18 000 adoring fans. Brenda and her bridegroom arrived to a rapturous reception in a helicopter. However, the two split two years later amid rumours that Mbambo assaulted Fassie. She later called him a leech, lecher and a wife-beater in the press.

01   In 1984, Brenda and *The Big Dude* pianist, Dumisani Ngubeni, became romantically involved. The following year they had a child together.

02   Brenda Fassie looks lovingly at her first and only child, Bongani, who was born in 1985.

03   Brenda Fassie had three wedding ceremonies. This photo was taken at the ceremony in Durban which was attended by nearly 2 500 people.

01

02

03

1985   Brenda Fassie had her first and only child, Bongani. A year later, the song, *Weekend Special*, entered the US Billboard Hot Black Singles Chart. As a result of the single's success, *The Big Dudes* embarked on a tour of the United States, Europe, Australia and Brazil.

1989   Fassie married Nhlanhla Mbambo in a spectacular ceremony. In the same year, she parted from *The Big Dudes* to launch a solo career and joined the producer, Sello 'Chico' Twala. They recorded the album *Too Late for Mama*, which was a massive hit.

LIFE CRUMBLES

Things started to go wrong for Brenda at this time. She was introduced to cocaine by a bodyguard and quickly became addicted to the drug. By 1993, she was in a downward spiral. Her son had been kicked out of school as she failed to pay his fees and Chico Twala dumped her as a result of her addiction. Her financial problems were worsened by her almost pathological generosity, as she later recalled in an interview in 2001:

> "I'd rather have happiness than money. People ask for money. Sometimes I don't have it. I make other people's problems my problem because they want me to; they ask me to. So sometimes I wish I didn't have the little money that I do."

Brenda also became famous for her mood swings. In public she would weep, get extremely angry and then become loving and sweet all in a matter of moments. Several journalists have said they were extremely scared of interviewing her.

Brenda reached her lowest point in 1995. She had run out of money and was living with her lesbian lover, Poppie Sihlahla, in Hillbrow's seedy Quirinal Hotel.

According to Twala, who remained connected to Brenda, it was a desperate situation:

> "My daily struggle was to rescue her from those around her. I literally dragged her screaming and kicking from a dingy R29 per night Hillbrow hotel...She never had a childhood. She should have been protected from herself first and those around her. There were just too many hangers-on in her life. She needed strong people who could discipline her."

Brenda finally acknowledged her situation in 1995 when she woke up next to Poppie, who had died of an overdose. She approached friends to help her out of her situation and entered rehab.

04   Brenda Fassie and Sello 'Chico' Twala, pictured here in 1987, were the South African version of Michael Jackson and Quincy Jones.

05   Fassie, like Madonna, courted controversy in the early 1990s by appearing in a music video in a priest's garb.

06   Brenda with her son, Bongani, in the recording studio in 1996 after cleaning up her act. Bongani has become an accomplished musician in his own right by mastering jazz piano.

1991   Nhlanhla Mbambo and Brenda Fassie divorced amid rumours of domestic abuse. The divorce started a downward spiral for Fassie, made worse by an addiction to cocaine.

1998   Fassie made her big comeback. She rejoined forces with Sello 'Chico' Twala to record the album *Memeza (Shout)*. She recorded five more albums: *Nomakanjani* (1999), *Amadlozi* (2000), *Mina Nawa* (2001), *Myekeleni* (2002) and *Mali* (2004). Each album reached platinum status, making Fassie one the biggest selling South African artists.

LONELINESS AND DESPAIR

When Brenda proved that she had cleaned up her act, she joined forces again with super-producer Sello 'Chico' Twala. They resurrected her career. Together with Twala, she recorded *Memeza (Shout)*. The album sold 50 000 units in the first four hours of its release and ultimately sold 560 000 units throughout Africa, going platinum 11 times. Over the next six years, she recorded a further six albums with Twala, all of which went platinum. This cemented her position as the Queen of Kwaito in the minds of South Africa's township hipsters.

But Brenda continued to struggle with her drug and alcohol addictions and was admitted to rehab a number of times. In 2003, a year before her death, she admitted that she was deeply depressed and had tried to commit suicide three times as journalist, Therese Owen, later recalled:

> "'Are you happy, Brenda?' I posed this question to Ms Fassie a few months before her untimely death. She blinked and her characteristic elfin charm disappeared. It was replaced by despair. 'No, no, I am not happy.' By this time the tears were streaming down her small face and she was sobbing…And here she was, sitting across from me in a coffee shop courtyard in Melville, crying will all the sadness in her soul…'Why are you so unhappy if you have everything?' I asked. There was a dramatic pause: 'Because I am so alone.'"

In May 2004, Brenda was admitted to hospital in a coma after suffering a heart attack. It was widely rumoured that the heart attack had been caused by a binge on crack-cocaine. Her hospitalisation provoked a massive outpouring of grief as both Nelson Mandela and Thabo Mbeki flew to visit a comatose Brenda. On the 9th of May, Brenda Fassie died, leaving behind her Bongani, 15 albums, over 150 songs and a grief-stricken nation.

Brenda's death was greeted with a nation-wide outpouring of grief. Her final resting place was the township from where she hailed, Langa. On 23 May, she was buried during a packed and emotional funeral.

01   Fassie continued to sing and record in the years before her death, notching up a string of hit albums. Here, she donned a new look hairstyle to record a music video in 2003, a year before her death.

2004   Fassie died in Johannesburg after spending two
9 May   weeks in a coma, thought to be caused by abusing crack cocaine. On 23 May, she was buried in Langa.

"Brenda Fassie came like a tycoon, and departed like Halley's comet. That natural. That strange. That wild. The first township wonder to defy South Africa's parochialism, Brenda belonged to the constellation of tragic black musical stars immortalised by Billie Holiday, Tupac Shakur and Miles Davis."

Bongani MADONDO

. . . .

ARTIST > ANGUS TAYLOR

. . . .

ADDRESS > Bassline, Newtown Precinct, Johannesburg

José Villa Soberon's sculpture of John Lennon in a park in Havana, Cuba, sparked Angus Taylor's concept of two performers' stools on a stage. Brenda sits on one, the other invites the visitor to sit alongside her.

Taylor started with research. "The better you understand the person you are working with, the better the sculpture will relay not just facial features." For weeks, Taylor's studio at his foundry in Pretoria was filled with photos of the singer. A DVD of her performing and being interviewed played continuously on a TV screen.

The text superimposed on the body of the life-sized bronze sculpture is all quotes by Fassie on her relationship with the media.

Ladysmith Black MAMBAZO

"We have won Grammy Awards, represented our homeland, travelled the world and, most importantly, spread a message of Peace, Love and Harmony to millions of people. This was never a dream a black South African could ever imagine."

Joseph SHABALALA

01

On a September night in 1967, Joseph Shabalala led his a cappella group, *The Blacks*, in their first performance of a unique style of harmonious singing he had heard in his dreams. Though the group was unknown, the audience demanded that they sing past midnight. *The Blacks* went on to win all the *isicathamiya* competitions around South Africa and renamed themselves *Ladysmith Black Mambazo – mambazo* meaning the axe that 'chopped down' all competition. They were soon barred from competing, but were always welcome to perform. The group, which today includes four of Joseph's six sons, has achieved unparalleled international fame and has won several Grammy awards.

Text from the Sunday Times memorial plaque

01 *Ladysmith Black Mambazo* is one of South Africa's most successful bands.

02 *Ladysmith Black Mambazo* won its second Grammy award in 2005.

MAMBAZO ON SONG

Grammy glory group is on roller coaster ride to success

BONGANI MAHLANGU

SOLOMON Linda and Joseph Shabalala deserve the credit for propelling *isicathamiya* music to great international heights since the development of the genre in the 1920s.

Linda was the lead singer of the Original Evening Birds, a group that began recording for Gallo Records in 1939.

He was ripped off and his family left with no more than the knowledge that their beloved gave the world *Mbube*, a spiritual awakening composition with a melody that spoke of an intense African culture.

But Shabalala and his outfit of energetic singers and dancers, Ladysmith Black Mambazo, have been on a roller coaster ride, reaping the fruits of their hard work and delectable craft.

The 10-member group is among the few African groups to have won two Grammy Awards and sold millions of records.

Last Sunday the group's latest album, *Wenyukela – Raise Your Spirit Higher*, won the award for Best World Album in the traditional category at the 47th Grammy Awards.

Amambazo Amnyama, as they are also affectionately known to their fans, continue to represent African culture through performances at packed venues worldwide.

The group is at present on a tour of the United States and has gigs planned until December.

Amambazo's first international release, *Shaka Zulu*, recorded in the United States and produced by Paul Simon, won a Grammy for the best World Music Recording in 1988.

Ladysmith Black Mambazo was initially signed by producer West Nkosi for Gallo Records and released their first recording, *Amabutho*, in 1973. It sold more than 25 000 copies.

Shabalala founded Ladysmith Black Mambazo in 1960 while he was a labourer.

The story goes that the original members of his group were not committed and willing to put in the work Shabalala demanded.

So the ambitious, determined and disciplined Shabalala recruited his own family members and friends.

Today the group consists of Shabalala's sons Msizi, Sibongiseni, Thamsanqa and Thulani, and relatives Jockey Shabalala, Albert Mazibuko, Abednego Mazibuko, Jabulani Dubazane and Russel Mthembu.

Other groups that have emerged from Ladysmith Black Mambazo include Woman of Mambazo, White Mambazo and *maskandi* outfit Shabalala Rhythm.

"Our country and its culture are the most important things to us," says Shabalala. "Each time we make a new CD we do so knowing we are keeping our culture alive."

Ladysmith Black Mambazo has successfully fused its *isicathamiya* music with genres such as gospel, R&B and pop.

The outfit's latest recording, *Raise Your Spirit Higher*, features the English Chamber Orchestra conducted by Ralf Gothóni. It will be released tomorrow.

Mambazo's achievements include:
● Recording more than 40 albums;
● Receiving a lifetime achievement award at the South African Music Awards in 2001; and
● Performing at two Nobel Peace Prize ceremonies.

ENERGETIC: Ladysmith Black Mambazo are touring the US in the wake of ther recent Grammy Award coup

A FEW ARTISTS WHO HAVE RECORDED WITH MAMBAZO

● Stevie Wonder
● The Wynans
● Dolly Parton
● Andreas Vollenweider
● Desiree
● Paul Simon
● Lou Rawls
● Nana "Coyote" Motijoane

MOVIE SOUNDTRACKS THEY HAVE FEATURED ON

● Moonwalker
● A Dry White Season
● Let's Do It A Cappella
● Coming To America
● Cry The Beloved Country
● The League of Gentlemen
● Disney's Lion King Part 2

THEIR TOP FIVE SONGS

● Unomathemba
● Homeless
● Siligugu Isiphambano
● Ilungelo ngelakho
● Hello My Baby

SINGALONG: Stevie Wonder. *Picture by Reuters*

DRIVER: Joseph Shabalala. *Picture by Siyabonga Mosonkulu*

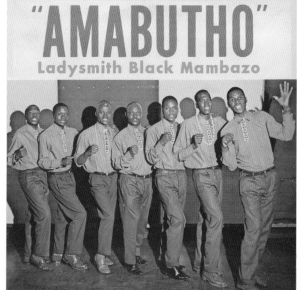

RURAL ROOTS

Bhekizizwe Joseph Shabalala was born on the 28th of August 1941 on a white-owned farm called Tugela just outside Ladysmith. He was the eldest of six children born to Mluwane Jonathan Nomandla and Elina Shabalala. Both of Shabalala's parents were musical: "My mother was a musician...my father was a musician and they had lovely beautiful voices. We used to sing together."

In 1945, when Shabalala was only four years old, his father died. Shabalala, the eldest child, was forced to take on many household responsibilities. He looked after the cattle and ran affairs on the farm.

01 Shabalala's first band, *The Blacks*, was inspired by the rural traditions of KwaZulu-Natal.

02 Ladysmith Black Mambazo's first album, *Amabutho*, was an immediate hit. It reached gold status and launched the band's illustrious career.

03 The members of the band were able to shift between the traditional rural world from where they came, and the world of popular modern music. Here, they are pictured in the late 1970s in dapper white suits.

04 *Ladysmith Black Mambazo's* celebration of its ethnic Zulu roots won many fans throughout the country.

'ISICATHAMIYA'

When he was of working age, Shabalala found employment making potato chips and pies at *The Guinea Fowl*, a Ladysmith tearoom.

While working in Ladysmith, Shabalala learned to play guitar from his father's cousin. He saved up to buy his first guitar.

> "During that time I always felt very passionate about music. I bought myself a brand new guitar for R1.45. I went back home with my new guitar...People on the farm asked me: 'What's this?' They said: 'No, no, maybe this is not good for you, it's a foreign something.' But when I played people cried because I played it very well." *Joseph Shabalala*

Before he was out of his teenage years, Shabalala moved to Durban to find work. He was employed at Frametex, a textile factory, where he oiled machines. Durban was a musical hotspot at the time. One musical style prevalent in Durban, *isicathamiya*, caught Shabalala's imagination. *Isicathamiya* was a rhythmic a cappella style of music, which was usually accompanied by a shuffle-dance known as *cothoza mfana*.

>> •

1941
28 August
Bhekizizwe Joseph Shabalala was born to Mluwane Jonathan Shabalala and Nomandla Elina Shabalala on a farm called Tugela near Ladysmith.

1960
Shabalala formed and directed the *isicathamiya* group *The Blacks*, composed largely of his family members. Four years later, Shabalala drew on many members of *The Blacks* to form *Ladysmith Black Mambazo*.

PERFECT HARMONY

Shabalala delved into this musical world, and joined a group called *Durban Choir*. Kalian Hlatswayo, a local choir director, took him under his wing. Under his able tutelage, Shabalala learnt the ins-and-outs of choir directing.

In 1960, Shabalala returned to Ladysmith and formed his first group, *The Blacks*, pictured on the previous page. It was largely made up of Shabalala's relatives and performed in the Ladysmith area. However, he was never entirely happy with the group: "I felt there was something missing...I tried to teach music that I felt, but I failed."

Over a period of six months in 1964, Shabalala had a series of dreams. He dreamed of a choir but unlike *The Blacks*, it sang in perfect harmony of a very particular kind:

> "The song was so harmonious it stayed in my mind. I knew then that our group was going to sing exactly the same way. It is difficult to explain. It was very nice and their voices were so collected and powerful."
> *Joseph Shabalala*

OPENING THE WAY

In order to make his dreams a reality, Shabalala reconstituted *The Blacks*, and included his brothers Headman and Jockey and his cousins Albert and Abednego Mazibuko.

After working on the new style for over three years, the group performed in public for the first time at the KwaMashu Community Hall in 1967. This was a major moment as the public responded wildly, encouraging the group to sing beyond midnight. In the same year, they recorded their first song, *Nomathemba*, which had been such a hit at their Community Hall concert. The band started to tour throughout South Africa and, along the way, changed its name to *Ladysmith Black Mambazo*.

Shabalala recalls, "I called them *Black Mambazo*, *Mambazo* means chopping axe. I wished their voices to open the way, to chop all the trees and open the big way to travel everywhere."

After receiving extensive radio play on Radio Zulu and other stations, and receiving rapturous receptions at concerts around the country, they were signed to Gallo Records by producer West Nkosi. He flew them to the Gallo studios in Johannesburg, and they started working on their first record. It was to be the start of an unforgettable musical journey.

1967 *Ladysmith Black Mambazo* made its debut performance at the KwaMashu Community Hall. The performance was an overwhelming success, and saw the group singing its now famous song, *Nomathemba*. *Nomathemba* was recorded as their first single and was played frequently on Radio Zulu.

1972 *Mambazo* signed its first record deal with West Nkosi, a producer at Gallo Records. The following year, the band recorded its first album, *Amabutho*. It was an immediate hit making them the first black group to have a gold-selling record.

HUGGING A WHITE MAN

Ladysmith Black Mambazo's major break on the international scene came in 1985. Paul Simon, the world-renowned musician, travelled to South Africa. He was looking for an African band with which he could collaborate. When he heard a tape of *Ladysmith Black Mambazo's* music, he was immediately won over. Simon contacted Shabalala, and set up a meeting in Johannesburg. The pair struck up an immediate connection, as Shabalala recalls:

> "It was easy to talk; it was easy to hug one another. It was my first time to hug a white man. I thought maybe as the time goes I'm going to be in jail but we just hugged one another. And then we talked about music and I said to him, 'If you talk about music to me, that is my life.'"

Simon flew *Ladysmith Black Mambazo* to New York, and they began working on an album together. The result was *Graceland*, one of the albums which defines Paul Simon's music. It was a major international hit, selling over 10 million copies worldwide. Shabalala contributed enormously to the album, writing the hit song *Homeless*. Although the band was criticised for breaking the apartheid cultural boycott, Shabalala later explained:

> "I am a musician. Paul Simon is a musician. He's not a politician. He was just trying to make something beautiful and take it somewhere else."

Soon after they worked with Simon, they started working with other music legends such as Stevie Wonder, Dolly Parton and Michael Jackson. Jackson was so impressed with the band that he included it in his hit film, *Moonwalker*. Shabalala wanted to expose Jackson to South African dancing: "When we saw him dancing, we wanted to show him that we have our dancing. That's why we did something with him and he was very happy."

01 Paul Simon with LBM in the early 1980s.

02 Members of the band are pictured here in the dashing suits they donned to appear in Michael Jackson's film, *Moonwalker*.

03 The response to LBM's Grammy award in 2005 was astounding, *Sowetan*, 15 February 2005.

1976   Shabalala converted to Christianity and the band recorded the album *Ukusindiwa*, a collection of hymns. It was a great success and was their first album to reach double platinum sales.

1985   Paul Simon, the internationally renowned musician, travelled to South Africa to seek fresh influences for his music. Simon found Shabalala, and they collaborated on the smash hit, *Graceland*.

1988   Ladysmith Black Mambazo received major recognition in the international musical arena, winning a Grammy Award for Best Traditional Folk Recording for the album *Shaka Zulu*.

In 1987, Paul Simon helped to produce *Mambazo's* album *Shaka Zulu*. It was released by Warner in the USA, and was another hit for the band. In 1988, *Shaka Zulu* won the Grammy award for Best Traditional Folk Album.

This feat was repeated in 2005, with the album *Raise Your Spirit Higher*. The headline of the newspaper article above, shows that *Ladysmith Black Mambazo's* success was central in helping South Africa construct a positive identity in the post-apartheid period.

A CAREER HIGHLIGHT

One of Joseph Shabalala's career highlights was playing at Nelson Mandela and FW de Klerk's Nobel Peace Prize ceremony. Mandela was a great fan of the band. As Shabalala later recalled: "It was beautiful. But when we finished the song, Mandela stood up, lifted his fist and said, '*Black Mambazo*! Black Power!'"

Ladysmith Black Mambazo continues to record and perform its most recent album. *Long walk to Freedom* was released in 2007. It received two further Grammy nominations.

"The people of the world love truth in music and one reason *Ladysmith* has remained popular abroad is that we try to remain truthful to our tradition. People see this and love it."

Joseph SHABALALA

. . . .

ARTIST > MAGWA LANGA

. . . .

ADDRESS > KwaMashu Hall, F Section, KwaMashu, KwaZulu-Natal

The concept is formed from a variety of influences within traditional Zulu ritual and *Ladysmith's* own experience as herd boys in their youth. The concept is based on *isiphandla*, a traditional arm band worn after ceremonial slaughtering, symbolising the presence of ancestors and providing protection for the wearer. Ancestors are a real connection as Joseph was 'given' melodies in his dreams and it is through dreams that we believe we are connecting with our ancestors. The shape of the piece is also reminiscent of headbands worn by Zulu leaders and by *Ladysmith Black Mambazo* when they are performing in traditional gear.

1 FREEDOM IN OUR TIME

1989 - 2004

This section captures the dying moments of apartheid and the birth of a new nation. The stories tell of those who were fortunate and courageous enough to play a leading role in shepherding the country away from the ruins of the past and into a much more hopeful, democratic future.

2 August 1989 — The Mass Democratic Movement (MDM), founded after the UDF was banned, launched a massive countrywide Defiance Campaign to protest against the 6 September election. The campaign was a major success with marches taking place in most cities.

15 August 1989 — PW Botha resigned from his post as President of South Africa. Former Minister of Education, FW de Klerk, took over as President.

2 September 1989 — Protestors marching through the Cape Town city centre as part of the MDM's Defiance Campaign were confronted by police and sprayed with purple dye. One protestor, Philip Ivey, jumped onto the water cannon and redirected the spray, painting the city centre purple.

15 October 1989 — Walter Sisulu, along with six other jailed senior ANC leaders, including Raymond Mhlaba and Govan Mbeki, was released from prison.

2 February 1990 — President FW de Klerk unbanned the ANC, PAC, SACP and other anti-apartheid organisations. He also announced that Nelson Mandela would be released from prison. Mandela walked from the gates of Pollsmoor Prison on the 11th of February as a free man.

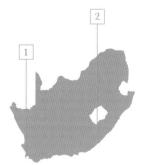

>> SAHA/*SUNDAY TIMES* MEMORIAL SITES:

1 The PURPLE MATCH
Corner Burg and Church Streets, Cape Town

1991   The last legal bastions of apartheid were destroyed. The Native Land and Trust Act, Group Areas Act and Population Registration Act were repealed. For the first time in four decades, South Africans of all colours could live, work and own land where they wished.

Late 1991   After nearly two years of talks between the ANC and the NP, the Convention for a Democratic South Africa (CODESA), a multi-party body, set about negotiating the nature of the post-apartheid state. In 1993, all negotiating parties agreed to a draft interim constitution.

1992   The sports boycott ended. South African athletes took part in the Barcelona Olympics. Three years later, SA won the Rugby World Cup. A year after that, SA cemented its place in the sporting world by winning the African Cup of Nations.

1993   Both FW de Klerk and Nelson Mandela were awarded the Nobel Peace Prize for their roles in ending apartheid.

27 April 1994   Around 20 million voters went to the polls in the country's first ever democratic elections. The ANC garnered 62.25% of the votes. The National Party became the official opposition with 20% of the votes. Nelson Mandela was inaugurated as South Africa's first black president.

1996   The Truth and Reconciliation Commission (TRC) began its first set of hearings in Port Elizabeth. After the second day of hearings, the Chairman of the TRC, Archbishop Desmond Tutu, was reduced to tears.

4 December 1996   South Africa's new democratic constitution was approved by the Constitutional Court, and took effect on the 7th of February 1997.

1999   Nelson Mandela stepped down as the head of the ANC and as President of the country. The ANC won the second multiracial election and selected Mandela's deputy, Thabo Mbeki, as the new President of the country.

2004   Thabo Mbeki was re-elected as President of the country.

The PURPLE MARCH

"Coming in to Cape Town on that day was really like entering a police state. I think there were more bright yellow police vehicles than any other vehicle. It was an overcast, cold-ish September day from what I recall. I just felt, *ja*, Cape Town was not my city."

Phillip IVEY
Acting Treasurer of the End Conscription Campaign

01

On 2 September 1989 anti-apartheid protesters marching on parliament were stopped by police near this spot in the centre of Cape Town. They mounted an impromptu sit-in and police retaliated with tear gas, batons and a new weapon - a water cannon laced with purple dye to stain demonstrators and make them easier to identify and detain. As they scattered, one protestor, Philip Ivey, climbed onto the armoured water cannon vehicle and turned the purple jet on police. Purple dye stained most of the surrounding buildings, including the National Party headquarters and the whitewashed walls of the historic Old Townhouse. The next day graffiti all over the city proclaimed "The Purple Shall Govern". This was one of the last protest marches outlawed by the apartheid government. Eleven days later, 30 000 people marched through the city without police intervention.

Text from the Sunday Times memorial plaque

01　Philip Ivey redirected the water cannon's nozzle. Ironically, the spray now painted the headquarters of the Western Cape National Party a deep, intense purple.

02　Philip Ivey was considered a hero amongst the Defiance Campaign protestors in Cape Town for taking an active stand against the police. This cartoon, found in Ivey's scrapbook, illustrates his bravery.

PURPLE MARCH

A NEW ERA

The 1980s were years unlike any other during apartheid. The apartheid state began to fray at the seams. By the late 1980s, popular protest dominated the headlines. South Africa was undergoing a revolution. In the words of Security Policeman, Paul Erasmus:

> "The struggle for liberation had intensified to the point that you had to be literally a bloody fool not to realise that this wasn't going to end up in chaos somewhere or that we were gonna give the country to the liberation movement."

At the beginning of the 1980's, the government accepted proposals made by the Wiehahn and Riekert Commissions, which recommended the scrapping of urban influx controls and allowed for the legalisation of unions for the first time in years. Black people flooded into the cities and joined the fight for freedom and democracy. Trade unions were formed and began to agitate for political freedom.

In 1983, a radical new political organisation was formed - the United Democratic Front (UDF). The UDF was set up as an umbrella body that provided a home for political groupings across the board, ranging from hardcore township militants to church and reading groups. At the peak of its power, roughly 700 civic organisations came together to fight apartheid under the banner of the UDF. The movement's affiliates set about organising school and rent boycotts and stay-aways.

One of the UDF's most successful campaigns was staged in 1984 in response to State President PW Botha's attempts to 'reform' apartheid. He had tabled the ludicrous idea of establishing three separate parliaments for whites, Coloureds and Indians. Blacks were completely excluded from the new deal. The UDF leaders were insulted by these 'reforms' and agitated for a boycott of the tri-cameral elections. The result was devastating. Only 20% of the potential electorate turned up to vote for the new houses of parliament.

THE STATE CRACKDOWN

The state retaliated swiftly by declaring a national State of Emergency (SOE) in June 1985. The army and police in caspirs and other military vehicles invaded the townships. But the SOE only fuelled the flames of popular resistance. The groundswell of opposition was heightened by the formation of a massive trade union organisation, the Congress of Trade Unions (COSATU), in December 1985.

COSATU embarked on a series of nationwide political campaigns that were hugely successful. On May Day 1986, over 1.5 million workers heeded COSATU's call to stay away from work. The following years proved even more successful. Over 2.5 million workers refused to go to work and over 3 million workers downed tools in June 1988.

In 1988, the UDF was banned and many of its leaders were imprisoned. The government placed severe restrictions on COSATU. As part of the SOE, hundreds of schools had been closed and thousands of children and adults were detained without trial. The army patrolled the streets and imposed order at all costs. Despite this crackdown, popular resistance could still not be quelled.

In response to the banning of the UDF, a new movement was formed called the Mass Democratic Movement (MDM). Closely aligned to the exiled ANC, the MDM picked up where the UDF had left off. In 1989, it launched the Defiance Campaign against apartheid laws. Inspired by the ANC's 1952 campaign and, in turn, by Gandhi's philosophy of non-violence, the MDM undertook a campaign of 'passive resistance' that was to culminate on the eve of the whites-only elections set for 6 September. A series of marches was organised, that intentionally broke apartheid's stringent security laws. In August 1989, restricted activists unbanned themselves. They declared the UDF unbanned. Thousands of people defied 'whites only' signs to reclaim the beaches for all race groups.

01 In September 1989, the police tried a new tactic of spraying protesters with purple dye so that they could be identified and arrested after they had dispersed.

02 In one of the few surviving photos of the day, we see Philip Ivey taking his life into his hands by taking control of the police water cannon.

>> . . . .

| 1983 | The United Democratic Front (UDF) was formed out of a diverse array of anti-apartheid organisations. For many, the UDF acted as the surrogate of the ANC in South Africa, providing direction and a centre for the resistance struggle. | 1985 | State President, PW Botha, declared a national State of Emergency (SOE). This increased the power of the state to arrest political activists for indefinite periods of detention without trial. | 1985 December | The Congress of South African Trade Unions (COSATU) was formed. |

FIGHTING BACK

On 2 September 1989, the MDM-led Defiance Campaign took to the streets of Cape Town. The protest attracted tens of thousands of supporters, who met at halls throughout the city to march along three separately planned routes that would converge outside the Houses of Parliament. A memorandum was to be delivered to the government to protest against the banning of political organisations and to announce that they would continue operating regardless. Laurie Nathan, an activist in the End Conscription Campaign, explains their expectations on the day:

"We were expecting a fight with the police… We were being provocative by virtue of promoting the ANC, which was a banned organisation. It was highly nerve-wracking. You're tense and you're anticipating a fight, a fight that physically we were bound to lose because we were not armed. But we would win it politically whenever they used excessive force. So the political victory was ours to be had."

Despite anticipating violence, the protestors were shocked at the police presence as they arrived in the city. A confrontation seemed inevitable. As one group marched down Burg Street, they were confronted by a heavy police presence that blocked their march across Green Market Square. After the police refused to move, and the crowd refused to disperse, the group sat down peacefully in an act of defiance. They were given ten minutes to disperse but six minutes later, a police vehicle with a mounted water cannon began to spray the protestors with a mixture of water and purple dye. The police ran into the crowd with *sjamboks*, batons and teargas. Laurie Nathan recalls:

"I was right in front of the police vehicle with the water cannon. Lo and behold, it was spraying purple! And at first it was surreal, because it had a colour and atmosphere of frivolity. It took a few seconds to dawn on us, but the point was then obvious: once you were stained you were clearly identifiable as having participated in this march."

02

| 1986 May | COSATU organised its first mass stay-away on May Day. 1.5 million workers heeded the call to stay away from work. The following year, 2.5 million workers stayed away. | 1988 February | The apartheid government banned the UDF and COSATU's growing power by imposing severe restrictions on their activities and by targeting key union leaders. The UDF responded by forming the Mass Democratic Movement (MDM). |

IVEY TAKES CONTROL

Phillip Ivey felt so angry that he decided to take action: "I clearly remember a couple of nuns being sprayed, their black and white habits getting progressively more purple ...I was quite affronted by the violence that was being imposed on us." Ivey decided to mount the police vehicle and take control of the spray.

"I came behind the vehicle, so the driver and the operator of the water cannon couldn't see me. It was three or four steps up a ladder and suddenly I was in control of the purple rain. I obviously didn't know how the contraption worked but grabbed the nozzle of the cannon and just lifted it off the marchers...to make sure that they weren't getting further damaged. The only thing I could really hear was the pounding of the blood in my ears...I managed to disconnect some of the pneumatic cables that operated the nozzle. And then without thinking, I jumped off the vehicle. There were policemen running towards me. Fortunately there were no gun shots and I knew that I had miraculously not been shot."

Ivey's action had a spectacular impact:

"It was absolutely amazing, I mean it was for us, really uplifting. He was so brave because he was obviously going to be arrested and beaten." *Jill Pointer*

01   Shortly after the march, Constable Marius Vivier received a medical certificate stating his eye had been damaged as a result of Phillip Ivey's assault. This cartoonist was amused by the claim.

02   This charge sheet for Phillip Ivey was drawn up after the Purple Rain March. It accused him of assaulting a police officer, Constable Marius Vivier, preventing a police officer of discharging his duties as well as malicious damage to police property.

Alison Ozinsky was one of the protestors. She later wrote an article for *Upfront* magazine describing the commotion and Ivey's brave action:

"Some are hit head on, full in the face. Some are knocked off their knees. Scramble and panic and somebody is shouting, 'Sit down, sit down.' Some are pinned against the wall and are painted like paper dolls as the jet sweeps past. A small remaining huddle in the road are covering their heads under the purple spray. The supply of purple dye seems endless and the machine sprays on and on. The gutters run with oily foam. The crowd is stunned into strange silence. All we can do is watch this weird purple blast sweep backwards and forwards...Then it stops. A lone protester has climbed on top of the truck and is diverting the nozzle away from the people. He is struggling with it, fighting with it and the purple jet streaks wildly across the building. The crowd stares for a moment in disbelief – then goes wild, cheering and shouting, and leaping in the air with delight for this brave young man. It is an indescribable moment. Even the police can simply stare, seeming to have momentarily lost their grip on the situation."

Ivey's singular act of bravery startled the police, but not for long. Ozinsky continues describing the events of the day:

"The (police) retaliate as teargas billows into the square. Marchers and policemen alike are stumbling and choking and fighting for breath. Spectators have become participants, willingly or not. Some collapse in the road. Eyes streaming, nose and mouth and lungs burning, we run up streets, into building, it's like a war. It is a war and it feels like the city is on our side. A friend of mine runs into a hairdressing salon and is washed clean of his purple stains. Another is rescued by taxi and is whisked off down the back streets.

1988
June

COSATU launched its own Defiance Campaign. Nearly 3 million South Africans took part in the campaign.

1988
October

PW Botha introduced the tri-cameral parliamentary system as an attempt to reform apartheid. This was a dismal failure and was boycotted by the majority of the population.

CASE NUMBER   13/945/89

COUNT 1

A N N E X U R E   'A'

STATE VERSUS PHILLIP JAMES IVEY

THAT the accused is guilty of an offence in terms of section 27(1)
read with Section 1 of Act 7 of 1958 as amended by section 7 of Act 90.

IN THAT upon or about) 2 September 1989, and at (or near) Burg Street,
Cape Town, the accused unlawfully assaulted Constable Marius Vivier
a member of the Force in the exercise of his powers or the performance
of his duties or functions by hitting him with his fist in his face,
kicking and/or stepping on his face with his feet and spraying dye in
his eyes.

IN THE ALTERNATIVE

THAT the accused is guilty of an offence in terms of Section 27(2)(a)
of Act 7 of 1958 as amended by Section 7 of Act 90 of 1977.

IN THAT upon (or about) 2 September 1989, and at (or near) Burg Street,
Cape Town, the accused unlawfully resisted or willfully hindered or
obstructed Constable Marius Vivier a member of the Force in the exercise
of his powers or the performance of his duties or functions, or in the
exercise of his powers or the performance of his duties or functions
by the said member of the Force, willfully intervered with such member
or his uniform or equipment or any part thereof by resisting when the
said member tried to remove him from a S A P Watercannon and/or preventing
him from taking control of the watercannon.

COUNT 2

A N N E X U R E

THAT the accused is guilty of the crime of MALICIOUS INJURY TO PROPERTY.

IN THAT upon (or about) 2/9/1989 and at (or near) CAPE TOWN in the
district of the Cape the accused did wrongfully and unlawfully and maliciously
break and damage the left headlight and the dye hose of a S A P watercannon
73804E (± R150.00) the property of S A P with the intent there and then
and thereby to injure the said SOUTH AFRICAN POLICE in their property.

"A department store is used as a hideout and a comrade emerges with a clean pair of trousers. We hear that all purple people are being rounded up and arrested. Jackets and jerseys are being turned inside out and incriminating stains are quickly concealed."

Many protestors took refuge in St George's Hall which was then surrounded by 13 police trucks, caspirs and a water cannon. Archbishop Tutu managed to negotiate with the police to withdraw their vehicles on condition that everyone inside the church would leave peacefully and in small groups.

THE AFTERMATH

In the aftermath of the confrontation, the police arrested roughly 500 protestors and 52 local and international journalists. Special courts were set up to process the detained. All photographic film was confiscated, explaining why photos of the day are so rare. Many were released soon after their arrest. Phillip Ivey, however, was brought under more serious charges, as detailed in the charge sheet above.

1988 Late	The Mass Democratic Movement announced its own Defiance Campaign against apartheid. Archbishop Desmond Tutu was one of the key figureheads in the campaign, which attracted international media attention.
1989 2 September	A mass march was organised through central Cape Town. The police responded by spraying the marchers with purple dye. One protestor jumped on the cannon, and redirected the spray onto the police.

Purple rain: Man in court

Staff Reporter

A BOTANIST, Mr Phillip Ivey, appeared in court yesterday in connection with an incident involving the "purple rain" cannon in the city centre during a protest in September.

During the protest in Burg Street on September 2 a man climbed on to the roof of a police riot-control truck and directed the nozzle, which was spraying purple dye on protesters, away from the crowd.

To page 2

Mr Phillip Ivey with his mother, Mrs Elspeth Ivey.

'Purple rain': Cannon damage charges dropped

By JOHN VILJOEN
Staff Reporter

CHARGES against a Kirstenbosch botanist who allegedly mounted and redirected a police water cannon during the "purple rain" protest march in Burg Street last September were dropped today.

Mr Philip Ivey, 26, of Bowwood Road, Claremont, pleaded not guilty to charges of assaulting a policeman, malicious damage to property and defeating the ends of justice. His trial was to have begun in the Magistrate's Court, Cape Town, today.

struck a police const face with his fist kicked and stepped to have sprayed dye while the constabl tempting to arrest of the cannon.

He was further have caused R150 the cannon by break headlight in the inci

Mr Ivey said he w but regretted not be clear his name. Hi Mr M James, said he fident" he would ha case.

The magistrate w Swanepoel Mr J Hobb

03

2/11/89

Dear P. Ivey,
I'm speaking for lots of us here in the lab when I say I really admire your courage. But you must look after yourself — this crazy country needs your idealism and energy badly, but you're no good to it in jail. Fight quietly and keep your cool and don't let the b....s get you down.
Much love from us all,
Jill

Royene
Maureen
Linoi

Strength to your arm!
love Di

01 Luckily for Ivey, he was released on bail after the charges of assault and destruction of property were heard in court. However, he would have to wait until 1990 for the charges to be dropped for good. *Cape Times*, 2 November 1989

02 In March 1990, the state finally dropped the charges against Phillip Ivey. Mandela's release the previous month presumably influenced the decision not to prosecute a local struggle hero.

03 Ivey's lab partners at the University of Cape Town expressed solidarity with his actions during the Purple March.

VICTORY AT LAST

Phillip Ivey's actions during the Purple Rain March proved to be deeply inspiring. During his time in police custody, he received many letters of support from friends and colleagues, as shown in this letter to the left.

Protestors in Cape Town were unperturbed by the violence of the police. Days after the Purple Rain March, graffiti began to appear throughout Cape Town proclaiming, "The Purple Shall Govern". On 13 September, the "Purple Shall Govern March" was organised. It attracted over 30 000 peaceful protestors.

This march was a key event. For the first time in decades, the police did not intervene. Protestors were allowed to freely walk the streets of Cape Town. They had finally unbanned themselves. Just a month after these large protests, and four decades after they had been arrested, Walter Sisulu and seven other long-terms prisoners were released from jail.

Early the following year, in February 1990, the new SA President, FW de Klerk, announced the release of Nelson Mandela and the unbanning of the ANC, SACP, PAC and other liberation movements. The resistance had finally ended apartheid.

In March 1990, the state dropped the charges against Ivey. He, too, was now a free man.

| 1989 13 September | On the 13 September, the "Purple Shall Govern March" took place through the centre of the city. Over 30 000 protesters took part. This time the police did not intervene. | 1989 October | Just after these large protest marches, Walter Sisulu and seven other long-term prisoners were released. | 1990 2 February | FW de Klerk unbanned the ANC, PAC and SACP. De Klerk also announced that he was to release Nelson Mandela, who finally walked free on the 11th of February, 1990. |

"There was a sense of triumphalism from the
people. We had faced the beast here. We faced
the beast and we had turned the cards on them."

Stan ABRAHAMS

. . . .

ARTIST > CONRAD BOTES

. . . .

ADDRESS > Corner Burg and Church Streets, Cape Town

Of all the colours in the spectrum, the artist Conrad Botes hates purple most. But it was an
aversion he had to overcome to interpret the events of September 1989 for the memorial
of "The Purple Shall Govern".

True to his roots as a graphic artist, Botes has drawn two sets of images for display on
either side of the notice board-like structure of the memorial. One side is a selection of
portraits of men and women in purple and black; the other side features a central image
of a Casspir - an armoured personnel carrier - surrounded by smaller images of keys, books
and even a Bible. These smaller images, says Botes, represent the different people who
took part in the march. They are also emblematic of the kinds of objects that would have
been in people's pockets as they gathered for the demonstration.

Desmond TUTU and the TRC

"There is no peace in Southern Africa. There is no peace because there is no justice. There can be no real peace and security until there be justice enjoyed by all the inhabitants of that beautiful land. God's *Shalom* – peace – involves righteousness, justice, wholeness, fullness of life, participation in decision-making, goodness, laughter, joy, compassion, sharing and reconciliation."

Desmond TUTU, *Nobel Peace Prize Acceptance Speech, 1984*

01

"In the East London City Hall, on 16 April 1996, Archbishop Desmond Tutu dropped his head in his hands and wept. It was Day Two of the Truth and Reconciliation Commission hearings; former Robben Island prisoner Singqokwana Ernest Malgas was describing his torture by security police. The TRC would hear from 21 000 people across South Africa, and Tutu, its chairman, would say of the process: 'We have looked the beast in the eye. Our past will no longer keep us hostage. We who are the rainbow people of God will hold hands and say, 'Never again! *Nooit weer! Ngeke futhi! Ga reno tlola!*'"

Text from the Sunday Times memorial plaque

01   At the end of the second day of hearings, Tutu broke down in tears after the devastating testimony of Sinqokwana Ernest Malgas.

02   When the TRC was launched, a massive newspaper campaign was undertaken to inform the public about the intention of the commission and to call for submissions.

TRUTH AND RECONCILIATION COMMISSION

A. THEEDFONAL 1 4 APR 1996

⇒ IN ORDER TO COME TO TERMS WITH THE PAST, THE TRUTH CONCERNING GROSS HUMAN RIGHTS VIOLATIONS IN OUR COUNTRY CANNOT BE SUPPRESSED OR FORGOTTEN. VIOLATIONS SHOULD BE INVESTIGATED, RECORDED AND MADE KNOWN.

⇒ THE COMMISSION SHALL GIVE VICTIMS THE CHANCE TO TELL OF THE VIOLATIONS THEY HAVE SUFFERED.

⇒ THE COMMISSION SHALL MAKE RECOMMENDATIONS TO THE PRESIDENT ABOUT REPARATION.

⇒ FOR PERSONS WHO MAKE A FULL DISCLOSURE OF ALL RELEVANT FACTS RELATING TO ACTS ASSOCIATED WITH A POLITICAL OBJECTIVE COMMITTED DURING THE CONFLICTS THAT TOOK PLACE BETWEEN 1/3/1960 AND 5/12/1993 – THE COMMISSION SHALL FACILITATE AMNESTY.

⇒ THE COMMISSION HAS AN INVESTIGATION UNIT WHICH HAS THE POWER TO SUBPOENA WITNESSES, SEARCH FOR EVIDENCE AND SEIZE ARTICLES WHICH MAY ASSIST IN THEIR INVESTIGATION.

THE TRUTH AND RECONCILIATION COMMISSION IS COMMITTED TO:

- The need for understanding but not for vengeance;
- The need for ubuntu but not victimisation;
- The need for reparation but not for retaliation.

IF YOU HAVE KNOWLEDGE OR EXPERIENCE OF HUMAN RIGHTS VIOLATIONS BETWEEN 1 MARCH 1960 AND 5 DECEMBER 1993 KINDLY CONTACT THE CHIEF EXECUTIVE OFFICER OR THE REGIONAL COMMISSIONER'S CONVENOR AT THE OFFICE CLOSEST TO YOU. YOU ARE ALSO WELCOME TO COME AND SPEAK TO US IN PERSON.

YOUR CONTRIBUTION WILL BE VALUED

CAPE TOWN REGIONAL OFFICE
(Western Cape and Northern Cape Province)

*Dr Wendy Orr (Convenor)
*Ms Ruth Lewin (Regional Manager)
9th Floor Old Mutual Building
106 Adderley Street
Cape Town 8001
Tel (021) 245 161
Fax (021) 245 225

TRC NATIONAL OFFICE

*The Most Reverend Desmond M Tutu (Chairperson)
*Dr Alex Boraine (Vice Chairperson)
*Dr Biki Minyuku (Chief Executive Officer)
7th Floor Old Mutual Building
106 Adderley Street
Cape Town 8001
Tel (021) 245 161
Fax (021) 245 225

EAST LONDON REGIONAL OFFICE
(Eastern Cape Province)

*Rev Bongani Finca (Convenor)
*Rev Vido Nyobole (Regional Manager)
5th Floor NBS Building
15 Terminus Street
East London 5201
Tel (0431) 432 885
Fax (0431) 439 352

GAUTENG REGIONAL OFFICE
(Gauteng, Mpumalunga, Northern Northwest Province)

*Dr Fazel Randera (Convenor)
*Mr Patrick Kelly (Regional Manager)
10th Floor Sanlam Centre
cnr Jeppe and von Wielligh Streets
Johannesburg 2001
Tel (011) 333 6330
Fax (011) 333 0832

DURBAN REGIONAL OFFICE
(KwaZulu/Natal and Free State Provinces)

*Mr Richard Lyster (Convenor)
*Ms Wendy Watson (Regional Manager)
9th Floor Metlife Building
391 Smith Street
Durban 4001
Tel (031) 307 6747
Fax (031) 307 6742

FROM 15 APRIL 1996 TO 10 MAY 1996 THE TRC WILL BE HOLDING ITS FIRST ROUND OF HEARINGS THROUGHOUT SOUTH AFRICA. HEARINGS WILL BEGIN IN THE FOLLOWING PROVINCES:

Eastern Cape	:	Week of 15 April 1996	Western Cape	:	Week of 22 April 1996
Gauteng	:	Week of 29 April 1996	KwaZulu/Natal	:	Week of 7 May 1996

FURTHER DETAILS AVAILABLE FROM OUR REGIONAL OFFICES ABOVE

AMNESTY FORMS AVAILABLE AT MAGISTRATES COURTS, THE MAIN POST OFFICES, ALL PRISONS AND ALL TRC OFFICES.

LET US BUILD A MORAL ORDER TOGETHER

'MPHILO' - LIFE

Archbishop Desmond Tutu is one of South Africa's most famous political figures. Like Nelson Mandela, Tutu is recognised throughout the world for his humane approach to politics and his outspoken attacks on injustice and inequality. As head of the Truth and Reconciliation Commission (TRC), his name became synonymous with healing and justice in the newly-democratic South Africa.

Tutu was the second son of Zacharia Zelilo Tutu and Aletta Dorothea Mavoertsek Mathlare. He was named 'Mpilo' which means life, because his parents feared that he was such a small baby that he may die. He survived against the odds as his grandmother had predicted. His father was typical of the middle-class black elite at the time. He studied at the University of Fort Hare, and he worked as a schoolteacher. Aletta was a domestic worker. Despite the family being relatively privileged, Tutu's childhood was not easy. Tutu later described Makoeteng Location in Klerksdorp where they lived as "a ghetto" where conditions were very rough. He was also a sickly child. He contracted polio and tuberculosis during his childhood and spent over a year in hospital when he was 14. One of the people who came to visit him was Trevor Huddlesone, the Anglican priest who became a well-known opponent of apartheid and was Tutu's friend until the day he died.

THE TRIUMPH OF HUMOUR

Tutu had a special quality that got him through his early traumas. From a young age, he had a great sense of humour and had an extraordinary capacity to make himself, and others around him, laugh. This talent is a hallmark of Tutu to this day.

At the age of 19, Tutu enrolled at the Pretoria Bantu College and trained to become a teacher. Initially, he wanted to study to be a doctor as a result of his childhood illnesses. His family, however, lacked the funds to pay for medical school. Tutu completed his studies in 1954 and began working as a teacher at the Johannesburg Bantu High School, his *alma mater*.

Tutu was shocked by the conditions under which he was forced to teach. The situation was made worse by the passing of the Bantu Education Act the previous year. As he later recalled:

> "I was teaching English and to think that we had 80 students in a class...To whom would you complain? Because the government's position was that Natives are a nuisance and the least you can do for them, the least you can get away with, the better...Our educational system was the pits."

>> . . . .

1931
7 October
Desmond 'Mpilo' Tutu was born near Klerksdorp in the North West Province. Tutu suffered from polio, for which there was no vaccine at the time. After completing his studies in 1954, Tutu worked as a teacher at the Johannesburg Bantu High School.

1957
Tutu resigned from teaching in protest against Bantu Education. He turned to study theology and completed his first stage of religious studies in 1960. He was appointed Chaplain at the University of Fort Hare.

A PRIEST FOR THE PEOPLE

Tutu resigned from his teaching post in 1957 in protest against Bantu Education. Inspired by Trevor Huddlestone, Tutu decided to enter the priesthood and went on to study at St Peter's Theology College in southern Johannesburg. By 1960, he had passed his theology exams with flying colours, and was ordained as an Anglican Minister. Tutu's first job was in Thokoza where he and his new wife, Leah Shenxane, and their young baby lived in a garage. The Church soon recognised his talents and compassion for those around him and sent Tutu to England to further his studies. Here, he received his Bachelors and Masters Degrees from Kings College in London. While studying, he ministered to a rich, predominately white community in Surrey. He used his special charms to win over the congregants who had never had a black priest before.

Over the next ten years, Tutu travelled between South Africa and London, continuing his theological studies and becoming a distinguished preacher. On his return to South Africa in 1975, he was appointed the Dean of St Mary's Anglican Cathedral in Johannesburg, the first black person appointed to the post. In typical style, Tutu rejected the luxury and trappings that came with this position and chose to stay in his modest house in Orlando in Soweto. The following year, he was appointed the Bishop of Lesotho.

AN OUTSPOKEN CRITIC

When Tutu was in Lesotho, he reflected on the shock he felt at the conditions of black people living in Johannesburg. He crystallised his own role in the political struggle:

"I had gone there to become bishop and I went there for a retreat. I don't know what happened but it seemed like God was saying to me, 'You've got to write a letter to the Prime Minister.'"

In May 1976, Tutu wrote a letter to then-Prime Minister, BJ Vorster, warning him of the discontent bubbling in the townships and that violence would erupt if the government did not scrap apartheid. Before he sent it, he gave the letter to a journalist, who published it in a prominent Sunday newspaper. The letter made Tutu into an overnight commentator on the anti-apartheid struggle.

01   Tutu married Leah Nomalizo in 1955. They had four children - Trevor (1956), Theresa (1957), Naomi (1960) and Mpho (1963).

02   Tutu in 1975, soon after being made the Dean of St Mary's Anglican Cathedral in Johannesburg.

03   Tutu travelled frequently between the United Kingdom and South Africa. Here he is pictured with a group of British children in 1976.

04   Tutu being inducted as Bishop of Lesotho, a year after being made Dean of St Mary's in Johannesburg.

1962   After two years as Chaplain, Tutu resigned to study theology at King's College in London. Four years later, Tutu received his Masters Degree in Theology.

1967   Tutu returned to South Africa, where he spent the next five years teaching theology. He also became an outspoken critic of apartheid.

A NEW PLATFORM

In 1978, Tutu's political position was strengthened when he was appointed secretary for the hugely influential lobby group, the South African Council of Churches (SACC). He used his new platform to attack the apartheid system, which he consistently characterised as "evil and unchristian".

Tutu's public profile continued to grow. He called for economic, sports and cultural sanctions rather than violence as a means of fighting apartheid. Despite his more reconciliatory approach, he was arrested and interrogated at the notorious John Vorster Square Police Station and was harassed by the police.

In 1984, his tireless and gallant fight was recognised when he was awarded the Nobel Peace Prize. He travelled to Oslo to receive the prize and, like Albert Luthuli before him, he used the platform to attack apartheid. His opposition was couched in the language of a common humanity and the need for peace and reconciliation, concepts that were to define much of the later work of the TRC:

"When will we learn that human beings are of infinite value because they have been created in the image of God, and that it is a blasphemy to treat them as if they were less than this and to do so ultimately recoils on those who do this? In dehumanising others, they are themselves dehumanised. Perhaps oppression dehumanises the oppressor as much as, if not more than, the oppressed. They need each other to become truly free, to become human. We can be human only in fellowship, in community, in peace.

Let us work to be peacemakers, those given a wonderful share in Our Lord's ministry of reconciliation. If we want peace, so we have been told, let us work for justice. Let us beat our swords into ploughshares."

```
ZCZC JXB036 LUJ866 TXR858
SAJH CO ZALU 165
LUASAKA 165/158 19 1140 PAGE 1/50
                                        '84 OCT 19  16  07

BISHOP DESMOND TUTU
BOX 4921
JOHANNESBURG/ 2000 SOUTH AFRICA

HERE WITH CORRECT VERSION OF MESSAGE SENT TO YOU ON
17/10/84
I PROUDLY CONVEY TO YOU DEAR BROTHER MY HEARTIEST CONGRATULATIONS
FOR THE HISTORIC ACHIEVEMENT OF BEING THE SECOND SOUTH AFRICAN
TO RECEIVE THE PRESITGIOUS NOBEL PEACE PRIZE FOR SERVICE TO
HUMANITY

COL 4921 2000 17/10/84

LUJ866 BISHOP PAGE 2/50

YOU ARE INDEED A WORTHY SUCCESSOR TO OUR VENERATED CHIEF
ALBERT LUTHULI THE AWARD IS A BRIBUTE TO THE TREMENDOUS
COURAGE AND SELFLESS DEVOTION WITH WHICH YOU OUR RELIGOUS
COMMUNITY AND OUR PEOPLE ARE CONFRONTING THE EVIL
HERRETICAL SYSTEM OF APARTHEID IT IS AN EXPRESSION OF THE
HORROR AND OUTRAGE

COL RELIGOUS

LUJ866 BISHOP PAGE 3/58

OF MANKIND AT THE CONTINUED BLATANT PERPETRATION OF THE WORST
SYSTEM OF MANS INHUMANITY TO MAN THE AWARD WILL
SURELY STRENGTHEN OUR RESOLVE AND DETERMINATION TO BRING ABOUT
A SPEEDY ELIMNATION OF THIS CRIMINAL SYSTEM
WE OWE IT TO OUR PEOPLE AND THE INTERNATIONAL COMMUNITY TO
CREATE A NEW DEMOCRATIC
NON-RACIAL' AND PEACEFUL SOUTH AFRICAN
O R TAMBO

COL NON-RACIAL
```

O.R. Tambo
Lusaka.

01   Oliver Tambo, President of the ANC in exile, sent this telegram of congratulations to Desmond Tutu when he heard that he had won the Nobel Peace Prize.

02   Tutu was a charismatic and forceful speaker. From the mid-1970s, he used his national political platform as head of the SACC to attack apartheid and gave rousing addresses in the townships and town halls across South Africa.

03   Tutu was swamped by well wishers at Jan Smuts airport when he arrived home after receiving the Nobel Peace Prize.

04   Chief Mangosuthu Buthelezi's letter, written in 1984, makes it clear that Tutu was considered South Africa's reconciler-in-chief long before the launch of the TRC.

1975   After teaching theology for three years in the UK, Tutu returned to South Africa. He was appointed Dean of St Mary's Anglican Cathedral in Johannesburg. The following year, he was appointed Bishop of Lesotho.

1978   Tutu was the first black South African to serve as secretary for the influential political lobby group, the South African Council of Churches (SACC).

04

KWAZULU

MINISTRY OF THE CHIEF MINISTER,
~~FINANCE~~ ECONOMIC AFFAIRS
AND POLICE.

Private Bag X01
Ulundi
3838

Bishop Desmond Tutu   14th December 1984
General Secretary
The South African Council of Churches
PO Box 4921
Johannesburg
2000

Dear Bishop Tutu,

I have not had the opportunity of congratulating you personally on
your being awarded the Nobel Peace Prize. It is a rare distinction
you have brought to our country, and I am sure you do so on behalf
of all Blacks who have for so long suffered so terribly under the
yoke of apartheid.

I enclose a copy of a Press Statement I issued on hearing of the
choice of yourself as this year's Laureate.

I find it most appropriate in our circumstances to remember that Mr.
Alfred Nobel grew fabulously rich as a result of him discovering
gun-powder. He was aware of its destructive force and quite rightly
dedicated a portion of his fortune to the eternal pursuit of peace.
In our situation, non-violence as a noble principle has a
particularly poignant meaning. Tyranny and oppression have produced
the anger which is the hand-maiden to violence, and the length of
that oppression has produced despair which is so easily exploited by
the forces of destruction.

You have served the Church in various capacities and now return to
the most important responsibility of all; the responsibility of
exercising national leadership from the base of pastoral care. I
believe somehow that the hand of God was in your election, because
never before have we needed an Anglican Bishop in Johannesburg who
serves all the race communities of this country, while at the same
time serves them without alienating them by partisan commitments and
ideological preferences.

In writing to congratulate you on your receiving the high honour of
the Nobel Peace Prize, may I at the same time write to you to

2

congratulate you on your election to the high office of the Bishop
of Johannesburg. As an Anglican, and a deeply committed Christian,
I wish you well in that demanding and awesome post, where you will
have to lay your hands in love and in charity on all race groups so
at variance with each other.

It is my special plea as a national leader that you approach your
new responsibilities with sensitivity and with the kind of care
which Christ would expect of those who are given special privileges
to act as mediators in high positions.

In this respect, I would plead with you to retain the present
Bishop's House and move into it as a Black reconciler drawing
Blacks, Indians and Coloureds into a White neighbourhood.

When ordinary people need love and tender pastoral care, the
Bishopry should be available and accessible to them. Suffering
Blacks can go to a White neighbourhood far more easily than
suffering Whites can go to a Black neighbourhood. To take up
residence in Soweto or some other such place, would I believe place
severe limitations on the reconciliatory nature of your role. I
raise this point, not knowing what you have finally decided, but in
response to reports in the press on the matter.

Now that you have vacated the contentious and perhaps highly
politicised position of General Secretary of the South African
Council of Churches, and are moving back into pastoral work, I
sincerely hope that you will use whatever influence you have for as
long as it may last, to discharge your Christian responsibility to
reconcile, reconcile and reconcile again. We have both seen how
difficult it has been for you to be reconciliatory this year, and
how it was not even possible for us to meet together to talk about
the things of God. There have been heavy demands on your time, and
you must have been under extremely heavy pressure not to have been
able to meet with me in fellowship. I look forward in 1985 to the
prospects of sharing with you thoughts about the deep aspirations of
Blacks like myself who are committed to the struggle for liberation.

Yours in Christ,

Sincerely,

MANGOSUTHU G. BUTHELEZI
CHIEF MINISTER KWAZULU
PRESIDENT OF INKATHA

1984
16 October

Tutu was awarded the Nobel Peace Prize for his
courageous stance against apartheid. He was the
second South African to receive the prize - the
first was Chief Albert Luthuli.

1980's

Tutu led the late 1980s Defiance Campaign
that eventually culminated in the "Purple
Shall Govern March" in Cape Town in 1989,
on the eve of the demise of apartheid.

A MORAL GIANT

When Mandela was released from prison in 1990, he spent his first night of freedom at the house of Tutu and his wife Leah. During the difficult years of the transition and the negotiated settlement, Tutu stood as a moral giant alongside Mandela. In 1995, the new government passed the Promotion of National Unity and Reconciliation Act which created the Truth and Reconciliation Commission (TRC). The TRC's mandate was to investigate gross human rights violations, which included torture, extreme ill-treatment, murder or its attempt, kidnapping and disappearances, between 1 March 1960 and 11 May 1994. Mandela appointed Tutu as the Chair of this difficult and painful process.

01 Tutu tries out the 'Mandela jive' outside Nelson Mandela's house after FW de Klerk's announced the release of Mandela and the unbanning of the ANC in 1990.

02 This cartoon by the well-known cartoonist Zapiro, depicts Minister of Justice, Dullah Omar, preparing to enter the haunted house of South Africa's past.

03 Tutu's actions were frequently in the headlines during the years of the TRC.

04 Winnie Mandela's refusal to answer many questions led some to question the efficacy of the TRC.

05 During his testimony to the TRC, President FW de Klerk refused to accept any responsibility for the atrocities carried out by the National Party. Many felt scandalised by de Klerk's denial.

THE TRUTH HURTS

Tutu promoted listening to the stories of gross human rights violations, as told by both the victims and the perpetrators, as crucial to the future of securing democracy for South Africans. He also advocated the honest and full disclosure of past crimes as the basis for reconciliation. But he warned, "The truth is going to hurt" as the TRC got down to business.

The TRC held its first hearing on 15 April 1996. From the start, the sessions were charged with emotion. On the second day of hearings, former Robben Island prisoner, Singqokwana Ernest Malgas, came before the Truth Commissioners in a wheelchair as a result of a stroke, probably caused by being repeatedly tortured at the hands of the East London Security Police. He spoke with difficulty of his assaults, arrests, detentions, imprisonment and the death of his son when his house was burned down. While describing how he was "suffocated with a mask…and a stick was put inside my knees", he broke down and wept. At this point, Tutu dropped his head into his hands and wept with him. Alex Borraine closed the proceedings for the day as Tutu felt too weak to talk. Tutu wondered if he was the right man for this arduous job, and if he would be able to bear the pain, despite his own warnings of how this job would be.

| 1995 December | Tutu was appointed Chairperson of the Truth and Reconciliation Commissoin (TRC), tasked with uncovering the story of South Africa's brutal past and giving amnesty to perpetrators of apartheid crimes on condition of full disclosure. | 1996 16 April | Tutu was reduced to tears during the devastating testimonies of Nomonde Calata and Singqokwane Malgas at the first human rights violations hearing in Port Elizabeth. |

03

TUTU WEEPS AT TRUTH PROBE

Harrowing stories by witnesses

EAST LONDON. — Archbishop Desmond Tutu laid his head on a table and wept yesterday at the end of a day of harrowing testimony about inhumanity, torture and murder under apartheid.

Archbishop Tutu, chairing Truth and Reconciliation Commission hearings into human rights abuses, gave in to his emotions when a wheelchair-bound former prisoner broke down crying as he recalled his torture at the hands of security police.

Singqokwana Malgas, sent to Robben Island for 14 years in 1963, said repeated police assaults and torture had resulted in epilepsy and a stroke that impairs his speech.

Mr Malgas was asked to detail the tortures. "I was always suffocated by a mask. Then there was helicopter training. They put a broomstick under your knees and then, and then . . ."

Mr Malgas broke into tears, his face contorted at the memory, before he could finish his sentence. The commission adjourned for the day, and Archbishop Tutu, dressed in his purple cassock, said afterwards: "I am weak . . . I thought I was tough, until today."

The testimony from Mr Malgas ended a day of evidence marked by frequent bouts of tears from widows of activists killed by security forces and one mother whose child never returned from a military camp of the African National Congress.

Archbishop Tutu adjourned the session for 15 minutes during the morning to allow one witness, Nomonde Calata, to compose herself.

Ms Calata collapsed backward into her chair, her cry of anguish hushing the packed assembly, as she described the moment in 1985 when she first suspected her teacher husband

TO PAGE 2

04

DR JACK

half-truths & recriminations
TRUTH & RECONCILIATION COMMISSION

BLOOD

AN INCREDIBLE PRIVILEGE

This was the first of many instances when the sheer horror and inhumanity described by the survivors overwhelmed the commissioners and their support staff – interpreters, counsellors, members of the public and witnesses. Emotions ran especially high during high-profile testimonies of people like Eugene de Kock, Winnie Mandela and FW de Klerk. By the end of the process, Tutu was able to write in the final report of the TRC that "It has been an incredible privilege for those of us who served the commission to preside over the process of healing a traumatised and wounded people."

Regardless of the difficulties of conducting the hearings, the TRC achieved a mammoth task. Between 1996 and 2003, the TRC received 7 700 amnesty applications and took over 20 000 victim's statements. In total, 7 115 amnesty applications were processed, of which 1 146 were accepted. The TRC was meant to last for two years, but worked for a total of six.

A GLORIOUS FUTURE

In 2003, the TRC concluded its investigation, and produced its five-volume final report. It was a remarkable piece of work which sought to provide a detailed account of 40 years of apartheid. Its findings were sometimes controversial, and the TRC attracted criticism.

In closing the TRC process, Desmond Tutu wrote the foreword to the TRC final report. He defended the TRC while recognising its weaknesses. Perhaps more importantly, he asked something of all South Africans:

"Having asked and received forgiveness and having made amends, let us shut the door on the past – not in order to forget it but in order not to allow it to imprison us. Let us move into the glorious future of a new kind of society where people count, not because of biological irrelevancies or other extraneous attributes, but because they are persons of infinite worth created in the image of God."

05

Tutu 'close to tears' in face of De Klerk's denial of liability

Stephen Laufer

CAPE TOWN — The truth commission and the National Party (NP) headed for their most serious showdown yet yesterday, with the NP again accusing the body of using unfair methods and commission chairman Desmond Tutu saying he was "devastated" at NP leader FW de Klerk's failure to accept responsibility for apartheid death squads.

At the same time, the commission's human rights violations committee said it would examine the possibility of a further recall of the NP.

Tutu choked back tears several times during a news conference yesterday.

Commissioner Yasmin Sooka said the committee would discuss the possibility of a hearing in which a number of former NP leaders — possibly including former security ministers — would be asked to explain systems and policies and their interpretations in a manner which added to the commission's overall understanding.

De Klerk was the only party functionary to answer questions from the commission during a five-hour hearing on Wednesday, and often said he could not answer questions through lack of personal information.

Tutu's deputy, Alex Boraine, said that the truth commissioners had been "baffled by how De Klerk could apologise for apart-

held policies, but not accept their inevitable consequences".

Tutu said he was "proud" of how the commission had handled the African National Congress (ANC) and NP submissions.

There had been "vigorous" questioning of both parties, and he was satisfied that the treatment of the NP had been "even handed". He had met De Klerk before the public hearing and had hoped he would display statesmanship in his approach.

Sapa reports Tutu said he could not understand how De Klerk could still insist that he had been unaware of apartheid atrocities when delegations from Lawyers for Human Rights and the Black Sash

among many others had told him of security force involvement in rights abuses.

Tutu said he himself had told De Klerk about allegations of security force involvement in the Boipatong massacre after visiting survivors and hearing their stories.

"There was an avalanche of information. To say I did not know ... I find that hard to understand. I have to say that I sat there (at Wednesday's hearing) and I was close to tears. I feel sorry for him. I am devastated. (For him) to make an impassioned apology ... and then to negate it."

The NP last night again attacked Glen Goosen, who had led evidence for the commission, for the manner in which he had

questioned De Klerk.

There would be "further developments in the next few days as persons whom ... Goosen involved in his attempts to implicate De Klerk take issue" with the commission, it said.

This appeared to be a reference to a lawyer's letter from former police commissioner Johan van der Merwe objecting to the manner in which Goosen had linked the former top cop to the Vlakplaas killer unit.

Boraine said Goosen had been referring to Van der Merwe's own amnesty submission. If there was a quarrel between Van der Merwe and De Klerk, they should sort it out themselves.

On the planned enlargement of the amnesty committee, Tutu said he was concerned that Parliament's justice committee had said it would be unable to pass the required amendment before the middle of next month. The amnesty committee has a backlog of several thousand cases.

The commission also said it would make public the contents of a set of confidential documents submitted by the ANC.

Included in the file were the names of government agents who had infiltrated the ANC and had been identified before 1981, the names of those executed for murder and rape, and of those suspected government agents killed by ANC security officials.

In October, the TRC presented its five-volume report. This was a landmark moment in South Africa's fledgling democracy. The work of the TRC ended four years later than expected, in 2002.

The idea of the Desmond Tutu Peace Centre was launched. The centre is due to be completed in 2010.

After nearly seven years of hard work, the TRC
presented its final report to President Thabo Mbeki
in 2003. Mbeki criticised the report for it's claim
that the ANC was guilty of human rights violations.
Mbeki argued that the ANC fought a "just war".

A NEW CENTRE FOR PEACE

Tutu established The Desmond Tutu Peace Trust in
1998. The trust received approval from the Cape Town
municipality to build the Desmond Tutu Peace Centre,
designed to house a library, peace museum, training centre
and conference facilities. It seeks to provide a public space
in which Tutu's principles of peace and spirituality can be
memorialised.

2008   Tutu has remained active in public life,
        speaking out against social ills. Most recently,
        he has mediated between warring parties in
        the 2008 Kenyan election dispute.

"Jesus did not say, 'If I be lifted up I will draw some'". Jesus said, 'If I be lifted up I will draw all, all, all, all, all.' Black, white, yellow, rich, poor, clever, not so clever, beautiful, not so beautiful. It's one of the most radical things. All, all, all, all, all, all, all, all. All belong. Gay, lesbian, so-called straight. All, all are meant to be held in this incredible embrace that will not let us go. All."

Desmond TUTU

ARTIST > ANTON MOMBERG

ADDRESS > East London City Hall, between Oxford and Argyle Streets, East London

"We all remember how Tutu sat at his table and listened to the stories at the Truth and Reconciliation Commission. My concept is simple - to see him sit again and remember him that way - to remind us all of what we heard," artist Anton Momberg says of his thinking behind the sculpture that commemorates day two of the very first TRC hearings at the East London City Hall in 1996. The powerful moment when Tutu wept with the anguish of a wounded nation brought the image and concept for this artwork to Momberg "overnight".

Momberg notes that "I would like people to come real close to my depiction of Desmond Tutu - the artwork is slightly smaller than life size - and I hope that they might find it irresistible to stroke his hand."

Endnotes

SECTION 1

Olive SCHREINER

"When I am strong…" - Schreiner, O. 1971. *Story of an African Farm*

"… despite having said… - Ibid

"The object of this society…" - Brown, J. 1923. *Olive Schreiner: Memories of a Friendship*

"If we could make you realise…our request." - Ibid

"What is left of this wonderful…events she helped to shape." - Lessing, D. "Introduction" in Schreiner, O. 1971. "Story of an African Farm", Century Hutchinson: Johannesburg

Mohandas GANDHI

"Truly speaking… no less than for India." - Reddy, E. S. "Mahatma Gandhi - South Africa's Gift to India?" in *Mainstream*, New Delhi, 21 January 1995

"…I was an insignificant…[I was] a Coolie." - Gandhi, M. 1947. "Speech at Inter-Asian Relations Conference, New Delhi", 2 April. www.ghandiserve.com

"…And if any Indian is put to trouble because of his refusal to register…I will appear in his case free of charge." - "Gandhi: Prisoner of Conscience", Permanent Exhibition at Constitution Hill, Johannesburg, October 2006

"…I have worn these sandals…so great a man. - Fischer, L. (ed.) 2002. *The Essential Ghandi*, Random House: New York

"…The spirit of Gandhiji…human survival in the twenty-first century." - Mandela, N. 1992. Speech Opening Gandhi Hall in Lenasia, September. www.anc.org.za

Isaac WAUCHOPE and the *SS Mendi*

"You are going to die …sons of Africa." - "*SS Mendi* - Historical Background", http://navy.mil.ac.za

"…Raise your war cries…left with our bodies…' - Ibid

"I hear myself say, 'Goodbye…so I am saved." - "Message from Dr. LE Hertslet, 23rd Anniversary Service, 25th February 1940", in *Souvenir of the Mendi Disaster*, African Ex-Servicemen's League, publication undated.

"[Stump] made no inquiries…his inaction was inexcusable." - *Report of Court and Annex: SS Mendi Disaster*, August 1917, National Archives: Pretoria

"It is highly undesirable to introduce raw Natives…friction in their relationships with whites…" - "Native Labour Contingents", The Star, 2 November 1916

"Compounds should be surrounded…handed over to the military police." - Willan, B. 1978. "The South African Native Labour Contingent, 1916 - 1918", *The Journal of African History*, Vol. 19, No. 1

"These people (the Natives) said…to their everlasting credit." - "Sinking of a Transport", *Rand Daily Mail*, 10 March 1917

Enoch MGIJIMA and the Bulhoek Massacre

"You are informing me…before you destroy me." - Letter from Enoch Mgijima to Col. Theo Truter, 22 May 1921. National Archives, Jus Vol. 288, Ref:2/853/20

"Mgijima's prophecies offered…God's chosen and blessed ones." - Edgar, R. *Because They Chose the Plan of God*, p. 13

"God sent us …necessary that we go." - Letter from Enoch Mgijima to Col. Theo Truter, 22 May 1921. National Archives, Jus Vol. 288, Ref:2/853/20

"…any resistance to lawful authority will be drastically dealt with". - Col. Theo Truter, ultimatum delivered to the Israelites, 21 May 1921. National Archives, Jus Vol. 288, Ref: 2/853/20

"…old ways of worship".- Edgar, R. 1982. "The Prophet Motive: Enoch Mgijima, the Israelites and the Background to the Bulhoek Massacre", *International Journal of African Historical Studies*, Vol. 15, No. 3

"I am a messenger…sink in blood…" - Letter from Enoch Mgijima to Col. Theo Truter, 22 May 1921. National Archives, Jus Vol. 288, Ref:2/853/20

"…resistance is offered…taught a lesson." - Letter from Col. Theo Truture to Secretary of Justice, 23 May 1921. National Archives, Jus Vol. 288, Ref: 2/853/20

"Despite the odds…all die here.' - Edgar, R. 1982. "The Prophet Motive: Enoch Mgijima, the Israelites and the Background to the Bulhoek Massacre", *International Journal of African Historical Studies*, Vol. 15, No. 3

"This was one of the first times…it has not been the last." - Interview with Denver Webb, SAHA Radio Documentary: The Bulhoek Massacre. Broadcast on SAFM in 2007.

Nontetha NKWENKWE

"We are not making war…a chance to pray" - Letter from Delanto Quashe to Secretary of Native Affairs, undated, National Archives, BAO 6605 11/328

"When she was asleep…brewing African beer." - SAHA Radio Documentary: Nontetha Nkwenkwe, Broadcast on SAFM in 2007

"She was saying, '*ibumbaya manyano*'…Devil he can go through." - Ibid

"The colonial authorities…Nontetha came to their attention." - Interview with Robert Edgar, SAHA Radio Documentary: Nontetha Nkwenkwe. Broadcast on SAFM in 2007

"Rather than bring her up on a trumped up charge…she must be crazy." - Ibid

"Disturbing element among the natives…carefully watched." - Maj. T Hutchons, Divisional Inspector, SAP, King William's Town to Deputy Commissioner, SAP, Grahamstown, 29 April 1923. National Archives, Jus 268 3/1064/18

"place(s) of confinement…sheer poverty and neglect." - Edgar, R. and Sapire, H. 2000. *African Apocalypse*

"One elderly gentleman…all the way to Pretoria." - Interview with Denver Webb, SAHA Radio Documentary: Nontetha Nkwenkwe. Broadcast on SAFM in 2007

"To rescue Nontetha…under the Urban Areas Act." - "'Prophetess' Among Philistines", *Rand Daily Mail*, 10 February 1927

"…visits from her relatives…make her mentally worse." - Edgar, R. and Sapire, H. 2000. *African Apocalypse*, p. 129

"Dear Major Herbst…admiration of her followers." - Letter from JT Dunston (Commissioner for Mental Hygiene) to Major Herbst (Department of Native Affairs), 11 June 1930, National Archives, BAO 6605 11/328

"The sad aspect…It was an open field." - Interview with Denver Webb, SAHA Radio Documentary: Nontetha Nkwenkwe. Broadcast on SAFM in 2007

"What made her story very poignant…taken out of circulation."- Ibid

SECTION 2

Albert LUTHULI

"I, together with thousands…peace and in brotherhood." - Luthuli, A. 1961. "Africa and Freedom", Nobel Peace Prize Acceptance Speech, Oslo, 11 December. www.anc.org.za

"I cannot be precise…certainly before 1900." - Luthuli, A. 1962. *Let My People Go*, p. 23

"We should rest content…struggle for freedom." - Luthuli, A. 1954. Speech to the First Natal Congress of the People, 5 September 1954. www.anc.org.za and www.sahistory.org.za

"I think that perhaps all the emphasis which Adams…going to their aid." - Luthuli, A. 1962. *Let My People Go*, pp. 54 - 55

"Now I saw, almost as though for the first time, the naked poverty of my people". - Ibid, p. 53

"Invidious…'servant of the people.'" - Luthuli, A. 1952. "Statement on his Dismissal from the Chieftainship of the Abase Mokolweni Tribe in the Umvoti Mission Reserve, Groutville, Lower Tugela District, Natal," 18 November. Luthuli Papers, UNISA, Ref: AAS135

"I settled into the routine…than was usually possible." - Luthuli, A. 1962. Let My People Go

"They took away his chieftainship…than those who had bound him." - Paton, A. 1967. "Speech on Behalf of the Liberal Party at Chief Albert Luthuli's Funeral" in *Christianity and Crisis*, 27 September. Alan Paton Centre and Struggle Archives: University of KwaZulu-Natal

Orlando PIRATES

"In their wildest dreams…People came and came…" - Interview with Lesley Shume, SAHA Radio Documentary: Orlando Pirates, broadcast on SAFM in 2007

'Mokgosinyane, a self-appointed social worker…'Buick' Buthelezi." - *Drum*, June 1980

"At the Boys Club… Orlando Boys Football Club." - Interview with Sam "Baboon" Shabungu, *Total Soccer Documentary Series*, broadcast on E-TV in 2007

"We were very selfish…very good understanding." - Ibid

"In our era…passionate about soccer." - SAHA Radio Documentary: Orlando Pirates, broadcast on SAFM in 2007

"In 1970, the Chairman of the soccer…Pirates was forced to let us go." - Ibid

"…the rise of Orlando Pirates…became settled in Soweto." - Interview with Professor Bonner, SAHA Radio Documentary: Orlando Pirates, broadcast on SAFM in 2007

"These people were icons….local people." - Interview with Lesley Shume, SAHA Radio Documentary: Orlando Pirates, broadcast on SAFM in 2007

"By association with club members…helped to be a Buccaneer faithful." - "The Man Who Made Bucs a Home", *Sunday Times*, 26 March 2006

"Remember the DRC war?…ground to inspire themselves." - Interview with Hitler Sobi and Mike Tseka, SAHA Radio Documentary: Orlando Pirates, broadcast on SAFM in 2007

"It was an institution…come to the funerals." - Interview with Lesley Shume, SAHA Radio Documentary: Orlando Pirates, broadcast on SAFM in 2007.

"If they're doing their tricks…black player himself." - Quoted in Kuper, S. 2003. *Football Against the Enemy*, Orion: London

Cissie GOOL

"Millions of people have died…the country is paralysed." - *Cape Times*, 22 July 1946

"At a time when woman's role…Cissie was out there." - Interview with Albie Sachs, SAHA Radio Documentary: Cissie Gool, broadcast on SAFM in 2007

"She and Sam Kahn…the love of his life." - Interview with Amy Thornton, SAHA Radio Documentary: Cissie Gool, broadcast on SAFM in 2007

"I heard our Auntie Cissie…the police thereafter carried arms." - Rassool, Y. 2000. *District Six - Lest We Forget*, p. 19

"She was handing out tickets…me as a boy." - Interview with Stan Abrahams, SAHA Radio Documentary: Cissie Gool, broadcast on SAFM in 2007

"Mrs Gool …hits straight from the shoulder…forefront to defeat it." - Letter to the Editor, Cape Standard, 29 August 1944

"Cissie was one of the best-known…People noticed her." - Interview with Albie Sachs, SAHA Radio Documentary: Cissie Gool, broadcast on SAFM in 2007

Alan PATON

"Cry, the beloved country…gives too much." - Paton, A. 1948. *Cry, The Beloved Country*

"The Ixopo countryside…hide it from the world." - Paton, A. 1980. *Towards the Mountain*, pp. 84 - 85

"A little girl in Standard V…came into the class." - Alexander, P. F. 1994. *Alan Paton: A Biography*, pp. 70 - 73

"…hated him like poison" - Ibid

"Of those four hundred boys…to be done with them…" - Paton, A. 1980. *Towards the Mountain*, pp. 162 - 163

"Small Offender…oh child, oh lost and lonely one." - Paton, A. "To A Small Boy Who Died at Diepkloof Reformatory", www.poetropical.co.uk

"I have one great fear…turned to hating." - Paton, A. 1948. *Cry, The Beloved Country*

"For it is the dawn…that is a secret." - Ibid

"My whole life has been a struggle…has not stopped." - "Alan Paton, Author and Apartheid Foe, Dies of Cancer at 85", New York Times, 12 April 1998

"One of South Africa's leading humanists…into a wasteland." - Nelson Mandela, quoted in www.kirjasto.sci.fi/apaton.html

Race CLASSIFICATION

"It was a total mix up… It's tragic man, I tell you." - Interview with Vic Wilkinson, SAHA Radio Documentary: Race Classification, Broadcast on SAFM in 2007

"In South Africa, a person's racial identity governed … odd as that sounds." - Interview with Deborah Posel, SAHA Radio Documentary: Race Classification, Broadcast on SAFM in 2007

"Tan-coloured Johannes Maynard…during the last war." - *Drum*, October 1955

"The 1950 Act affected my family…it was wrong to be mixing." - Interview with Zayne Adams, SAHA Radio Documentary: Race Classification, Broadcast on SAFM in 2007

"These bloody laws come out…to leave the country?" - Interview with Vince Kolbe, SAHA Radio Documentary: Race Classification, Broadcast on SAFM in 2007

"The big family break up happens…variety of ways." - Interview with Craig Soudien, SAHA Radio Documentary: Race Classification, Broadcast on SAFM in 2007

"Apartheid was in many senses a shambles…aspiration of a non-racial society." - Interview with Deborah Posel, SAHA Radio Documentary: Race Classification, Broadcast on SAFM in 2007

Bessie HEAD

"If I had to write one day…important as human beings." - Head, B. 1962. "Let Me Tell You a Story Now", *New African*, September

'Things I Don't Like…But going to fight - OKAY?" - Head, B. 1962. "Things I Don't Like", *New African*, July

"The child is coloured, in fact quite black and native in appearance." - Starfield, J. 1997. "Review: The Return of Bessie Head", *Journal of Southern African Studies*, Vol. 23, No. 4

"I have always just been me…fitting in or belonging." - Eilersen, G. 1993. "A Skin of Her Own", *New Internationalist*, Issue 247, September

"When Miss Cadmore came…right-about turn for us." - Eilersen, G. 1995. *Thunder Behind Her Ears*, pp. 29 - 45

"So sheer and lovely I am afraid to wear them". - Ibid

"I detest snobbery…ashamed of what I am!" - Ibid

"Self-Portrait…Idealist…THAT is I." - Coetzee, P. and MacKenzie, C. 1996. "Bessie Head: Rediscovered Early Poems", *English in Africa*, May

"I was not well…pain for other people." - Letter from Bessie Head to Randolph Vigne, 15 July 1971 in Vigne, R. *A Gesture of Belonging*, pp. 143 - 144

"First they received you…Its mother is white." - Head, B. *A Question of Power*, p. 17

"From the confusions…a brief common purpose." - Van Rensburg, P. 2007. "What Bessie Had to Say for, and of, herself in mid-1985 (Part 2)", *Mmegi Online*, 13 July

SECTION THREE

Raymond MHLABA

"I led the very first group…we were making history." - Mhlaba, R. and Mufumadi, T. 2001. *Raymond Mhlaba's Personal Memoirs: Reminiscing from Rwanda and Uganda*, pp. 83 - 84

"proud, confident and attractive woman…independent and assertive". - Ibid, p. 8

"One of the memorable lessons…against white domination." - Ibid, p. 5

"They regarded me…week of commencing work." - Ibid, p. 22

"Many of us certainly were not graduated…university of life." - Ibid, p. 77

"What struck me…superior to another in the meeting." - Ibid, p. 31

"I must say that if there is one area…as I consider myself to be.'" - Mandela, N. "Foreword" in Mhlaba, R. and Mufumadi, T. 2001. *Raymond Mhlaba's Personal Memoirs: Reminiscing from Rwanda and Uganda*

"fired from my job for my involvement in the workers' struggle." - Mhlaba, R. and Mufumadi, T. 2001. *Raymond Mhlaba's Personal Memoirs: Reminiscing from Rwanda and Uganda*, p. 32

"We prayed the whole night…defy an unjust system." - Ibid, p. 83

"Indeed we too should exult…white minority rule." - Mbeki, T. 2005. Speech at Funeral of Raymond Mhlaba, Port Elizabeth, 27 February. www.dfa.gov.za

"Oom Ray and the other titans…apartheid state could vanquish." - Ibid

George PEMBA

"I was always able…building up my art." - Hudlestone, S. 1996. *Against All Odds*, p. 40

"But I never thought you could draw souls" - Lee, D. 2006. *George Pemba: Painter of the People*, p. 12

"I had no idea…my own entertainment." - George Pemba Personal Diaries, Courtesy of Bobo Pemba

"recommended that I revert to oil…to go independent…" - Ibid

"It was during the year 1944…to create truthfully." - Hudlestone, S. 1996. *Against All Odds*, p. 40

"I think there is nothing connecting them…the thought of getting rich." - Ibid, p. 41

"I certainly was very keen to paint…essence of native South Africa." - Ibid, pp. 43 - 44

"The history of my drinking…in my drunken stupor." - George Pemba Personal Diaries, Courtesy of Bobo Pemba.

"I felt addiction to liquor…I was completely cured." - Ibid

"Draw from life and imagination…strong drink and distractions." - Ibid

"With Pemba's death…African art in the 20th century." - "George Milwa Mnyaluza Pemba (South African 1912 - 2001)", www.michaelstevenson.com

Duma NOKWE

Are we to lose an opportunity to break the (racial) barrier for lack of a cup of tea?" - Bizos, G. 2007. *Odyssey to Freedom*, pp. 138 - 140

"His name remained…felt safer at the advocates' chambers." - Ibid

"until the millennium" - Mandela, N. 1994. *Long Walk to Freedom*, pp. 291 - 296

"The armed wing…DEATH TO IMPERIALISM!" - "Duma Nokwe: Honourable Son of Africa", 1978, *Sechaba*, Vol. 12, April

Lilian NGOYI

"Strydom, stop and think…sooner than you expect" - Ngoyi, L. Presidential Address delivered at the Annual Conference of ANC Women's League, Soweto, 11 November 1956, Wits Historical Papers

"I realised that here…when we first met her." - Interview with Amina Cachalia, SAHA Radio Documentary: Lilian Ngoyi, Broadcast on SAFM, 2007

"Dr Malan…Mussolini in Italy" - Interview with Sophie Williams, SAHA Radio Documentary: Lilian Ngoyi, Broadcast on SAFM, 2007

"She challenged them a lot…behind a woman's skirt?" - Ibid

She can toss an audience…with renewed courage." - "Lilian Ngoyi - The Most Talked-Of Woman in Politics", *Drum*, March 1956

"…police coming in to come and fetch my mum to jail." - Interview with Memory Mphahlele, SAHA Radio Documentary: Lilian Ngoyi, Broadcast on SAFM, 2007

"I walked up to the amphitheatre…women coming from all around." - Interview with Amina Cachalia, SAHA Radio Documentary: Lilian Ngoyi, Broadcast on SAFM, 2007

"This was the first time…we've brought these petitions." - Interview with Sophie Williams, SAHA Radio Documentary: Lilian Ngoyi, Broadcast on SAFM, 2007

"*Strijdom, Wathint Abafazi*…You are going to die." "Wathint Abafazi" as sung by Frances Baard, Mayibuye Archives

"Lilian led everybody…Nobody could frighten Lilian." - Interview with Phyllis Naidoo, SAHA Radio Documentary: Lilian Ngoyi, Broadcast on SAFM, 2007

"In solitary confinement…you wouldn't eat." - Interview with Albertina Sisulu, SAHA Radio Documentary: Lilian Ngoyi, Broadcast on SAFM, 2007

"The thing that makes me so sad…such dire poverty." - Interview with Nthato Motlana, SAHA Radio Documentary: Lilian Ngoyi, Broadcast on SAFM, 2007

"For the past 300 years…Mrs Ngoyi." - "Hamba Kahle 'Ma-Ngoyi!", *Sechaba*, Vol. 14, 1980

"For 18 years…great energies totally suppressed." - Bernstein, H. 1982. "Isitwalandwe for Ma-Ngoyi", *Sechaba*, August

Athol FUGARD

"Theatre is a very powerful agent…were replacing words"- *Star Tonight*, 19 June 1989

"…flesh and blood…poor enough for too much hope…" - Fugard, A. 1994. *Cousins: A Memoir*

"New Brighton…spoils the approach to Port Elizabeth". - Ibid

"a place where we all came together… family's unique history". Ibid, p. 33

"My relationships with women…dominant and affirmative voice." - Ibid, pp. 10 - 11

"They have now finally succeeded…grow up in." Benson, M. (ed.) 1983. *Notebooks 1960/1977 Athol Fugard*, p. 129

"…the ugliest thing I've ever been part of." - "Fugard - Profile", www.africana.com

"the blood knot…race classification laws. - Christie, R. 1976. "Fugard in Focus", *The Star*, 7 September

"After watching the first few seconds…spontaneous debate I have ever heard." - "When Brecht and Sizwe Banzi Met in New Brighton", *Observer* (UK), 8 August 1982

"The passion for the truth…with incredible fondness." - Robert Woodruff Interview with John Kani, 2005, American Repertory Theatre, www.amrep.org

SECTION 4

Ingrid JONKER

"I saw the mother…my sense of bereavement." - "Rebel S.A. Poet Writes of Sharpeville, Orlando, Langa, and…The Child That Died at Nyanga", *Drum*, May 1963

"The Child…Without a pass." - Jonker, I. "The Child", *Drum*, May 1963. Translated from the original Afrikaans by Jack Cope

"Ingrid and I played…Granny's little 'heartbroken child'. - Meterlekamp, P. 2003. *Beeld Van 'n Digterslewe*, p. 31

"At home nobody mentioned…our adolescent years…" - Ibid, p. 48

"We are and have been fighting…with the enemy." - Ibid, p. 127

"It grew out of my own experience…thank me for it…" - "Rebel S.A. Poet Writes of Sharpeville, Orlando, Langa, and…The Child That Died at Nyanga", *Drum*, May 1963

"After what you have done to me…From Dad. Abraham H. Jonker." - Meterlekamp, P. 2003. *Beeld Van 'n Digterslewe*, p. 132

"The truth is, I can no longer go on living like this." - Ibid, pp. 184 - 185

"I have never read the poetry of Ingrid Jonker…'young housewife.' - "Jonker Threatened Writers", *Sunday Times*, 25 July 1965

"Ingrid had something of her own…long time beyond her grave." - Krige, U. 1965. "Her Voice Will Still Be Heard", *Sunday Times*, 25 July

"LADYBIRD (A memory about my mother)" - Jonker, I. 1963. *Rook en Oker*, translated from the original Afrikaans by William Stewart

"She was both a poet…the beauty of life." - Mandela, N. 1994. Inaugural Address to Parliament, 24 May. www.anc.org.za

John VORSTER SQUARE

"John Vorster Square was the pinnacle of torture chambers." - Tymon Smith Interview with Jackie Seroke, 9 March 2007, SAHA/Sunday Times Heritage Project

"In Detention…a piece of soap while washing" - Van Wyk, C. "In Detention", www.thetimes.co.za

"state-of-the-art modern police station…one roof " - De Witt Dippenaar, M. 1988. *The History of the South African Police*

"…the breakdown of law…circumstances whatsoever." - "Mandela - An Audio History", www.radiodiaries.org

"Perhaps it is not inappropriate…concern for communists in South Africa?'" - Vorster, B. 1962. Speech made in House of Assembly, 21 May. www.sahistory.org.za

"Whenever you were there, you knew you were between death and life." - Tymon Smith Interview Tsanki Leagkotla, 25 May 2007, SAHA/Sunday Times Heritage Project

"The Security Police had a cruel calmness of people with no souls." - Tymon Smith Interview with Molefe Pheto, 22 May 2007, SAHA/Sunday Times Heritage Project

"The pressure was tremendous…unfortunate that these things happened." - Tymon Smith Interview with Hennie Heymans, 25 May 2007, SAHA/Sunday Times Heritage Project

"Those offices upstairs…absolutely no protection." - Tymon Smith Interview with Barbara Hogan, 4 April 2007, SAHA/Sunday Times Heritage Project

"I was slapped and kicked…what would it help?" - Tymon Smith Interview with Penelope Baby Twaya, 26 May 2007, SAHA/Sunday Times Heritage Project

"It was winter…speak or to say anything." - Tymon Smith Interview with Jabu Ngwenya, 22 May 2007, SAHA/Sunday Times Heritage Project

"To me and the rest of the Timol family…he was murdered." - Tymon Smith Interview with Imtiaz Cajee, 26 May 2007, SAHA/Sunday Times Heritage Project

"It's probably the iconic institution…the mad forces." Tymon Smith Interview with Barbara Hogan, 4 April 2007, SAHA/Sunday Times Heritage Project

Basil D'OLIVEIRA

"In 1966, I achieved something…land of my birth." - D'Oliveira, B. with Murphy, P. 1980. *Time to Declare*, p. 33

"We needed four runs…thrill of exultation." - D'Oliveira, B. 1960. "Sports is my Whole Life", *Drum*, June

"We were never coached…skills on display." - D'Oliveira, B. with Murphy, P. 1980. *Time to Declare*, p. 3

"I played for my father's club…we changed for the match." - Ibid, p. 2

"I was an absolute disaster…everyone knew it." - Ibid, pp. 6 - 13

"The dropping of Basil D'Oliveira…never mind believe it." - Morgan, B. 2007. "Not Just Cricket", March. www.southafrica.info

"We are not prepared to accept…attempt to hide." - Gemmell, J. 2002. *The Politics of South African Cricket*, p. 151

"These laws which degrade non-whites…being a black man." - D'Oliveira, B. with Murphy, P. 1980. *Time to Declare*, p. 113

"Last Wednesday a group of Englishmen…never mind believe it." - Morgan, B. 2007. "Not Just Cricket", March. www.southafrica.info

Tsietsi MASHININI

'Students today want to be recognised as human beings…" - Interview with Tsietsi Mashinini, *Intercontinental Press*, 14 March 1977, ANC Archives, University of Fort Hare

"As a youngster…charmed everyone he met." - Schuster, L. 2004. *A Burning Hunger*, p. 39

"as a teenager…with high shoes." - "Tsietsi Mashinini - Profile', www.sahistory.org

Tsietsi was forever frightening…they adored him." - Schuster, L. 2004. *A Burning Hunger*, p. 40

"The pupils used…This was the school." - "Humble Façade of Morris Isaacson Belies Important Role Played in SA History", *Saturday Star*, 17 June 1995

"was a highly disciplined school, almost military in its discipline." - TRC Hearings on Human Rights Violations: Soweto. Testimony of Mr. Fanyana Mazibuku, 22 July 1996. www.doj.gov.za

"Tsietsi would take a stage…no question about that." - Tshepo Maloi Interview with David Kutumela, 14 June 2007, SAHA/Sunday Times Heritage Project

"His social life…a well-dressed Casanova." - "Tsietsi Mashinini - Profile', www.sahistory.org

"If students are not happy…compulsory for Africans." - "The Afrikaans Medium Decree", www.africanhistory.about.com

"…the best, shortest, simplest and (most) easy to understand". - "Tsietsi Mashinini", www.thetimes.co.za/heritage

"The main thing…we'll disperse." - Ibid

Tsietsi le Vorster…Tsietsi has passed" - Hlongwane, A. "The Mapping of the Soweto Uprising Student Routes: Past Recollections and Present Reconstruction(s)"

"cheerfully swung his pick…premises for him." - Ndlovu, N. "Amandla! The Story of the Soweto Student's Representative Council", Wits Historical Papers

"I saw Tsietsi pass between me…off he went." - TRC Hearings on Human Rights Violations: Soweto. Testimony of Mr. Fanyana Mazibuku, 22 July 1996. www.doj.gov.za

"One night, the police surrounded a house…laughing women." - Ndlovu, N. "Amandla! The Story of the Soweto Student's Representative Council", Wits Historical Papers

"Mashinini's daredevil courage…urge pupils on in their *mzabalazo* (fight/struggle)." - Maseko, L. "A Nightmare Revisited", *Sowetan*, 16 June 1995

"Tsietsi became the darling…Miriam Makeba." - Schuster, L. 2004. A Burning Hunger, p. 120

"As far as the students in South Africa are concerned…they are not doing anything." - Interview with Tsietsi Mashinini, *Intercontinental Press*, 14 March 1977, ANC Archives, University of Fort Hare

"He had heard about this Miriam Makeba… sat with them and asked about home." - Makeba, M. 2004. *The Miriam Makeba Story*, pp. 157 - 162

"Tsietsi…spends a lot of time in Lagos…psychiatric institution." - Schuster, L. 2004. *A Burning Hunger*, p. 320

"Tsietsi could not have died…he had marks on his face." - *Sowetan*, 9 August 1990

"He didn't do it for the ANC…for our liberation." "Tsietsi Mashinini", *Sunday Times Heritage Project*, www.thetimes.co.za/heritage

Brenda FASSIE

"I have done more than 25 videos…oh, I'll survive!" - *Sunday Independent*, 8 November 1999

"Fassie used to lead…She always liked attention." - *This Day*, 11 May 2004

"I met Brenda… treat her like my own daughter.'" - "That Voice Sent Goosepimples Down My Spine", *This Day*, 11 May 2004

"I went and fetched her…she embraced the job." - Paul Holden Interview with Melvyn Matthews, 16 August 2007, *SAHA/Sunday Times Heritage Project*

"I went to the rehearsal room…from her boyfriend." - Ibid

"Why should we pretend…political by definition." - "What Brenda Meant to SA', This Day, 11 May 2004

"In a minute…She was gold." - "How I Battled to Keep Brenda Safe", *Star*, 11 May 2004

"Never have I experienced anything…it was wonderful." - Anstey, G. "Once in a Generation", www.thetimes.co.za/heritage

"I'd rather have happiness…money that I do." - "The Madonna of the Townships", *Time*, 17 December 2001

"My daily struggle…could discipline her." - "How I Battled to Keep Brenda Safe", *Star*, 11 May 2004

"'Are you happy, Brenda?'…I am so alone.'" - "How Brenda Terrified Me Most - With Her Tears", *Saturday Star*, 15 May 2004

"Brenda Fassie came like a typhoon…Miles Davis." - Madondo, B. 2007. "Life is Goin' On", *Sunday Times Lifestyle*, 6 May

Ladysmith BLACK MAMBAZO

"There were three choirs… started being known." - Joseph Tshabalala Interview with Shelley Seid, 2007, *Sunday Times Heritage Project*

"My mother was a musician…We used to sing together." - Marion Isaacs Interview with Joseph Tshabalala, 16 September 2007, SAHA Archives

"During that time…people cried because I played it very well." - Ibid

"I felt there was something missing...but I failed." - Ibid

"…song was so harmonious…so collected and powerful." - Ibid

"I called them Black Mambazo…big way to travel everywhere." - Ibid

"It was easy to talk…that is my life.'" - Ibid

"I am a musician…take it somewhere else." - "Somebody Say…", *Memphis Flyer*, 9 February 1998

"When we saw him dancing…he was very happy." - Marion Isaacs Interview with Joseph Tshabalala, 16 September 2007, SAHA Archives

"It was beautiful…'Black Mambazo! Black Power!'" - Ibid

"The people of the world…and love it." - *Sunday Times*, 16 February 2005

SECTION 5

Purple MARCH

"Coming in to Cape Town…not my city." - Interview with Philip Ivey, SAHA Radio Documentary: The Purple March, Broadcast on SAFM, 2007

"The struggle for liberation…gonna give the country to the liberation movement." - Tymon Smith Interview with Philip Erasmus, 2007

"We were expecting a fight…political victory is ours to be had." - Interview with Laurie Nathan, SAHA Radio Documentary: The Purple March, Broadcast on SAFM, 2007

"I was right in front of the police vehicle…identifiable as having participated in this march." - Ibid

"I clearly remember a couple of nuns…imposed on us." - Interview with Philip Ivey, SAHA Radio Documentary: The Purple March, Broadcast on SAFM, 2007

"I came behind the vehicle…arrested and beaten." - Ibid

"Some are hit head on…lost their grip on the situation." - Ozinsky, A. 1989. "Purple Reign", *Upfront*, November

"The (police) retaliate…incriminating stains are quickly concealed." - Ibid

"There was a sense of triumphalism…turned the cards on them." - Interview with Stan Abrahams, SAHA Radio Documentary: The Purple March, Broadcast on SAFM, 2007

"Those that saw Philip…it was a fine moment, it really was." - Interview with Laurie Nathan, SAHA Radio Documentary: The Purple March, Broadcast on SAFM, 2007

Desmond TUTU and the TRC

"There is no peace…sharing and reconciliation." - Tutu, D. 1984. Nobel Prize Acceptance Speech, Oslo, 11 December. www.nobelprize.org

"I was teaching English…Our educational system was the pits." - Interview with Desmond Tutu, Academy of Achievement, Chicago, 12 June 2004. www.achievement.org

"I had gone there…write a letter to the Prime Minister.'" - Ibid

"When will we learn…beat our swords into ploughshares." - Tutu, D. 1984. Nobel Prize Acceptance Speech, Oslo, 11 December. www.nobelprize.org

"suffocated with a mask…and a stick was put inside my knees" - Singqokwana Ernest Malgas testimony before the Truth and Reconciliation Commission, Human Rights Violations Hearings, East London, 16 April 1996. www.doj.gov.za/trc

"It has been an incredible privilege…wounded people." - Tutu, D. 2003. "Foreword" in *TRC Final Report*

"Having asked and received forgiveness…image of God." - Harper, G. 2001. *Colonial and Post-Colonial Incarceration*, p. 233

"Jesus did not say…embrace that will not let us go. All." - "Tutu Calls on Anglicans to Accept Gay Bishop", *Spero* News, 14 November 2005

Bibliography

SECTION 1

Olive SCHREINER

Walker, C. 1979. "The Woman's Suffrage Movement in South Africa", Centre for African Studies, University of Cape Town

First, R. and Scott, A. (eds.) 1989. *Olive Schreiner*, The Women's Press

Brown, J. 1923. *Olive Schreiner: Memories of a Friendship*, Cape Town

Cronwright-Schreiner, S.C. (ed.) 1924. *The Letters of Olive Schreiner*, T. Fisher Unwin Limited: London

Clayton, C. (ed.) 1983. *Olive Schreiner*, McGraw-Hill Book Company: Johannesburg

Schoeman, K. 1992. *Only an Anguish to Live Here: Olive Schreiner and the Anglo-Boer War, 1899–1902*, Human & Rousseau: Cape Town

7th Annual Report, Women's Enfranchisement League, 1 April 1914, Centre for African Studies, University of Cape Town

Schreiner, O. 1971. *The Story of an African Farm*, Penguin Books: London

Draznin, Yaffa C. (ed.) 1992. *My Other Self: The Letters of Olive Schreiner and Havelock Ellis, 1884–1920*, Peter Lang Publishing: New York

Olive Albertina Emilie Schreiner Collection, Historical Papers, Cullen Library, University of the Witwatersrand

Horton, Susan R. 1995. *Difficult Women, Artful Lives: Olive Schreiner and Isak Dinesen, In and Out of Africa*, The John Hopkins University Press: Baltimore

Barash, C. "Introduction to 'The Woman Question'" in Barash, C. (ed.) 1997. *An Olive Schreiner Reader: Writings on Women and South Africa*, Pandora Press: London

Mohandas GANDHI

Fischer, L. (ed.) 2002. *The Essential Gandhi*, Random House: New York

Gandhi, M. 1993. *An Autobiography or My Experiments with the Truth*, translated from the original Gujarati by Mahadev Desai, Gandhi Book Centre: Bombay

Gandhi, M. *Satyagraha in South Africa*, Navajivan Publishing House: Ahmedabad.

Itzkin, E. 2000. *Gandhi's Johannesburg: Birthplace of 'Satyagraha'*, University of the Witwatersrand Press: Johannesburg

Reddy, E.S. and Gandhi, G. 1993. *Gandhi and South Africa, 1914–1948*, Navajivan Publishing House: Ahmedabad

Reddy, E.S. "Mahatma Gandhi: South Africa's Gift to India?" in *Mainstream*, New Delhi, 21 January 1995

Gandhi Collection, Brenthurst Library, Johannesburg

Gandhi Collection, Wits Historical Papers, Johannesburg

www.sahistory.org.za

www.ghandiserve.com

www.anc.org.za

SS MENDI

Clothier, N. 1987. *Black Valour: The South African Native Labour Contingent, 1916–1918*, University of KwaZulu-Natal Press: Pietermaritzburg

Odendaal, A. 1983. "African Political Mobilization in the Eastern Cape, 1880–1910", PhD Thesis, University of Cambridge

Opland, J. 1998. *Xhosa Poets and Poetry*, David Philip: Cape Town

Report of Court and Annexures: SS Mendi Disaster, August 1917, National Archives: Pretoria

Souvenir of the Mendi Disaster, 21 February 1917, Mendi Memorial Bursary Fund

Souvenir of the Mendi Disaster, African Ex-Servicemen's League, undated

Thomson, T. *Touching the Heart: Xhosa Missionaries to Malawi* (forthcoming)

Uys, I. 1993. *Survivors of Africa's Oceans*, Fortress Publishers: London

Willan, B. 1978. "The South African Native Labour Contingent, 1916–1918", *Journal of African History*, Vol. 19, No. 1

Bulhoek MASSACRE

Edgar, R. 1988. *Because They Chose the Plan of God: The Story of the Bulhoek Massacre*, Ravan Press: Johannesburg

Edgar, R. 1982. "The Prophet Motive: Enoch Mgijima, the Israelites and the Background to the Bulhoek Massacre", *International Journal of African Historical Studies*, Vol. 15, No. 3

Makobe, D.H. 1996. "The Bulhoek Massacre: Origins, Causalities, Reactions and Historical Distortions", *Militaria*, Vol. 26, No. 1–2

McCracken, J. 1977. *Politics and Religion in Malawi, 1875–1940*, Cambridge University Press: Cambridge

Interview with Denver Webb, *Sunday Times Heritage Project*

Interview with Bishop N.E. Shweni, *Sunday Times Heritage Project*

Interview with Evangelist M.M. Mtimkulu, *Sunday Times Heritage Project*

Interview with Evangelist E.T. Nkopo, *Sunday Times Heritage Project*

Nontetha NKWENKWE

Daily Dispatch, 16 and 24 June 1998

Edgar, R. and Sapire, H. 1999. *African Apocalypse: The Story of Nontetha Nkwenkwe, a Twentieth Century South African Prophet*, University of the Witwatersrand Press: Johannesburg

Interview with Mzimkhulu Bungu, *Sunday Times Heritage Project*

Interview with Eric Tole, *Sunday Times Heritage Project*

SAHA Radio Documentary: Nontetha Nkwenkwe, Broadcast on SAFM, 2007

SECTION 2

Albert LUTHULI

Luthuli, A. 1962. *Let My People Go*, Collins: London

Luthuli A. 1954. "The Challenge of Our Time", Speech to the First Natal Congress of People Held in Durban, 5 September

Luthuli, A. 1961. "An Honour to Africa", Albert Luthuli's Acceptance Speech on Receiving the Nobel Peace Prize, Oslo, 10 December

Mandela, N. 1994. *Long Walk to Freedom*, MacDonald Purnell: South Africa

Paton, A. 1986. *The Long View*, Pall Mall Press: London

Rule, P. 1993. *Nokukhanya: Mother of Light*, The Grail: South Africa

Pillay, J. 1993. *Voices of Liberation: Albert Luthuli* (Vol. 1), Human Sciences Research Council Publishers: cape Town and Johannesburg

Sisulu, E. 2003. *Walter and Albertina Sisulu: In Our Lifetime*, David Philip: Cape Town

"13th Anniversary of Chief Albert Luthuli's Death: Remember Him in Action", *Mayibuye*, No. 6, 1982

Albert Luthuli Collection, University of South Africa, Pretoria

South African Institute of Race Relations Collection, Wits Historical Papers, Johannesburg

www.anc.org.za

Orlando PIRATES

Alegi, P. 2004. *Laduma! Soccer, Politics and Society in South Africa*, University of KwaZulu-Natal Press: Pietermaritzburg

Bonner, P. and Segal, L. 1998. *Soweto: A History*, Maskew Miller Longman: Cape Town

Maguire, R. 1991. "The People's Club: A History of Orlando Pirates", Honours Dissertation, University of the Witwatersrand

The Fifties People of South Africa, 1989. Bailey's Africa Photo Archive Production: Johannesburg

"Orlando Pirates: 65th Anniversary, 1937–2002", *KickOff Magazine*

SAHA Radio Documentary: Orlando Pirates, Broadcast on SAFM, 2007

www.joburg.org.za

www.orlandopiratesfc.com

www.sasoccer365.com

Cissie GOOL

Van der Spuy, P. 2002. "Not Only the Younger Daughter of Doctor Abdurahman", PhD Thesis, University of Cape Town

Everett, E. 1978. "Zainunnissa Cissie Gool 1897–1963: A Biography", BA Honours Essay, University of Cape Town

Field, S. (ed.) 2001. *Lost Communities, Living Memories: Remembering Forced Removals in Cape Town*, David Philip: Cape Town

Jeppie, S. and Soudien, C. (eds.) 1990. *The Struggle for District Six Past and Present*, Buchu Books: Cape Town

Hirson, B. "A Short History of the Non-European Unity: An Insider's View", www.sahistory.org.za

Paleker, G. 2002. "She Was Certainly Not a Rosa Luxemborg: A Biography of Cissie Gool in Images and Words", MA Thesis, University of Cape Town

Rassool, Y. 2000. "District Six – Lest We Forget: Recapturing Subjugated Histories of Cape Town", University of the Western Cape: Cape Town

Schuster, A. 2000. "Piecing Together the Past: Writings from a Workshop on Memory and Narrative Held at the District Six Museum during August and September 2000", District Six Museum: Cape Town

The Fifties People of South Africa, 1989. Bailey's Africa Photo Archive Production: Johannesburg

Abdurahman Collection, Manuscripts and Archives, University of Cape Town

Cissie Gool Collection, Manuscripts and Archives, University of Cape Town

Alan PATON

Alexander, P.F. 1994. *Alan Paton: A Biography*, Oxford University Press: Oxford

Paton, A. 1948. *Cry, the Beloved Country: A Story of Comfort in Desolation*, Scribner's Sons: New York

Paton, A. 1975. *Knocking on the Door: Shorter Writings*, David Philip: Cape Town

Paton, A. 1980. *Towards the Mountain*, David Philip: Cape Town

Paton, A. 1990. *Journey Continued*, Penguin Books: London

Alan Paton Centre and Struggle Archives, University of KwaZulu-Natal

Alan Paton Collection, Wits Historical Papers, Johannesburg

www.imdb.com

www.britanica.com

www.suntimes.co.za/bookawards/faqs.asp

www.kirjasto.sci.fi/apaton.htm

www.library.unp.ac.za/paton/index.htm

Race CLASSIFICATION

Armstrong, S. 1991. "Forum: Watching South Africa's 'Race' Detectives – The Results of South Africa's Race Classification Laws", *New Scientist Print Edition*, 20 April

Erasmus, Y. 2007. "The Race Classification Boards and the Negotiation of Racial Boundaries", PhD Thesis, St. George's University of London

Horrell, M. 1958. "Race Classification in South Africa: Its Effects on Human Beings", Fact Paper, South African Institute of Race Relations

Horrell, M. 1978. "Laws Affecting Race Relations in South Africa", South African Institute of Race Relations

Lewis, G. 1987. *Between the Wire and the Wall: A History of South African "Coloured" Politics*, David Philip: Cape Town

Parrow, C.P. *Statutes of the Union of South Africa*, Government Publications

Pilger, J. 1986. *Heroes*, Jonathan Cape: London

Pirie, G. 1984. "Race Zoning in South Africa: Board, Court, Parliament, Public", *Political Geography Quarterly*, Vol. 3, No. 3

Posel, D. 2001. "Race as Common Sense: Racial Classification in Twentieth Century South Africa", *African Studies Review*, Vol. 44, No. 2

Suzman, A. 1960. *Race, Classification and Definition in the Legislation of the Union of South Africa, 1910–1960*, South African Institute of Race Relations: Johannesburg

Venter, A.L. 1974. *Coloured: A Profile of Two Million South Africans*, Human & Rousseau: Cape Town

Legal Resources Centre Collection, Wits Historical Papers, Johannesburg

Betty Kennedy interview with Tshepo Maloi, 16 May 2007, *SAHA/Sunday Times Heritage Project*

Stanley Grant interview with Tshepo Maloi, 30 November 2006, *SAHA/Sunday Times Heritage Project*

Vic Wilkinson interview with Sue Valentine, 19 May 2006, *SAHA/Sunday Times Heritage Project*

Bessie HEAD

Coetzee, P. and MacKenzie, C. 1996. "Bessie Head: Rediscovered Early Poems", *English in Africa*, May

Cullinan, P. 2005. *Imaginative Trespasser*, University of the Witwatersrand Press: Johannesburg

Eilersen, G.S. 1996. *Bessie Head: Thunder Behind Her Ears*, Heinemann: London

MacKenzie, C. 1989. *Bessie Head: An Introduction*, NELM Introductions

Vigne, R. (ed.) 1991. *A Gesture of Belonging: Letters from Bessie Head, 1965–1979*, S.A. Writers: London

Jean Marquard Papers, Wits Historical Papers, Johannesburg

www.bessiehead.org

SECTION 3

Raymond MHLABA

Baines, G. 2002. "The Shadow of the City: A History of New Brighton, Port Elizabeth, 1903–1953", Edwin Mellen Press: London

Lodge, T. 1983. *Black Politics in South Africa since 1945*, Ravan Press: Johannesburg

Mandela, N. 1994. *Long Walk to Freedom*, MacDonald Purnell: South Africa

Mhlaba, R. and Mufumadi, T. 2001. *Raymond Mhlaba's Personal Memoirs: Reminiscing from Rwanda to Uganda*, HSRC and Robben Island Museum: Cape Town and Johannesburg

Naicker, MP. 1972. "The Defiance Campaign Recalled", www.anc.org.za

Sisulu, E. 2003. *Walter and Albertina Sisulu: In Our Lifetime*, David Philip: Cape Town

The Road to Democracy in South Africa, Vol. 1. 2004. SADET: Johannesburg

Tomas Karis interview with Raymond Mhlaba, 7 December 1989, Karis-Gerhart Collection, Wits Historical Papers

Philip Bonner interview with Raymond Mhlaba and Barbara Harmel, 27 October 1993, Phil Bonner personal collection

George PEMBA

Berman, E. 1993. *Art and Artists of South Africa*, Southern Book Publishers: Halfway House

De Jager, J. 1992. *Images of Man: Contemporary South African Black Art and Artists*, Fort Hare University Press: Alice

Hudlestone, S. 1996. *Against All Odds: George Pemba, His Life and Works*, Jonathan Ball: Johannesburg

Mangani, N. 1996. *A Man Called Sekoto*, University of the Witwatersrand Press: Johannesburg

Mhlaba, R. and Mufumadi, T. 2001. *Raymond Mhlaba's Personal Memoirs: Reminiscing from Rwanda to Uganda*, HSRC and Robben Island Museum: Cape Town and Johannesburg

Proud, H. and Feinberg, B. 1996. "Pemba Retrospective Exhibition Catalogue", South African National Gallery and Mayibuye Centre, University of the Western Cape

Diaries of George Pemba, courtesy of Bobo Pemba

Janette Bennett interview with Bobo Pemba, *SAHA/Sunday Times Heritage Project*

Janette Bennett interview with Lizo Pemba, *SAHA/Sunday Times Heritage Project*

South African Institute of Race Relations Collection, Wits Historical Papers, Johannesburg

Rev. Shepherd Collection, Cory Library, University of Grahamstown

Duma NOKWE

Bizos, G. 2007. *Odyssey to Freedom*, Random House: Johannesburg

Huebner, M. 1993. "Who Decides? Restructuring Criminal Justice for a New South Africa", *Yale Law Journal*, Vol. 102, No. 4

Hunt, P.M.A. 1963. "The Faculty of Law, University of the Witwatersrand, Johannesburg", *Journal of African Law*, Vol. 17, No. 2

Mandela, N. 1994. *Long Walk to Freedom*, MacDonald Purnell: South Africa

Selvan. R. L. "Early Days at the Johannesburg Bar", www.johannesburgbar.co.za

"Duma Nokwe: Honourable Son of Africa", *Sechaba*, Vol. 12, April 1978

"History of the BLA [Black Lawyers Association]", www.bla.org.za

"The Legal Profession after Ten Years of Democracy", *De Rebus*, May 2004

www.anc.org.za

www.sacp.org.za

www.sahistory.org.za

Lilian NGOYI

Bonner, P. and Segal, L. 1998. *Soweto: A History*, Maskew Miller Longman: Cape Town

Daymond, M. "From a Shadow City: Lilian Ngoyi's Letters, 1971–1980, Orlando, Soweto" in *Post Colonial Cities: Africa*, Lilian Ngoyi Collection, Wits Historical Papers, Johannesburg

Frederikse, J. 1995. *Helen Joseph: They Fought for Freedom*, Maskew Miller Longman: Cape Town

Joseph, H. 1963. *If This Be Treason*, André Deutsch: London

Joseph, H. 1986. *Side by Side: The Autobiography of Helen Joseph*, Zed Books: London

Mpahle, E. "Lilian Ngoyi: The Most Talked-of Woman in Politics", www. anc.org.za

Lilian Ngoyi Collection, Wits Historical Papers, Johannesburg

SAHA Radio Documentary: Lilian Ngoyi, Broadcast on SAFM, 2007

www.sahistory.org.za

www.liberation.org.za

Athol FUGARD

Benson, M. (ed.) and Fugard, A. 1983. *Notebooks 1960–1977*, Faber and Faber: London

Christie, R. 1976. "Fugard in Focus", *The Star*, 7 September

Eve, J. 2003. *A Literary Guide to the Eastern Cape*, Double Storey Books: Cape Town

Fugard, A. 1983. *"Master Harold" and the Boys*, Oxford University Press: Oxford

Fugard, A. 1994. *Cousins: A Memoir*, University of the Witwatersrand Press: Johannesburg

Gray, S. 1991. *File on Fugard*, Methuen Drama: London

Walder, D. 2000. *Athol Fugard: Township Plays*, Oxford University Press: Oxford

Zack, J. W. 2008. "My Brother's Keeper: An Interview with Athol Fugard" in *Words on Plays*, American Conservatory Theatre, 28 January. www.act-sf.org

Athol Fugard Collection, Wits Historical Papers, Johannesburg

http://www.info.gov.za/aboutgovt/orders/2005/fugard.html

http://www.zar.co.za/athol.html

http://www.roundabouttheatre.org

SECTION 4

Ingrid JONKER

Jonker, I. 1963. "The Child That Died at Nyanga" in *Drum*, May

Jonker, I. 1963. *Rook en Oker*, Afrikaanse Pers-Boekhandel: Johannesburg

Jonker, I. 1988. *Selected Poems*, translated by Jack Cope and William Plomer, Human & Rousseau: Cape Town

Lytton, D. 1967. "Ingrid Comes to Stratford", *Contrast*, Vol. 4

Meterlekamp, P. 2003. *Beeld van 'n digterslewe*, Hemel in See: Vermont

Smit, B. 1963. "Ter Inleiding", *Sestiger*, Vol. 1, No. 1

Van Wyk Louw, N.P. 1964. "Sestig, Sestiger, Sestigste", *Sestiger*, Vol. 1, No. 3

Sestiger, Vol. 1, No. 2, February 1964

John VORSTER SQUARE

Bizos, G. 1998. *No One to Blame? In Pursuit of Justice in South Africa*, David Philip: Cape Town

Breytenbach, B. 1984. *The True Confessions of an Albino Terrorist*, Taurus Books: Johannesburg

Cronin, J. 1983. *Inside*, Ravan Press: Johannesburg

D'Oliveira, J. 1977. *Vorster the Man*, E. Stanton: Johannesburg

First, R. 1965. *177 Days*, Penguin: Harmondsworth

Feinberg, B. (ed.) 1980. *Poets to the People: South African Freedom Poets*, Heinemann: London

Lewin, H. 1976. *Bandiet*, Penguin Books: London

Niehaus, C. 1993. *Fighting for Hope*, Human & Rousseau: Cape Town

Pheto, M. 1985. *The Night Fell*, Heinemann: Johannesburg

Sachs, A. 1990. *The Jail Diary of Albie Sachs*, David Philip: Cape Town

Seroke, J. 2002. "We Presume (for Our Expected Baby)" in Mapanje, J. (ed.) *Gathering Seaweed*, Heinemann: Johannesburg

De Witt Dippenaar, M. 1988. *The History of the South African Police 1913–1988*, Promedia Publications: Silverton

Sanders, J. 2006. *Apartheid's Friends: The Rise and Fall of South Africa's Largest Secret Service*, John Murray: London

Critical Health, April 1982 (special edition tribute to Neil Aggett)

John Vorster Square Collection, SAPS Archives, Pretoria

Neil Aggett Collection, Wits Historical Papers, Johannesburg

Interviews conducted by Tymon Smith with the following individuals:
George Bizos (10 March 2007)
Imtiaz Cajee (26 May 2007)
Max and Audrey Coleman (10 April 2007)
Paul Erasmus (22 May 2007)
Dr Elizabeth Floyd (24 May 2007)
Hennie Heymans (25 May 2007)
Barbara Hogan (14 April 2007)
Catherine Hunter (11 April 2007)
Reverend Cedric Mayson (8 March 2007)
Commissioner Simon Mpembe (25 May 2007)
Dr Kantilal Naik (5 March 2007)
Jabu Ngwenya (22 May 2007)
Molefe Pheto (22 May 2007)
James Sanders (25 May 2007)
Jackie Seroke (9 March 2007)
Zwelinzima Sizane (9 March 2007)
Penelope Baby Twaya (26 May 2007)
Chris Wilken (24 May 2007)
Helen Suzman (6 March 2007)
Koos van der Merwe (31 May 2007)

www.sahistory.org.za

www.anc.org.za

www.joburg.org.za

www.info.gov.za

Basil D'OLIVEIRA

D'Oliveira, B. 1980. *Time to Declare: An Autobiography*, London

Gemmell, J. 2004. *The Politics of South African Cricket*, Routledge: London

Odendaal, A. 2003. *The Story of an African Game*, David Philip: Cape Town

Murray, B.K. 2001. "Politics and Cricket: The D'Oliveira Affair of 1968", *Journal of Southern African Studies*, Vol. 27, No. 4

Murray, B.K. and Merrett, C. 2004. *Caught Behind: Race and Politics in Springbok Cricket*, University of the Witwatersrand Press: Johannesburg

United Cricket Board Collection, Wits Historical Papers, Johannesburg

Tsietsi MASHININI

Bonner, P. and Segal, L. 1998. *Soweto: A History*, Maskew Miller Longman: Cape Town

Brink, E., Malungane, G. and Lebelo, S. 2001. *Soweto, 16 June 1976: It All Started with a Dog*, Kwela: Cape Town and Global: London

Glaser, C. 1998. "'We Must Infiltrate the Tsotsis': School Politics and Youth Gangs in Soweto, 1968–1976", *Journal of Southern African Studies*, Vol. 24, No. 2

Hlongwane, A. "The Mapping of the Soweto Uprising Student Routes: Past Recollections and Present Reconstruction(s)", Paper presented at the Annual Teachers' Workshop, University of the Witwatersrand

Makeba, M. with Mwamuka, N. 2004. *Makeba: The Miriam Makeba Story*, STE Publishers: Johannesburg

Schuster, L. 2004. *A Burning Hunger: One Family's Struggle against Apartheid*, Jonathan Cape: London

Helena Pohiand-McCormick Collection, Wits Historical Papers, Johannesburg

Karis-Gerhart Collection, Wits Historical Papers, Johannesburg

http://www.doj.gov.za/trc/hrvtrans/soweto/mashinin.htm

www.joburg.org.za

www.mg.co.za

www.suntimes.co.za/2004/02/15/insight/in17.asp

www.news24.com

www.alternatives.ca/article1244.html

www.annalog.co.za

www.sahistory.org.za

Brenda FASSIE

Whaley, A. 2004. *Brenda Remembered*, Spearhead: Cape Town

"Madonna of the Townships", *Time*, 15 September 2001

The Star (2004)

Saturday Star (2003–2004)

This Day (2004)

Sunday Times (2003–2004)

City Press (2004)

The Citizen (1995)

Paul Holden interview with Melvyn Matthews, 16 August 2007, *SAHA/Sunday Times Heritage Project*

Ladysmith BLACK MAMBAZO

Sowetan (1996–2007)

Newsweek (1987)

Drum (1987)

The Star (1988–2007)

New Nation (1987)

Marion Isaacs interview with Joseph Tshabalala, 9 August 2007, *SAHA/Sunday Times Heritage Project*

Joseph Tshabalala Personal Archive

Ladysmith Black Mambazo Collection, Gallo Records, Johannesburg

www.mambazo.com

www.ladysmithblackmambazo.com

www.africanmusic.org

www.afropop.org

www.jazzreview.com

www.alternatemusicpress.com

www.jazzusa.com

www.durban.gov.za

SECTION 5

Purple MARCH

Lodge, T. and Nasson, B. 1991. *All Here and Now: Black Politics in South Africa*, David Philip: Cape Town

Seekings, J. 2000. *The UDF: A History of the United Democratic Front, 1983–1991*, David Philip: Cape Town, Ohio University Press: Athens and James Currey: Oxford

Smuts, D. and Westcott, S. (eds.) 1991. *The Purple Shall Govern: A South African A–Z of Non-Violent Action*, Oxford University Press: Oxford

SAHA Radio Documentary: The Purple March, broadcast on SAFM, 2007

Philip Ivey Personal Collection

Sue Valentine Interview with Philip Ivey, 4 September 2006, *SAHA/Sunday Times Heritage Project*

Upfront (1989)

Sunday Times (1989)

Sunday Star (1989)

Weekend Argus (1989)

Weekly Mail & Guardian (1989)

The Cape Times (1989)

Desmond TUTU and the TRC

Allen, J. 2006. *Rabble Rouser for Peace: The Authorized Biography of Desmond Tutu*, Rider Books: London

Boraine, A. 2000. *A County Unmasked*, Oxford University Press: Oxford

Gobodo-Madikizela, P. 2003. *A Human Being Died That Night: A South African Story of Forgiveness*, Houghton Mifflin: New York

Hamber, B. 1998. "How Should We Remember? Issues to Consider When Establishing Commissions and Structures for Dealing with the Past", Centre for the Study of Violence and Reconciliation, December

Krog, A. 2001. *Country of My Skull*, Random House: Johannesburg

Seekings, J. 2000. *The UDF: A History of the United Democratic Front, 1983–1991*, David Philip: Cape Town, Ohio University Press: Athens and James Currey: Oxford

Simpson, G. 1998. "A Brief Evalution of South Africa's Truth and Reconciliation Commission: Some Lessons for Societies in Transition", Centre for the Study of Violence and Reconciliation, December

Sarkin, J. 2004. *Carrots and Sticks*, Inter Sentia: Oxford and Antwerp

Sparks, A. 2003. *Beyond the Miracle*, Jonathan Ball: Johannesburg

Villa-Vicencio, C. and Verwoerd, W. (eds.) 2000. *Looking Back, Reaching Forward: Reflections on the Truth and Reconciliation Commission of South Africa*, University of Cape Town Press: Cape Town

Rand Daily Mail (1984)

The Star (1984, 1996–1998)

Die Beeld (1984)

Sowetan (1984 and 1996–1998)

Sunday Times (1996–2000)

Business Day (1996–1998)

The Citizen (1996–1998)

Diocese of Johannesburg Collection, Wits Historical Papers, Johannesburg

www.nobelprize.org

www.doj.gov.za/trc

Photographic Credits

All photos of the memorials were provided by *Sunday Times* photographers

ANC Archives (University of Fort Hare):
p. 104 (01), p. 107 (02), p. 108 (02), p. 110 (01; 02), p. 164 (01)

Avusa Library: p. 4 (01); p. 46 (02), p. 48 (01), p. 50 (01; 02), p. 51 (03), p. 52 (01), p. 53 (02), p. 54 (01; 02), p. 66 (01; 02), p. 70 (01; 02; 03), p. 72 (01), p. 88 (01), p. 102 (01), p. 115 (01), p. 116 (01; 02), p. 120 (01), p. 121 (02), p. 123 (01; 02), p. 125 (03; 04), p. 126 (01; 02; 03), p. 130 (01), p. 133 (03), p. 135 (02; 03), p. 138 (01), p. 140 (02), p. 141 (03), p. 144 (01), p. 148 (01), p. 151 (01; 02; 03), p. 152 (01; 02), p. 156 (01), p. 159 (01), p. 163 (02; 03), p. 164 (02), p. 166 (01), p. 169 (01; 02; 03), p. 170 (01; 02; 03), p. 171 (01; 02; 03), p. 172 (01), p. 174 (01), p. 177 (03; 04), p. 178 (01; 02), p. 190 (01), p. 191 (02), p. 192 (01, 02), p. 193 (03, 04), p. 195 (02; 03), p. 196 (01; 02), p. 198 (01)

Baileys African History Archives: p. 42 (01), p. 46 (01), p. 49 (02), p. 64 (01), p. 75 (01; 02), p. 80 (01), p. 82 (01; 02), p. 96 (01), p. 98 (01, 02), p. 101 (02), p. 106 (01), p. 112 (01), p. 152 (03)

Brenthurst Library: p. 11 (02)

British Thames: p. 162 (01)

EMI Music Publishing (South Africa): p. 167 (02)

Gallo Music Publishing (South Africa): p. 177 (02)

Johannesburg Bar Association Archives: p. 108 (01), p. 109 (02)

Joseph Tshabalala Personal Collection: p. 176 (01)

King George VI Art Gallery (Port Elizabeth): p. 97 (02)

Lizo Pemba Personal Collection: p. 32 (01)

Manuscripts and Archives (University of Cape Town): p. 57 (02), p. 61 (02)

Museum Africa: p. 7 (03), p. 12 (01; 02), p. 13 (03), p. 14 (01), p. 24 (01), p. 26 (01), p. 30 (01; 02; 03)

National Afrikaans Literary Museum (Bloemfentein): p. 132 (01; 02), p. 135 (01)

National Archives (Pretoria): p. 17 (02), p. 22 (01), p. 25 (02), p. 27 (02), p. 28 (01), p. 29 (02), p. 32 (02), p. 35 (01), p. 36 (01), p. 37 (02), p. 105 (02), p. 117 (03), p. 160 - 161 (01 - 07)

National English Literary Museum (Rhodes University): p. 84 (01)

Philip Ivey Personal Collection: p. 182 (01), p. 183 (02), p. 185 (03), p. 187 (01; 02), p. 188 (03)

South African History Archives: p. 146 (01)

South African National Museum of Military History: p. 18, p. 19, p. 20 (02; 03), p. 21 (01; 02; 03)

South African National Library (Cape Town): p. 10 (01), p. 16 (01), p. 56 (01), p. 61 (01)

South African Police Service Archives (Pretoria): p. 143 (04), p. 145 (02), p. 146 (03)

Thembeka Mufamadi Personal Collection: p. 90 (01; 02; 03), p. 91 (01), p. 93 (01)

Trace Images: p. 184 (01; 02)

Unisa Archives: p. 43 (02), p. 44 - 45 (01), p. 46 (03), p. 60 (01, 02, 03), p. 63 (03)

Wits Historical Papers: p. 6 (01; 02), p. 68 (01), p. 69 (02), p. 76 - 77 (01; 02; 03), p. 78 (01), p. 113 (02), p. 118 (01), p. 124 (02), p. 142 (01; 02), p. 157 (02), p. 194 (01), p. 195 (04)

Index